175 Best Superfood Blender Recipes

Using Your **NutriBullet**®

Marilyn Haugen
& Doug Cook, RD, MHSc

Robert
ROSE

For complete cataloguing information, see page 217.

Disclaimers
175 Best Superfood Blender Recipes is an independent publication of Robert Rose Inc. and has not been
authorized, sponsored or otherwise approved by any other party, including Capbran Holdings, LLC, and
Robert Rose Inc. is not a licensee of or otherwise associated with Capbran Holdings, LLC.

The recipes in this book have been carefully tested by our kitchen and our tasters. To the best of our
knowledge, they are safe and nutritious for ordinary use and users. For those people with food or other
allergies, or who have special food requirements or health issues, please read the suggested contents of each
recipe carefully and determine whether or not they may create a problem for you. All recipes are used at
the risk of the consumer. Consumers should always consult their manufacturer's manual for recommended
procedures and cooking times. We cannot be responsible for any hazards, loss or damage that may occur
as a result of any recipe use. For those with special needs, allergies, requirements or health problems, in the
event of any doubt, please contact your medical adviser prior to the use of any recipe.

Design and production: Alicia McCarthy & Kevin Cockburn/PageWave Graphics Inc.
Editor: Sue Sumeraj
Recipe editors: Kelly Jones and Jennifer MacKenzie
Proofreader: Wendy Potter
Indexer: Gillian Watts
Photography: Tango Photography
Food stylist: Éric Régimbald
Prop stylist: Véronique Gagnon-Lalanne

Cover image: © istockphoto.com/Svetl

The publisher gratefully acknowledges the financial support of our publishing program by the Government
of Canada through the Canada Book Fund.

Published by Robert Rose Inc.
120 Eglinton Avenue East, Suite 800, Toronto, Ontario, Canada M4P 1E2
Tel: (416) 322-6552 Fax: (416) 322-6936
www.robertrose.ca

Printed and bound in USA

1 2 3 4 5 6 7 8 9 LSC 25 24 23 22 21 20 19 18 17

Contents

Introduction 4

PART ONE
Promoting Health with Blended Superfoods

Chapter 1: Principles of Healthy Eating 6

Chapter 2: The Health Benefits of Superfoods 11

Chapter 3: The Health Benefits of Blended Foods 37

PART TWO
Superfood Recipes for Your NutriBullet

Blending and NutriBullet Basics 58

Breakfast Smoothies 61

Anytime Smoothies 89

Dressings, Dips and Spreads 115

Soups and Sauces 143

Kid-Friendly Recipes 167

Desserts 189

Appendix 1: General Health Benefits of Superfoods 210

Appendix 2: Managing Health Conditions with Superfoods 212

Resources 216

Index 218

Introduction

If you are reading this book, then you value health. Whether you want to maintain the good health you already have or are looking for ways to improve your health, you understand that health is worth investing in. The Greek physician Herophilus said it best: "When health is absent, wisdom cannot reveal itself, art cannot manifest, strength cannot fight, wealth becomes useless, and intelligence cannot be applied."

It's fitting, then, to see health as true wealth, because without it, most of the things we take for granted — such as the ability to work, be independent, be active and enjoy traveling — simply could not happen. Health is an investment and, as with monetary investments, we need to invest and invest often if we want to have robust dividends both in the short term (today) and in the long term (years and decades from now).

Health doesn't just happen, nor is it something that suddenly disappears; we are building it, maintaining it or gradually giving it away every day, based on the sum of our choices. Health challenges often appear to "come out of nowhere," but in most cases, the wear and tear has been brewing below the surface, sometimes for decades.

It shouldn't come as a surprise that nutrition is the foundation of health. Our magnificent bodies are made up of the three macronutrients — protein, fat and carbohydrate — as well as some 25 micronutrients, and food is the source of all of these nutrients. In the human body, function follows form: the foods we choose influence the structure of our tissues and organs. In turn, structure affects function across all aspects of health: mind, body and spirit, or mood.

Because nutrition has a profound impact on overall health, influencing every organ system, it is one of the most important variables in reducing the risk for chronic degenerative disease (or for managing it) and in promoting healthy aging. According to the World Health Organization, chronic diseases are responsible for the deaths of an estimated 38 million people globally each year. While the majority of these deaths are in low- and middle-income countries whose citizens may lack access to appropriate and timely health care, chronic diseases are still a major killer of people worldwide. The top four chronic diseases — cardiovascular disease, cancer, respiratory disease and diabetes — account for 82% of all deaths from chronic disease. Lifestyle risk factors that increase the risk of dying of chronic disease include tobacco use, physical inactivity, the harmful use of alcohol and, of course, an unhealthy diet.

The very good news is that study after study has clearly demonstrated that including more plant foods, such as fruits, vegetables, whole grains, nuts and seeds, in your diet can go a long way toward reducing your risk of developing the most common chronic diseases, and can help you manage pre-existing health conditions.

Everyone knows they should be following a balanced diet that includes a variety of healthy foods. But the reality is, that's often easier said than done. Government agencies around the world routinely find that, while people know what to do, they miss the mark when it comes to getting the minimum recommended intake of vitamins and minerals on a daily basis. People are time-crunched, and it has become commonplace to choose fast food, takeout and prepared meals over home-cooked meals.

That's where the NutriBullet comes in. This compact, space-saving blender makes it incredibly easy to whip up nutrient-dense single-serving smoothies, soups, dips, sauces and desserts that are packed with wholesome ingredients and bursting with flavor. Adding fresh plant foods to your diet doesn't get any simpler than this. For just a small investment of time each day, you'll be rewarded with huge dividends in your health and quality of life.

PART ONE

Promoting Health with Blended Superfoods

CHAPTER 1

Principles of Healthy Eating

It's easy to get lost in the minutiae when it comes to talking about what is, and what is not, a healthy diet. The truth is, there are many paths to the same destination, and no one diet, food guide or cultural model has it all. There are no essential foods, but there *are* essential nutrients, and we get those nutrients from food. Suffice it to say, it's much easier to get the 50-plus nutrients we need every day for optimal health and wellness when we eat a variety of minimally processed, nutrient-dense whole foods.

For most people, a diet that includes a variety of both plant- and animal-based foods, both cooked and raw, ensures that they'll get the nutrients they need in an easy-to-digest and easy-to-absorb form. The human body needs protein, fat, carbohydrate, vitamins, minerals, water and electrolytes every day for growth, maintenance, repair and healing. And in order to truly thrive, it needs plenty of phytonutrients from a variety of plant foods.

Because nutrition is the greatest influence on health throughout the life cycle, the quality of our food choices matters. It isn't enough to focus on calories, milligrams of sodium or grams of fat, protein, carbohydrate or fiber; doing so misses the mark when optimal health is the goal. A reductionist approach like that tells you nothing about the quality of a food in terms of its nutrient density: how rich it is in vitamins, minerals and phytonutrients.

Yes, calories still matter, especially in the enticing food environment most of us face every day. Food is available almost everywhere, and portion sizes are out of control, so it's natural that we've become a society of calorie-counters. But at what cost? Calorie counts alone don't make the best nutritional compass when it comes to staying the course on your journey to better health. For example, a typical coffee shop muffin can have 350 calories (mostly from refined white flour, sugar and vegetable oil); for the same calorie count, you could have a poached egg on a slice of whole-grain toast, half a medium avocado and a small piece of fruit. Either breakfast fits into almost any caloric budget, but the muffin offers little in the way of nutrition — it is a very expensive purchase because of the poor quality of its calories.

How do blended foods fit into a healthy lifestyle?

Blended foods are one of the easiest ways to pack a lot of nutrition into a small serving size. You can get several servings of fruits and/or vegetables, a good source of fiber, protein and even some grains, all in a 16-ounce (500 mL) cup! You can boost the nutrients even more with easy additions such as wheat germ, cacao powder or nut butter. Blended meals made from wholesome foods can be an effective way to increase the overall nutrient density

What are phytonutrients?

Phytonutrients are unique compounds found only in plant foods (*phyto* is from the Greek *phuton*, meaning "from a plant"). Phytonutrients have been shown in study after study to reduce the risk for many chronic degenerative diseases and are responsible for the health-promoting properties of plant foods. Phytonutrients are non-essential nutrients: you can get by on just protein, fat, carbohydrate, vitamins and minerals. But why just "get by" when you can thrive?

of your diet, helping to bridge the gap between the nutrients you are getting and the nutrients you actually need.

Blended foods are also convenient and easy to make. They don't require any significant cooking skills and take little time to prepare. They can be prepared in the morning before you leave home or can be made the night before and stored in the fridge. Sealed in a portable container, they can be tossed into a briefcase, gym bag, tote or knapsack. They offer meal flexibility, too: for example, you can drink a smoothie when it best suits you, whether that's as soon as you get to work or school or right after a workout. No need to rush to get something to eat or deal with lineups at the coffee shop or food court.

In addition, blended foods allow for personalized nutrition: they can be tailored to suit both your individual needs and your taste preferences. If you need to eat more vegetables, you can include spinach, pumpkin, carrots or sweet potatoes in a soup; if you want to eat more fruit, you can load a smoothie with blueberries, strawberries and mango. And if you want to target a specific health condition, you can fine-tune your blended recipes to

fit the bill, perhaps using anti-inflammatory foods such as ginger or turmeric, or adding potassium-rich foods such as coconut water and banana to help lower blood pressure.

How do blended foods fit into a healthy diet?

The basic principles of variety, balance and moderation offer the perfect template for building a healthy diet.

- **Variety:** No one food has all the essential nutrients needed for health. Carrots have vitamins, minerals and phytonutrients that celery doesn't provide, but celery offers unique compounds of its own. Eating a variety of foods is the best way to ensure that you're getting enough of the macronutrients, vitamins, minerals and phytonutrients that help us not only survive but thrive.
- **Balance:** Balanced eating helps ensure that you're not overeating one food or nutrient at the expensive of another. There's nothing wrong with enjoying a large chicken breast or steak fillet, but if a big portion of protein is leaving you with little room for a few different vegetables, then you won't be reaping the benefits of other choices.
- **Moderation:** It all boils down to avoiding extremes. An ultra-low-fat, high-fat, high-protein or low-carb diet rarely works in the long run. For long-term health and happiness, it's best to enjoy a little bit of everything, in the right amounts.

By incorporating a variety of different foods and liquids, blended foods, such as smoothies and soups, can provide a balance from all of the food groups: fruits and vegetables; grains; dairy (milk, yogurt, kefir) or nondairy alternatives (soy, almond, hemp beverage); and meat alternatives (pasteurized egg whites, whey or hemp protein, nuts or seeds), in amounts that meet one's nutritional needs and/or goals.

Guidelines for incorporating smoothies into your diet

Incorporating smoothies into your daily fare is easy. The key is to pay attention to your ingredients and how much you use. Our recipes can help you in this regard, as they provide portion sizes to ensure that you're getting the nutrition you need without going overboard on calories. It's best to follow recipes as you get started with using your NutriBullet, and you'll want to measure all of your ingredients to get a sense of what a serving size is. As you become more familiar with making smoothies, you'll be able to "eyeball" amounts more easily.

Blended foods can easily be incorporated into anyone's diet, whether as part of a meal, as a meal replacement or as a snack. They may be just what you're looking for to improve your diet and personal nutrition.

- **As a meal:** A smoothie can be enjoyed as a quick breakfast, a portable lunch or even dinner if you're not in the mood to cook but also don't want to succumb to a takeout meal.
- **As part of a meal:** A smoothie can be reduced in size and consumed as part of a meal, but you'll want to reduce the other components of your meal as well so that you're not taking in too many calories. For example, if your breakfast typically includes a piece of toast with 1 tsp (5 mL) of butter, 2 poached eggs and an orange, try half a smoothie and 1 soft-cooked egg.
- **As a snack:** As when enjoying a smoothie as part of a meal, you'll want to reduce your portion if using a smoothie as a snack.

Who can benefit from blended foods?

In a word: everyone. People of all ages, from toddlers to seniors, can enjoy the best that blended foods have to offer.

CHILDREN (AGES 2 TO 8)

Growing bodies need lots of protein and calories to support normal development. During this time, bones lengthen and become denser, muscles grow, brains continue to grow (by the age of 2, a child's brain is only about 80% of adult size), blood volume increases and more. This time of rapid growth demands a lot of nutrition, including all of the macronutrients, vitamins and minerals. Nutritional surveys show that, while the diets of most children provide adequate amounts of calories, protein and fat, children in this age range may not be getting enough vitamin D, calcium or fiber.

Blended foods are an easy, convenient and effective way to pack in the nutrients that growing bodies need, helping to fill any nutritional gaps. Smoothies, for example, can easily be customized to suit the often finicky tastes of kids, incorporating ingredients such as peanut butter, bananas, berries and even chocolate (using a good-quality raw cacao powder for better nutrition).

TWEENS AND TEENS (AGES 9 TO 18)

Growth spurts happen throughout the tweens and teens, and these growing bodies still need a lot of high-quality nutrition, especially if the child is involved in activities that increase energy requirements. Studies show that people in this age group are more likely to eat "junk foods": foods that are high in refined and free sugars, sodium, calories and processed fats, including trans fats, and low in fiber, vitamins and minerals. In fact, some of the highest intakes of trans fats are among teenagers, with teenage boys typically consuming the most. Many adolescents also have inadequate intakes of fiber, calcium, iron, magnesium and vitamins A, B_6, B_9 (folate), C and D.

As with younger children, taste preferences strongly influence what a teenager will eat. Soups, smoothies, dips and dressings can easily be customized to include their favorite flavors, and it is quite easy to add foods they might normally turn their noses up at, because in blended foods both tastes and textures can be masked. Carrots, beets, sweet potatoes, spinach, kale, lentils and chickpeas are all fairly neutral in taste and take on the flavors of the other ingredients they are blended with.

Fueling the brain

Study after study shows that nutrition has a profound impact on learning. Students of all ages who eat breakfast perform better in school, are better behaved and are less likely to be absent. Breakfast provides the brain with the carbohydrate it needs to be at its best. After an overnight fast, the tank is empty and needs to be refilled with a balanced meal that includes protein, fat, carbohydrate, vitamins and minerals.

Growing children need a lot of sleep, and getting out of bed can be legitimately difficult for them, leaving them little time to get ready for school, let alone have something nutritious to eat. Skipping breakfast or grabbing something quick along the way isn't a good solution, but a convenient, portable smoothie is.

ADULTS (AGES 19 TO 65)

It's not only children and teenagers who struggle to get the recommended minimum intake of nutrients; many adults also routinely miss the mark, for a variety of reasons. People seem busier than ever today, and our eating habits often suffer when we feel we can't spare the time for grocery shopping and meal prep. More and more, people are relying on fast foods and prepared foods, including takeout and delivery.

It is estimated that about a quarter of the calories we consume are from foods of poor nutritional quality that are heavy on calories, added sugars, refined flours, sodium and fat. Not surprisingly, surveys of adult eating habits reveal that many of us are not getting enough fiber, magnesium, iron, calcium and vitamins A, B_1, B_6, B_9 (folate), B_{12}, C and D. That's quite a list.

Blended foods can help those who want to eat healthier but who are short on time. They take little time to make and, because they can be made ahead and stored in the fridge, they're easy to grab as you head out the door.

OLDER ADULTS (AGE 65 AND UP)

Aging has an impact on many aspects of nutritional health. As people age, they need less energy (fewer calories) but still need the same amount of vitamins, minerals, protein and fiber. The challenge is to eat a nutrient-dense diet without excessive calories. It's also common for seniors to experience a decrease in their ability to sense thirst and hunger, as well as decreased appetite. As a result of changes in their eating habits, it's not uncommon for the elderly to experience muscle loss, dehydration and an inadequate intake of nutrients. Changes in the digestive tract can lead to more frequent constipation, too.

Single seniors may also lose motivation to cook for themselves. Cooking for one can be a chore at any age, but the elderly can find it even more challenging, leading to the so-called tea and toast stereotype. As a result, good nutrition can suffer.

Soups, sauces and dips packed with nutrients can raise the nutritional bar of everyday meals. A chickpea dip on toast, for example, will add fiber, protein, calcium and

B vitamins to a lunch that otherwise might just be chicken noodle soup. And seniors can really benefit from smoothies made with lower-calorie, nutrient-dense foods — they're like a multivitamin in a glass, and can easily be customized with high-protein and high-fiber add-ons. In addition, because all smoothies are made with a fluid base, they're great for helping to prevent dehydration.

Fueling the active body

Active living, whether you're a novice sports enthusiast or an elite athlete, requires optimal nutrition. Eating well will ensure that you have enough fuel for high-energy activities while providing the essential nutrients needed for the repair and maintenance of muscles and other tissues, allowing you to perform at your peak.

Whole-food smoothies, soups and dips provide good-quality carbohydrate, which supplies energy during an activity and replenishes glycogen (the storage form of carbohydrate in muscles) post-workout. Fruits, fruit juices, milk, yogurt, starchy vegetables and pulses are good sources of carbohydrate, as well as vitamins, minerals and electrolytes such as potassium. Those who are involved in endurance activities may wish to add a pinch of salt to their blended foods, to replace the sodium lost through sweating.

Active individuals also need more protein than sedentary people, to repair and maintain muscle protein that gets damaged during exercise. There are many ways to add protein to blended foods, including legumes, yogurt, pasteurized egg products, nut butters and protein powders.

CHAPTER 2

The Health Benefits of Superfoods

There is a lot of buzz around the word "superfood." It implies a food with superpowers, able to prevent and treat disease in a single bound. But the reality is, no one food can do it all; it's the sum of *all* our dietary choices — the total diet concept — that either moves us toward health or away from it. At the end of the day, week, month or year, what is your nutritional bottom line?

When reviewing the foods in this chapter, keep in mind the context of the total diet concept. Don't think of them as individual items that you can use to treat a particular health condition; rather, consider how they can contribute to the sum total of nutrients that have been shown to help reduce the risk for chronic diseases or manage their symptoms. Eating a single avocado won't prevent macular degeneration, but a regular diet of lutein-rich foods, including avocado, kale and spinach, just might.

Think of these foods and their nutrients as a buffet to help you build a health-promoting pattern of eating that will reduce your risk for chronic disease.

Celery: A neglected superfood?

When we hear the word "superfood," celery is not what typically springs to mind. Yet celery contains a naturally occurring phytochemical called 3-n-butylphthalide, and the amount in four celery stalks can lower blood pressure in a meaningful way. So why haven't we heard about this? In short, celery hasn't enjoyed the benefits of a good PR campaign. But celery is a nutritious food and deserves a place in a healthy diet just as much as more widely touted superfoods such as açaí berries and kale.

FRUITS

AVOCADOS

Key nutrients: Fiber, folate, potassium, alpha- and beta-carotene, lutein and zeaxanthin, proanthocyanidins.

Health-promoting properties: The nutrients in avocados offer antioxidant protection; have anti-inflammatory properties; control appetite and help manage weight; support gut bacteria; promote regularity; support healthy skin; support fetal development and a healthy pregnancy; balance blood sugar, cholesterol and triglycerides; lower homocysteine; support a healthy heartbeat; maintain healthy blood pressure; and reduce the risk for cancer, dementia, insulin resistance, type 2 diabetes and cardiovascular disease (CVD).

Health conditions that benefit: Constipation, diverticular disease, hemorrhoids, kidney stones, megaloblastic anemia, osteoporosis, overweight and obesity, as well as any condition in which significant inflammation and oxidative damage can occur, such as CVD, cataracts, dementia, macular degeneration, prediabetes and diabetes, and possibly autoimmune diseases like asthma and rheumatoid arthritis.

Blended foods to try: Rejuvenating Spinach, Cucumber and Avocado Smoothie (page 85); Avocado and Pineapple Salsa (page 126); Avocado Lentil Chocolate Pudding (page 201).

Purchasing tips: To choose a ripe avocado, place it in the palm of your hand and squeeze gently. The avocado should be firm, but should give slightly. Color does not indicate ripeness, as some varieties turn dark green or black while others have a lighter green skin. Avoid avocados with dark blemishes.

BANANAS

Key nutrients: Fiber, potassium, inulin and oligosaccharides, proanthocyanidins.

Health-promoting properties: The nutrients in bananas promote the growth of healthy gut bacteria and therefore gut health, which, in turn, supports healthy moods, digestive health and immune function; promote healthy bowel function and the natural elimination of toxins; soften stools and help to prevent and manage hemorrhoids; help move nutrients into cells and waste products out; support fetal development and a healthy pregnancy; lower cholesterol and blood sugar; support healthy blood pressure; provide antioxidants; support healthy cognitive function and offer neuroprotection; positively influence gene expression and cell growth, reducing the risk for cancer; and may help with weight maintenance and loss.

Health conditions that benefit: Diseases associated with high blood pressure, such as cardiovascular disease, kidney disease and kidney stones.

Blended foods to try: Banana, Peach, Citrus and Goji Berry Smoothie (page 75); Berry Banana Smoothie Bowl (page 112); Chocolate Banana Butterscotch Milkshake (page 192).

Purchasing tips: Choose bananas that are firm and free of bruises. The stem and tip should be intact. Completely yellow bananas and yellow bananas with some spots are fully ripened. When purchasing bananas, select those at varying stages of ripeness if you want to use them over several days. A banana typically moves daily from one stage of ripeness to the next.

BLACKBERRIES

Key nutrients: Fiber, potassium, beta-carotene, flavan-3-ols (epicatechin), flavonols (quercetin), proanthocyanidins.

Health-promoting properties: The nutrients in blackberries promote the growth of healthy gut bacteria and regularity, thereby supporting natural detoxification; promote satiety (a sense of fullness after eating) and can help one achieve and maintain a healthy body weight; support healthy nerve function; lower blood pressure; lower and balance blood sugar, cholesterol and triglycerides; protect blood vessels from damage; support fetal development and a healthy pregnancy; have broad antioxidant and anti-inflammatory properties, including the ability to regulate gene expression; and bind excess metal ions, like iron and copper, to prevent free radical damage, which can reduce the risk for cancer.

Health conditions that benefit: Constipation, dyslipidemia (elevated LDL cholesterol and triglycerides), hemorrhoids, metabolic syndrome, osteomalacia, osteoporosis, overweight and obesity, and possibly health conditions with underlying inflammation, such as arthritis, asthma, cardiovascular disease, dementia and diabetes.

Blended foods to try: Blackberry Pear Smoothie (page 62); Blackberry, Beet and Chia Seed Smoothie (page 90); Chocolate, Blackberry, Banana Superfood Smoothie Bowl (page 113).

Purchasing tips: Choose blackberries that are deeply colored, with no stems attached. They should not be bruised or have signs of mold. Blackberries are best when eaten freshly picked. Store unwashed blackberries in a single layer, lightly covered, in the refrigerator for up to 3 days.

BLUEBERRIES

Key nutrients: Fiber, anthocyanidins, flavan-3-ols (epicatechin), flavonols (quercetin), proanthocyanidins.

Health-promoting properties: The nutrients in blueberries lower cholesterol and triglycerides; balance blood sugar; increase the amount and diversity of gut bacteria to promote digestive health; promote satiety and help to control appetite; and have potent antioxidant and anti-inflammatory properties that regulate gene expression and cellular activity, growth and differentiation.

Health conditions that benefit: Autoimmune disorders, cardiovascular disease, depression, diabetes, diverticular disease, dyslipidemia, hemorrhoids, high blood pressure, and overweight and obesity; diseases associated with inflammation may benefit from the anti-inflammatory and antioxidative properties.

Blended foods to try: Blueberry and Coconut Protein Smoothie (page 63); Creamy Banana, Blueberry and Papaya Smoothie (page 74); Just Peachy Blueberry and Almond Sorbet (page 196).

Purchasing tips: Choose blueberries that are deeply colored and have a slight frosty-white hue. They should not be damaged or show signs of mold. Blueberries can be stored, unwashed, in their original container in the refrigerator for up to 7 days.

CRANBERRIES

Key nutrients: Fiber, anthocyanidins, flavan-3-ols (epicatechin), flavonols (quercetin), proanthocyanidins.

Health-promoting properties: The nutrients in cranberries promote satiety and control appetite, helping one achieve and maintain a healthy body weight; lower and balance blood sugar, cholesterol and triglycerides; promote healthy gut bacteria, mood and immune function; have antioxidant and anti-inflammatory properties that protect cells and tissues from free radical damage; promote healthy cell division, gene expression and communication between cells; provide neuroprotection; and bind excess metal ions, such as copper and iron.

Health conditions that benefit: Constipation, dyslipidemia, metabolic syndrome, overweight and obesity, prediabetes and diabetes, as well as any health condition with increased inflammation, such as cancer, cardiovascular disease, dementia, depression, and possibly autoimmune diseases like asthma and rheumatoid arthritis.

Blended foods to try: Pumpkin Cranberry Protein Smoothie (page 103); Cranberry, Pineapple and Almond Relish (page 125); Cranberry Pear Splash (page 177).

Purchasing tips: Choose cranberries that are firm, plump and deep red. They should not be shriveled, soft or discolored. Fresh cranberries can be refrigerated for up to 7 months or frozen for up to a year.

DATES

Key nutrients: Fiber, potassium, anthocyanidins, proanthocyanidins.

Health-promoting properties: The nutrients in dates promote satiety; support the amount and diversity of gut bacteria; support the bowel's role in detoxification; provide bulk to the stool, helping to promote regularity; help balance blood sugar, lower cholesterol and triglycerides, lower blood pressure and support a normal heartbeat; have anti-inflammatory and antioxidant properties; support healthy cell division and growth; bind excess metal ions, such as copper and iron; support fetal development and a healthy pregnancy, and may reduce the risk for pre-eclampsia and eclampsia; support a healthy mood; and improve immune function.

Health conditions that benefit: Constipation, diverticular disease, dyslipidemia, hemorrhoids, high blood pressure, metabolic syndrome, overweight and obesity.

Blended foods to try: Cooling Avocado, Cucumber and Grapefruit Smoothie (page 102); Spicy Moroccan-Inspired Tomato Dip (page 130); Spiced Pineapple and Maca Energy Balls (page 188).

Purchasing tips: Choose fresh dates that are plump and moist and have glossy skins. They should not be wrinkled or cracked. Medjool dates are more tender and moist than many other varieties, which makes them ideal for smoothies.

Sweeteners

To sweeten or enhance the flavors of blended food, consider adding a small amount of agave nectar, cane sugar, coconut sugar, dates, honey, maple syrup, molasses, stevia or turbinado sugar.

GOJI BERRIES

Key nutrients: Fiber, potassium, anthocyanidins, proanthocyanidins, zeaxanthin.

Health-promoting properties: The nutrients in goji berries provide broad antioxidant and anti-inflammatory properties; promote regularity and digestive health; support gut bacteria; control appetite; help the nerves and cells communicate via nerve impulses; lower blood pressure; help move nutrients into cells and waste products out; maintain a healthy heartbeat; support normal cell division and growth; support the liver's detoxification pathways; promote skin health, maintenance and repair; lower high blood pressure; support healthy mood; and reduce the risk for cardiovascular disease, cancer and possibly other inflammation-associated chronic diseases, such as cataracts, dementia, depression, Alzheimer's disease, arthritis and diabetes.

Health conditions that benefit: Age-related macular degeneration, constipation, hemorrhoids, and overweight and obesity.

Blended foods to try: Pineapple, Mango and Goji Berry Smoothie (page 77); Kiwi, Goji Berry and Cacao Green Smoothie (page 78); Chocolate Pudding with Goji Berries (page 200).

Purchasing tips: Choose dried goji berries that have a long, flat shape and are dark red, not bright red. Goji berries should taste sweet, but not overly sweet; they should not have a bitter taste, which would indicate that other chemicals have been added.

GRAPES, RED

Key nutrients: Potassium, flavonoids.

Health-promoting properties: The nutrients in grapes have anti-inflammatory and antioxidant properties; positively influence gene expression and cell division and growth; bind metals to reduce free radical production; help the nerves and cells communicate via nerve impulses; lower blood pressure and help maintain a healthy heartbeat; help move nutrients into cells and waste products out; and support fetal development and a healthy pregnancy, possibly reducing the risk for pre-eclampsia and eclampsia.

Health conditions that benefit: Any health condition with pronounced inflammation and oxidation, such as arthritis, cardiovascular disease, prediabetes and diabetes.

Blended foods to try: Red and Green Smoothie with Pepitas (page 70); Hydrating Spinach, Berry and Orange Smoothie (page 106); Raspberry, Peach and Grape Ice Pops (page 184).

Purchasing tips: Choose grapes that are predominantly red, without any green or yellow patches. The grapes should be firm, plump and firmly attached to the stem. The stems should be green and flexible and not dried out. If the grapes have a powdery white coating, it is a good sign that the grapes are moist and fresh, but this is not a necessary feature.

KIWIFRUIT

Key nutrients: Fiber, vitamins C and K_1, magnesium, potassium.

Health-promoting properties: The nutrients in kiwis promote regularity and satiety; lower cholesterol; balance blood sugar; support collagen production; improve blood vessel function; reduce inflammation; reduce oxidation and damage from free radicals; increase the absorption of iron; support neurotransmitter production and function; lower blood pressure; support bone and tooth health; support insulin metabolism and help to improve insulin sensitivity; improve arterial stiffness; support the health of the adrenal glands; and support fetal development and a healthy pregnancy.

Health conditions that benefit: Acute and chronic stress, constipation, diabetes, dyslipidemia, insulin resistance, low bone density and osteoporosis, metabolic syndrome, as well as health conditions with inflammation, increased oxidation and impairment of healthy blood vessel function, such as age-related macular degeneration, cardiovascular disease, cataracts and depression.

Blended foods to try: Pear, Kiwi and Key Lime Smoothie (page 71); Tropical Kiwi, Coconut and Chia Seed Smoothie (page 101); Grape Kiwi Kid-Power Smoothie (page 170).

Purchasing tips: Choose kiwis that are firm, with unblemished skin. The size of the kiwi does not indicate ripeness or flavor, so choose any size that looks best to you. The kiwi should give slightly when pressed with your thumb.

MANGOS

Key nutrients: Fiber, vitamin C, potassium, beta-carotene, proanthocyanidins.

Health-promoting properties: The nutrients in mangos promote satiety and regularity; support healthy gut bacteria and the bowel's role in detoxification; may help with weight loss and maintenance; lower cholesterol and triglycerides; have antioxidant and anti-inflammatory properties; lower blood pressure and help to maintain a healthy heartbeat; help move nutrients into cells and waste products out; support normal cell division and growth; support the immune system, skin health and wound repair; stimulate collagen production; support fetal development and a healthy pregnancy, possibly reducing the risk for pre-eclampsia and eclampsia; and support mood.

Health conditions that benefit: Constipation; skin conditions such as acne and psoriasis; diseases with underlying inflammation, such as cardiovascular disease, asthma, dementia, cataracts and diabetes.

Blended foods to try: Mango Agua Fresca (page 96); Mango Guacamole (page 140); Mango Almond Lassi (page 194).

Purchasing tips: To choose a perfectly ripened mango, squeeze it gently to make sure it gives slightly. Occasionally, the base of the stem will have a fruity aroma. Do not choose a mango by color, as different varieties display a spectrum of red to yellow colors.

PEACHES

Key nutrients: Fiber, potassium, beta-carotene, anthocyanidins, flavan-3-ols (catechins, epicatechin), proanthocyanidins.

Health-promoting properties: The nutrients in peaches promote satiety and regularity; support healthy gut bacteria and the bowel's role in detoxification; may help with weight loss and maintenance; support overall liver health and its natural detoxification pathways; help the nerves and cells communicate via nerve impulses; lower blood pressure and help to maintain a healthy heartbeat; help move nutrients into cells and waste products out; lower cholesterol and triglycerides; have antioxidant and anti-inflammatory properties; support normal cell division and growth; support fetal development and a healthy pregnancy, possibly reducing the risk for pre-eclampsia and eclampsia; support immune function, skin health and wound repair; stimulate collagen production; reduce the risk for cardiovascular disease (CVD); and reduce the risk for and may slow the progression of macular degeneration, cataracts and atherosclerosis.

Health conditions that benefit: Constipation, diverticular disease, hemorrhoids, high blood pressure, as well as conditions with underlying inflammation, such as age-related macular degeneration and cataracts, CVD, prediabetes and diabetes.

Blended foods to try: Oatmeal, Peach and Yogurt Smoothie (page 72); Peach, Blueberry and Chia Parfait (page 182); Raspberry, Peach and Grape Ice Pops (page 184).

Purchasing tips: Choose peaches that have a sweet fragrance. The particular mix of yellow and/or red coloration indicates variety of peach, not ripeness. Peaches should be soft, but not mushy; do not squeeze peaches, as they bruise easily.

PEARS

Key nutrients: Fiber, potassium, anthocyanidins, flavan-3-ols (epicatechin), proanthocyanidins.

Health-promoting properties: The nutrients in pears help to slow the rate of digestion and promote satiety; may help one achieve and maintain a healthy body weight; promote regularity; lower cholesterol; lower blood pressure and support a healthy heartbeat; have antioxidant and anti-inflammatory properties; improve blood vessel function; bind excess metals, such as copper and iron, reducing free radical production; support normal cell division and growth; support the liver's normal detoxification pathways; provide neuroprotection and can help to preserve cognitive function; and reduce the risk for cardiovascular disease (CVD), diabetes and cancer.

Health conditions that benefit: Diverticular disease, hemorrhoids, high blood pressure, overweight and obesity, as well as any health condition with increased oxidation and inflammation, such as CVD and diabetes.

Blended foods to try: Pear, Camu Camu and Arugula Smoothie (page 72); Pear, Cranberry and Bok Choy Smoothie (page 95); Fall Cranberry Pear Sorbet (page 198).

Purchasing tips: Fully ripened pears will be slightly soft when you press a finger near the stem. They should not have any soft spots or blemishes in other areas. Pears are picked before they are fully ripened, so if you press near the stem and it is firm, that is okay; pears will ripen at room temperature within a few days. To speed up ripening, place them in a paper bag and store at room temperature. Once ripened, pears should be refrigerated.

PINEAPPLE

Key nutrients: Fiber, vitamin C, potassium.

Health-promoting properties: The nutrients in pineapple help to control appetite and achieve a healthy body weight; support healthy gut bacteria and overall digestive health; lower cholesterol and triglycerides; support the body's detoxification process; lower blood pressure; support healthy nerve transmission; reduce inflammation and oxidation, including the oxidation of LDL cholesterol; stimulate the production of collagen; promote healthy blood vessel function; support a healthy mood; support fetal development and a healthy pregnancy, possibly reducing the risk for pre-eclampsia and eclampsia; support healthy skin and wound, ligament, tendon and cartilage repair; reduce the risk for cardiovascular disease (CVD) and possibly inhibit its progression.

Health conditions that benefit: Constipation, CVD, overweight and obesity.

Blended foods to try: Blueberry, Pineapple and Spinach Boost (page 65); Pineapple, Ginger and Peanut Butter Marinade (page 124); Coconut Pineapple Cream Pie (page 205).

Purchasing tips: Choose a pineapple that is yellow-orange in color, with bright skin. A ripe pineapple will smell very fragrant, and the leaves will pull off easily when tugged. Do not choose even a slightly green or unripe pineapple, as they do not ripen well after being picked.

PRUNES

Key nutrients: Fiber, vitamin K_1, potassium, beta-carotene, polyphenols.

Health-promoting properties: The nutrients in prunes lower blood pressure; help move nutrients into cells and waste products out; enable nerves to transmit impulses; support a healthy heartbeat; promote satiety, help to control appetite and support regularity; help one to achieve and maintain a healthy body weight; lower cholesterol; support appropriate blood clotting to help wound healing; help to build and maintain bone tissue; provide broad antioxidant and anti-inflammatory protection; support healthy skin; support fetal development and a healthy pregnancy; reduce the risk for cancer and cardiovascular disease (CVD); and may reduce the risk for and progression of cataracts and age-related macular degeneration.

Health conditions that benefit: Constipation, diverticular disease, hemorrhoids, high blood pressure, and overweight and obesity, as well as any health condition with increased inflammation, such as CVD, depression and diabetes.

Blended foods to try: Red and Green Smoothie with Pepitas (page 70); Garden Basket Veggie and Fruit Smoothie (page 174); Blueberry Chia Parfait (page 203).

Purchasing tips: Choose prunes that are moist and slightly flexible. They should be blue-black and blemish-free. Select prunes that are free of preservatives. Store prunes in a sealed container in a cool, dark place for up to 6 months.

RASPBERRIES

Key nutrients: Fiber, vitamin C, magnesium, potassium, flavonoids.

Health-promoting properties: The nutrients in raspberries promote satiety and support regularity and healthy gut bacteria; support bone and tooth development; lower blood pressure; stimulate collagen production; have anti-inflammatory, antioxidant and antihistamine properties; aid in insulin metabolism and blood sugar regulation; lower cholesterol and triglycerides; enable protein synthesis and vitamin D metabolism; balance blood sugar balance; support neurotransmitter production and function; support skin health and repair, wound healing and the repair of cartilage, tendons and ligaments; and support fetal development and a healthy pregnancy.

Health conditions that benefit: Age-related macular degeneration, cardiovascular disease, cataracts, dyslipidemia, high blood pressure, metabolic syndrome, osteoporosis, prediabetes and diabetes.

Blended foods to try: Carrot, Raspberry and Oatmeal Breakfast (page 80); Raspberry Poppy Seed Dressing (page 119); Raspberry Chocolate Milkshake (page 191).

Purchasing tips: Choose raspberries that are plump and deeply colored and that have a soft gloss. They should be free of bruises, discoloration and mold. Avoid raspberries with stems attached. Raspberries are best when eaten freshly picked. Store unwashed raspberries in a single layer, lightly covered with paper towels, in the refrigerator for up to 3 days.

STRAWBERRIES

Key nutrients: Fiber, vitamin C, potassium, anthocyanidins, catechins, proanthocyanidins.

Health-promoting properties: The nutrients in strawberries promote satiety and support regularity and healthy gut bacteria; help one achieve and maintain a healthy body weight; support bone and tooth development; lower blood pressure; stimulate collagen production; have anti-inflammatory, antioxidant and antihistamine properties; aid in insulin metabolism and blood sugar regulation; lower cholesterol and triglycerides; enable protein synthesis and vitamin D metabolism; balance blood sugar balance; offer neuroprotection and can help to preserve cognitive function; and reduce the risk for cardiovascular disease (CVD), blood vessel dysfunction, high blood pressure, diabetes and cancer.

Health conditions that benefit: Diverticular disease, hemorrhoids, overweight and obesity, as well as any health condition with increased oxidation and inflammation, such as CVD and diabetes.

Blended foods to try: Strawberry, Camu Camu and Oolong Smoothie (page 93); Strawberry Almond Dressing (page 120); Cold Strawberry and Tomato Soup (page 151).

Purchasing tips: Strawberries are fully ripe when picked. Choose berries that are bright red and have a natural sheen and fresh green leaves and stems. Store strawberries in the refrigerator. Rinse berries in cold water, with stems intact, just before serving and blot dry with a paper towel.

VEGETABLES

ARUGULA

Key nutrients: Vitamin K, calcium, magnesium, potassium, beta-carotene, chlorophyll, flavonols, glucosinolates, lutein and zeaxanthin.

Health-promoting properties: The nutrients in arugula have antibacterial properties; lower homocysteine; support overall healthy gene expression and cell division; lower blood pressure; support appropriate blood clotting for wound repair; stimulate the conversion of carcinogens into less harmful compounds and facilitate their elimination; help to bind various carcinogens, providing general risk reduction; positively influence estrogen metabolism, helping to keep it and its metabolites within a healthy range; support the overall health of the liver and its natural detoxification pathways; may help to improve the quality and appearance of skin and to slow skin aging and wrinkle formation; reduce the risk for and may slow the progression of macular degeneration, cataracts and atherosclerosis; and reduce the risk for cardiovascular disease (CVD).

Health conditions that benefit: Constipation, diverticular disease, hemorrhoids, high blood pressure, low bone density and osteoporosis; conditions with underlying inflammation, such as age-related macular degeneration, cataracts, CVD, and prediabetes and diabetes; may help treat *H. pylori* infection.

Blended foods to try: Ginger, Lime and Arugula Pick-Me-Up (page 82); Spicy Tomato Avocado Smoothie (page 105); Chilled Peppery Avocado and Arugula Soup (page 146).

Purchasing tips: Choose arugula that is bright green and has no yellow or bruised spots. Younger arugula is milder and has a less peppery taste. Store arugula in a produce bag or lightly wrapped in paper towels in the refrigerator for up to 1 week.

BEETS

Key nutrients: Fiber, folate, potassium, magnesium, alpha- and beta-carotene, betaine, lutein and zeaxanthin.

Health-promoting properties: The nutrients in beets help the nerves and cells communicate via nerve impulses; lower and manage blood pressure, improve blood vessel function and help maintain a healthy heartbeat; help move nutrients into cells and waste products out; lower homocysteine; support liver health and normal detoxification pathways in the liver; provide potent and broad antioxidant protection; reduce inflammation; promote and maintain healthy bones and teeth; support the metabolism of protein and vitamin D; support neurotransmitter production; support digestive health, promote regularity and control appetite; and may improve the appearance and health of skin.

Health conditions that benefit: Anemia (megaloblastic and microcytic), dyslipidemia, high blood pressure, metabolic syndrome, and prediabetes and diabetes, as well as any health condition where significant inflammation and oxidative damage can occur, such as cardiovascular disease, cataracts, dementia, diabetes, macular degeneration and possibly autoimmune diseases like asthma and rheumatoid arthritis.

Blended foods to try: Beet, Citrus and Açaí Berry Smoothie (page 80); Creamy Beet, Ginger and Almond Dip (page 129); Cold Beet Soup (page 147).

Purchasing tips: Select beets that are firm and heavy for their size, with no nicks or soft spots. The greens (which are also edible) should be fresh-looking and not wilted. Store beets, separated from their greens, gently wrapped in paper towels in the refrigerator for up to 2 weeks.

BOK CHOY

Key nutrients: Vitamins C and K_1, calcium, potassium, beta-carotene, chlorophyll, glucosinolates.

Health-promoting properties: The nutrients in bok choy have antibacterial properties; lower blood pressure and improve blood vessel function; lower homocysteine; support overall healthy gene expression and cell division; stimulate the conversion of carcinogens into less harmful compounds and facilitate their elimination; help to bind various carcinogens, providing overall general risk reduction; positively influence estrogen metabolism, helping to keep it and its metabolites within a healthy range; support the overall health of the liver and its natural detoxification pathways; reduce the risk for cardiovascular disease (CVD), bone loss, osteoporosis, colon cancer and oxalate-based kidney stones.

Health conditions that benefit: Atherosclerosis, constipation, diverticular disease, hemorrhoids, high blood pressure; conditions with underlying inflammation, such as age-related macular degeneration, cataracts, CVD, and prediabetes and diabetes; may help treat *H. pylori* infection.

Blended foods to try: Cucumber Pineapple Green Smoothie (page 82); Pear, Cranberry and Bok Choy Smoothie (page 95); Pineapple, Mango and Bok Choy Smoothie (page 99).

Purchasing tips: Choose bok choy with rigid and firm leaves and stems with no dark spotting. The leaves can be dark green or yellow-green, depending upon the variety. The stalks can be yellow-green or off-white.

CARROTS

Key nutrients: Fiber, vitamin B_1, potassium, alpha- and beta-carotene, falcarinol.

Health-promoting properties: The nutrients in carrots promote satiety and control appetite; promote regularity and support overall gut health and gut bacteria diversity; support the colon's role in detoxification; support immune function and healthy mood; lower and balance blood sugar; lower inflammation and provide antioxidant protection; lower blood pressure and help maintain a healthy heartbeat; help the nerves and cells communicate via nerve impulses; help move nutrients into cells and waste products out; help with the metabolism of carbohydrate for energy production; and support healthy skin and help to prevent accelerated skin aging.

Health conditions that benefit: Constipation, hemorrhoids, diverticular disease, and high blood pressure, as well as any condition in which significant inflammation and oxidative damage can occur, such as cardiovascular disease, cataracts, dementia, macular degeneration, diabetes and possibly autoimmune diseases like asthma and rheumatoid arthritis.

Blended foods to try: Refreshing Mango, Strawberry and Carrot Smoothie (page 97); Carrot Ginger Dressing (page 121); Roasted Vegetable Pasta Sauce with Tomatoes, Carrots and Mushrooms (page 161).

Purchasing tips: Choose carrots that have their green stems on and are not peeled. The stems should look fresh and not wilted. Carrots come in a variety of colors; choose those with intense, deep color. The root should be slightly thin, with thin stem ends. Carrots should not have splits, cracks or hairy roots.

KALE

Key nutrients: Folate, vitamins C and K_1, calcium, potassium, beta-carotene, chlorophyll, flavonols, glucosinolates, lutein and zeaxanthin.

Health-promoting properties: The nutrients in kale have antibacterial properties; lower high blood pressure and homocysteine; support overall healthy gene expression and cell division; stimulate the conversion of carcinogens into less harmful compounds and facilitate their elimination; help to bind various carcinogens, providing overall general risk reduction; positively influence estrogen metabolism, helping to keep it and its metabolites within a healthy range; support healthy skin; enable appropriate blood clotting for wound repair; help to preserve bone mass; support overall liver health; and provide broad risk reduction for cancer, Alzheimer's disease, dementia and possibly depression.

Health conditions that benefit: High blood pressure; any condition in which significant inflammation and oxidative damage can occur, such as cardiovascular disease, cataracts, dementia, diabetes, macular degeneration and possibly autoimmune diseases like asthma and rheumatoid arthritis; may help treat *H. pylori* infection.

Blended foods to try: Dreamy Berry and Kale Smoothie (page 66); Creamy Kale and Feta Dip (page 131); Kale and Roasted Pepper Pesto (page 164).

Purchasing tips: Choose kale with smaller leaves that are moist, crisp and free of tiny holes. The leaves should be a rich green, with no yellow or brown spots. To store kale, wrap unwashed leaves in damp paper towels and refrigerate for up to 3 days. Kale may stay fresh longer, but will develop a stronger taste the longer it is stored.

MUSHROOMS

Key nutrients: Vitamins B_3 and B_5, potassium, beta-glucan, l-ergothioneine.

Health-promoting properties: The nutrients in mushrooms are needed for the synthesis of steroid compounds, such as cholesterol, estrogen, testosterone and vitamins A and D; help convert food into energy; help the nerves and cells communicate via nerve impulses; lower blood pressure and help maintain a healthy heartbeat; help move nutrients into cells and waste products out; support neurotransmitter production and function; support the adrenal glands; support healthy moods; and reduce the risk for cardiovascular disease.

Health conditions that benefit: Arrhythmia; high blood pressure and associated conditions such as stroke, heart disease and kidney disease.

Blended foods to try: Wild and Button Mushroom Soup (page 152); Zesty Chickpea, Tomato and Mushroom Soup (page 158); Creamy Mushroom Sauce (page 163).

Purchasing tips: Choose mushrooms that are not bruised, shriveling or slimy-feeling. The stems should be firm and uniform in color. The gills should be dry and almost fanlike.

Unique mushroom phytonutrients

L-ergothioneine is a sulfur-containing amino acid antioxidant found in mushrooms. It accumulates in the red blood cells, bone marrow, liver, kidney, skin and eyes, where it appears to prevent oxidation from metals, such as iron and copper.

Beta-glucan is a type of fiber found in fungi that supports immune function and the activity of natural killer cells (major white blood cells of the immune system). Beta-glucan may help reduce the risk for hormone-dependent cancers, such as prostate and breast cancer, balance blood sugar in diabetes and lower cholesterol.

PUMPKIN

Key nutrients: Fiber, vitamins B_3 and E, iron, potassium, alpha- and beta-carotene, lutein and zeaxanthin.

Health-promoting properties: The nutrients in pumpkin slow digestion and provide a sense of fullness; support the amount and diversity of gut bacteria; balance blood sugar by slowing down the absorption of carbohydrate; can help to lower cholesterol by binding to bile acids; support normal detoxification; help to build and maintain red blood cells; provide energy; provide broad antioxidant and anti-inflammatory protection of cells and tissues; lower blood pressure, improve blood vessel function and blood flow, and support a healthy and normal heartbeat; improve gene expression; promote healthy-looking skin; may reduce skin inflammation and help decelerate skin aging; and may reduce the risk for skin cancer.

Health conditions that benefit: Arterial stiffness and high blood pressure; constipation, hemorrhoids and possibly diverticular disease; any disease with generalized underlying inflammation, such as Alzheimer's disease, asthma, cardiovascular disease, dementia, and prediabetes and diabetes; may slow the progression of cataracts, age-related macular degeneration and atherosclerosis.

Blended foods to try: Pumpkin, Date and Flaxseed Smoothie (page 104); Pumpkin, Oat and Pomegranate Smoothie Bowl (page 114); Roasted Pumpkin and Carrot Juice Soup (page 153).

Purchasing tips: Choose pumpkins that are labeled "pie pumpkin" or "sweet pumpkin." These are smaller than the typical carving pumpkin, and their flesh is sweeter and less watery. Avoid pumpkins with either no stem or a stem that is shorter than 1 inch (2.5 cm). A pumpkin should be free of blemishes, mold and soft spots and should feel firm and heavy for its size.

SEAWEEDS (DULSE, KELP, NORI, WAKAME)

Key nutrients: Folate, calcium, iodine, potassium, beta-carotene, chlorophyll.

Health-promoting properties: The nutrients in seaweeds provide potent antioxidant and anti-inflammatory properties; support thyroid hormone metabolism and the overall health of the thyroid gland; support energy metabolism and energy production; lower and maintain homocysteine and blood pressure; support neurotransmitter production and function; provide bone- and tooth-building minerals; support healthy breast tissue; help to bind various carcinogens, providing overall general risk reduction; support healthy skin; support fetal development and a healthy pregnancy, helping to reduce the risk for cretinism-related maternal iodine deficiency.

Health conditions that benefit: Cardiovascular disease, diabetes, depression and high blood pressure; thyroid hormone dysfunction in those with iodine deficiency or insufficiency; may reduce the progression of cataracts and age-related macular degeneration.

Blended foods to try: Pineapple, Mango and Bok Choy Smoothie (page 99); Sweet Chile Dipping Sauce (page 127); Enchilada Sauce with Poblano Peppers and Black Beans (page 162).

Purchasing tips: Choose seaweeds from a trusted and reliable source. The ideal sea vegetables are handpicked and sustainably harvested for the best nutrition levels, and should be tested for harmful chemicals or metals. You can purchase seaweed whole, flaked, granulated or powdered. Our recipes use flaked, granulated and powdered seaweed.

SPINACH

Key nutrients: Folate, vitamin K_1, calcium, iron, magnesium, potassium, beta-carotene, chlorophyll, flavonols, lutein and zeaxanthin.

Health-promoting properties: The nutrients in spinach lower and maintain healthy homocysteine and blood pressure levels; support overall healthy gene expression and cell division; support insulin metabolism and healthy blood sugar and lipid (cholesterol and triglyceride) levels; provide broad antioxidant and anti-inflammatory protection; help to maintain bone tissue and teeth; ensure appropriate blood clotting for wound repair; help to bind various carcinogens, providing overall general risk reduction; support healthy skin; and support fetal development and a healthy pregnancy.

Health conditions that benefit: High blood pressure, iron deficiency and osteoporosis, as well as any condition in which significant inflammation and oxidative damage can occur, such as cardiovascular disease, cataracts, dementia, diabetes, macular degeneration and possibly autoimmune diseases like asthma and rheumatoid arthritis.

Blended foods to try: Spinach, Hot Pepper and Yogurt Hummus (page 139); Spicy Spinach Cilantro Sauce (page 165); Bountiful Berry, Spinach and Cashew Smoothie Bowl (page 178).

Purchasing tips: Choose spinach with thin, flexible leaves — indicators that they are younger and more tender. The leaves should be bright green, with no dark spots or yellowing.

TOMATOES

Key nutrients: Fiber, vitamins B_1 and B_3, folate, vitamin C, calcium, iron, magnesium, potassium, beta-carotene, lycopene.

Health-promoting properties: The nutrients in tomatoes support gut health and gut bacteria, promote regularity and help prevent constipation; help convert food into energy; lower blood pressure and homocysteine; aid in the production of red blood cells; support immune function; have antihistamine action; reduce vascular damage and LDL cholesterol oxidation; support bone and tooth development; provide neuroprotection; and may improve mood and reduce symptoms of depression.

Health conditions that benefit: Chronic diseases associated with increased oxidation and inflammation, such as accelerated skin aging, Alzheimer's disease, breast and prostate cancer, cardiovascular disease, dementia, depression, diabetes and osteoporosis.

Blended foods to try: Romesco Dipping Sauce with Tomatoes and Almonds (page 128); Guacamole with Tomatoes and Cilantro (page 141); Creamy Tomato Coconut Soup (page 154).

Purchasing tips: Choose tomatoes that have a rich color and a sweet, woody smell. They should have smooth skin with no cracks, bruises or soft spots.

The power of lycopene

Lycopene, a potent antioxidant and anti-inflammatory carotenoid, is found in fruits and vegetables with a red pigment, including tomatoes, watermelon and pink guava and grapefruit. It concentrates in the liver, blood, lungs, prostate, colon cells and skin, supporting their health.

WATERCRESS

Key nutrients: Fiber, folate, potassium, alpha- and beta-carotene, chlorophyll, glucosinolates, lutein and zeaxanthin, proanthocyanidins.

Health-promoting properties: The nutrients in watercress provide antioxidant protection from free radicals; have anti-inflammatory and antibacterial properties; promote regularity and support gut bacteria; balance blood sugar and blood lipids (cholesterol and triglycerides); maintain healthy blood pressure; support nerve transmission; lower homocysteine; support overall healthy gene expression and cell division; stimulate the conversion of carcinogens into less harmful compounds and facilitate their elimination; help to bind various carcinogens, providing overall general risk reduction; positively influence estrogen metabolism, helping to keep it and its metabolites within a healthy range; support overall liver health and its natural detoxification pathways; and reduce the risk for cancer, cardiovascular disease (CVD), dementia, insulin resistance and type 2 diabetes.

Health conditions that benefit: Atherosclerosis, constipation, diverticular disease, hemorrhoids and high blood pressure; any condition with underlying inflammation, such as age-related macular degeneration and cataracts, CVD and prediabetes and diabetes; may help treat *H. pylori* infection.

Blended foods to try: Oats, Greens and Matcha Smoothie Bowl (page 87); Land and Sea Green Smoothie with Chocolate and Berries (page 107); Pea Soup with Mushrooms, Watercress and Mint (page 155).

Purchasing tips: Choose watercress that is crisp and bright green, with no yellowing. Watercress is delicate and is best eaten within 1 day of purchase. Both the leaves and stems are edible, but the stems tend to get tougher later in the season.

LEGUMES

BLACK BEANS

Key nutrients: Protein, carbohydrate, fiber, vitamins B_1 and B_3, folate, vitamin E, calcium, iron, magnesium, phosphorus, potassium, zinc.

Health-promoting properties: The nutrients in black beans promote satiety and help convert food into energy; support the growth, maintenance and repair of muscles and other body tissues; slow age-related muscle loss (sarcopenia); help build bones and teeth; increase the number and diversity of gut bacteria; support bowel health and regularity; support the immune system; help to achieve and maintain healthy blood pressure; lower homocysteine; support the adrenal glands; protect fats, cell membranes and other body tissues from oxidation; lower inflammation; help produce healthy red blood cells and build iron stores in the bone marrow; support cognitive health, mood and normal stress response.

Health conditions that benefit: Cardiovascular disease, constipation, depression, dyslipidemia, diverticular disease, hemorrhoids, high blood pressure, overweight and obesity, metabolic syndrome, osteoporosis, prediabetes and diabetes, and sarcopenia.

Blended foods to try: Time-Out Black Bean Dip (page 134); Enchilada Sauce with Poblano Peppers and Black Beans (page 162).

Usage tips: If using canned beans, drain and rinse them until the water runs clear. If using dried beans, discard any that are split or cracked or have off-color spots.

CANNELLINI (WHITE KIDNEY) BEANS

Key nutrients: Protein, carbohydrate, fiber, vitamins B_1 and B_3, vitamin E, choline, calcium, copper, iron, magnesium, manganese, phosphorus, potassium, flavan-3-ols.

Health-promoting properties: The nutrients in white kidney beans promote satiety and help convert food into energy; support the growth, maintenance and repair of muscles and other body tissues; slow age-related muscle loss (sarcopenia); help build bones and teeth; provide bulk to stool, promoting regularity; support healthy glucose metabolism and blood sugar levels; lower cholesterol and blood pressure; are involved in the production of red blood cells; have antioxidant and anti-inflammatory properties; promote the production and support the function of neurotransmitters; support general cognitive health; support mood and normal stress response; support fetal development and a healthy pregnancy; support overall healthy gene expression and cell division; and reduce the risk for cancer.

Health conditions that benefit: Cardiovascular disease, constipation, dyslipidemia, hemorrhoids, high blood pressure, overweight and obesity, metabolic syndrome, osteoporosis, prediabetes and diabetes, and sarcopenia.

Blended foods to try: Spicy White Bean Dip (page 135); Avocado Almost-Vichyssoise (page 145); Tuscan White Bean Soup (page 159).

Usage tips: If using canned beans, drain and rinse them until the water runs clear. If using dried beans, discard any that are split or cracked or have off-color spots.

CHICKPEAS

Key nutrients: Protein, carbohydrate, fiber, vitamins B_3 and B_6, folate, calcium, iron, magnesium, manganese, phosphorus, potassium, zinc.

Health-promoting properties: The nutrients in chickpeas promote satiety, help control appetite and help convert food into energy; support the growth, maintenance and repair of muscles and other body tissues; help build bones and teeth; increase the number and diversity of gut bacteria; support bowel health and regularity; support the immune system; help to achieve and maintain healthy blood pressure; lower homocysteine; protect fats, cell membranes and other body tissues from oxidation; lower inflammation; help produce healthy red blood cells and build iron stores in the bone marrow; support cognitive health, mood and normal stress response; and support fetal development and a healthy pregnancy.

Health conditions that benefit: Cardiovascular disease, constipation, dyslipidemia, hemorrhoids, high blood pressure, metabolic syndrome, osteoporosis, overweight and obesity, and prediabetes and diabetes.

Blended foods to try: Chickpea and Yogurt Dip (page 136); Pesto Almond Hummus (page 138); Zesty Chickpea, Tomato and Mushroom Soup (page 158).

Usage tips: If using canned chickpeas, drain and rinse them until the water runs clear. If using dried chickpeas, discard any that are split or cracked or have off-color spots. (Note: Chickpeas may also be labeled "garbanzo beans.")

GREEN PEAS

Key nutrients: Protein, carbohydrate, fiber, vitamins B_1, B_3 and B_5, folate, choline, iron, magnesium, manganese, phosphorus, potassium, zinc, beta-carotene, lutein and zeaxanthin.

Health-promoting properties: The nutrients in split peas promote satiety, control appetite and help convert food into energy; support digestive health and maintain gut bacteria; support the growth, maintenance and repair of muscles and other body tissues; slow age-related muscle loss (sarcopenia); help build and maintain bones and teeth; help balance blood sugar and lipids (cholesterol and triglycerides); support insulin metabolism; lower blood pressure and homocysteine levels; support the adrenal glands; support skin health and wound repair; are involved in the production and function of neurotransmitters; support cognitive health, mood and normal stress response and may reduce symptoms of depression; and support fetal development and a healthy pregnancy.

Health conditions that benefit: Cardiovascular disease, constipation, diverticular disease, dyslipidemia, hemorrhoids, high blood pressure, metabolic syndrome, osteoporosis, overweight and obesity, and prediabetes and diabetes.

Blended foods to try: Pea Soup with Mushrooms, Watercress and Mint (page 155); Arugula and Sweet Pea Pesto (page 163); Zingy Green and Fruity Energy Boost (page 174).

Usage tips: Frozen sweet green peas are the most convenient choice for these recipes.

LENTILS

Key nutrients: Protein, carbohydrate, fiber, vitamins B_1, B_3 and B_6, folate, choline, calcium, copper, iron, magnesium, manganese, phosphorus, potassium, zinc.

Health-promoting properties: The nutrients in lentils promote satiety and help convert food into energy; support the growth, maintenance and repair of muscles and other body tissues;

slow age-related muscle loss (sarcopenia); help build bones and teeth; provide bulk to stool, promoting regularity; support healthy glucose metabolism and blood sugar levels; lower cholesterol and blood pressure; support the adrenal glands; are involved in the production of red blood cells; have antioxidant and anti-inflammatory properties; promote the production and support the function of neurotransmitters; support skin health and wound repair; support cognitive health, mood and normal stress response; support overall healthy gene expression and cell division; and reduce the risk for cancer.

Health conditions that benefit: Cardiovascular disease, constipation, depression, dyslipidemia, diverticular disease, hemorrhoids, high blood pressure, overweight and obesity, metabolic syndrome, osteoporosis, prediabetes and diabetes, and sarcopenia.

Blended foods to try: African-Inspired Lentil Dip (page 133); Red Lentil, Chickpea and Tomato Soup (page 157); Banana Coconut Lentil Balls (page 187).

Usage tips: Sort through dried lentils before use to choose lentils that are firm, are not shriveled and are uniform in color. Lentils come in a variety of colors with slightly different flavors. Store dried lentils in an airtight container in a cool, dry place for up to 1 year.

SOYBEANS

Key nutrients: Protein, carbohydrate, fiber, vitamins B_1 and B_3, folate, vitamin C, calcium, iron, magnesium, manganese, phosphorus, potassium, zinc, isoflavones.

Health-promoting properties: The nutrients in soybeans convert food into energy; help build and maintain muscles; provide bulk to stool, promoting regularity; increase satiety; help control appetite and may help with weight loss and maintenance; support healthy glucose metabolism and blood sugar levels; lower cholesterol and blood pressure; are involved in the production of red blood cells; support immune function; support skin health and wound repair, including collagen production; help build bones; have antioxidant, antihistamine and anti-inflammatory properties; help with healthy cell division and gene expression, reducing the risk for cancer; promote the production and support the function of neurotransmitters; support cognitive health, mood and normal stress response; and support fetal development and a healthy pregnancy.

Health conditions that benefit: Cardiovascular disease, constipation, dyslipidemia, hemorrhoids, high blood pressure, metabolic syndrome, osteoporosis, overweight and obesity, and prediabetes and diabetes.

Blended foods to try: Zesty Edamame Dip (page 179); Spaghetti Beanballs (page 181).

Usage tips: If using canned soybeans, drain and rinse them until the water runs clear. Unripened green soybeans are called edamame; look for shelled edamame in the frozen food section of the grocery store.

Isoflavones

Soybeans contain unique polyphenols called isoflavones that weakly mimic estrogen (in both men and women) and bind to estrogen receptors on body tissues. Isoflavones support cells that benefit from estrogen, such as bone and liver cells, and inhibit estrogen's activity in cells where estrogen can be a problem, such as reproductive tissue in the prostate, breast and uterus. Isoflavones from whole foods reduce the risk for hormone-dependent cancers, such as breast, endometrial and prostate; support bone health; and improve blood flow by reducing arterial stiffness and supporting blood vessel function.

SPLIT PEAS

Key nutrients: Protein, carbohydrate, fiber, vitamins B_1, B_3 and B_5, folate, choline, calcium, copper, iron, magnesium, manganese, phosphorus, potassium, zinc.

Health-promoting properties: The nutrients in split peas promote satiety, control appetite and help convert food into energy; support digestive health and maintain gut bacteria; support the growth, maintenance and repair of muscles and other body tissues; slow age-related muscle loss (sarcopenia); help build and maintain bones and teeth; help balance blood sugar and lipids (cholesterol and triglycerides); support insulin metabolism; lower blood pressure and homocysteine levels; support the adrenal glands; support skin health and wound repair; are involved in the production and function of neurotransmitters; support cognitive health, mood and normal stress response and may reduce symptoms of depression; and support fetal development and a healthy pregnancy.

Health conditions that benefit: Cardiovascular disease, constipation, diverticular disease, dyslipidemia, hemorrhoids, high blood pressure, metabolic syndrome, osteoporosis, overweight and obesity, and prediabetes and diabetes.

Blended foods to try: Yellow Split Pea and Pumpkin Soup (page 156).

Usage tips: Sort through dried yellow or green split peas before use to remove any foreign particles and choose peas that are uniform in color. Rinse and drain split peas before cooking.

GRAINS AND SEEDS

ROLLED OATS

Key nutrients: Protein, carbohydrate, fiber, iron, magnesium, phosphorus, potassium.

Health-promoting properties: The nutrients in oats support the growth, maintenance and repair of muscles and other body tissues; help to preserve muscle during weight loss and throughout the lifecycle; promote satiety and (with higher intakes) help one to achieve and maintain a healthy body weight; provide bulk to stool, promoting regularity; support healthy cholesterol and triglyceride levels; support the number and diversity of gut bacteria, which, in turn, support immune function and mood; aid in the production of red blood cells and in energy production; lower blood cholesterol and balance blood sugar by slowing the digestion of carbohydrate; lower and maintain healthy blood pressure; and support the development of healthy bones and teeth.

Health conditions that benefit: Dyslipidemia, high blood pressure, iron-deficiency anemia, kidney disease, metabolic syndrome, osteoporosis, overweight and obesity, prediabetes and diabetes, and sarcopenia.

Blended foods to try: Oatmeal, Peach and Yogurt Smoothie (page 72); Oats, Greens and Camu Camu Smoothie Bowl (page 86); Gooey Almond Oat Balls (page 186).

Purchasing tips: Choose large-flake (old-fashioned) rolled oats from a reliable source. Check the package to ensure there are no additional additives, such as sugars or flavoring. Do not use quick-cooking or instant oats, as they have gone through additional processing and will not have the same flavor and texture.

CHIA SEEDS

Key nutrients: Protein, alpha-linolenic acid, carbohydrate, fiber, vitamin B_3, calcium, copper, iron, magnesium, manganese, phosphorus, potassium, selenium, zinc.

Health-promoting properties: The nutrients in chia seeds support the growth, maintenance and repair of muscles and other body tissues; support the growth and maintenance of bone and teeth; help slow age-related muscle loss (sarcopenia) and bone loss; support mood; help convert food into energy; promote satiety and slow the digestion of carbohydrate; may help with weight control; support the immune system; lower cholesterol and blood pressure; balance blood sugar; reduce inflammation; help the liver with normal detoxification; support red blood cell, collagen and cartilage formation; help repair damaged ligaments, cartilage and tendons; support skin health and wound healing; assist in the production of glutathione (the "master antioxidant"); and reduce the risk for cardiovascular disease, colon and breast cancer, and type 2 diabetes.

Health conditions that benefit: Constipation, diverticulosis, dyslipidemia, essential fatty acid deficiencies, hemorrhoids, high blood pressure, low ferritin stores and iron deficiency, metabolic syndrome, prediabetes and diabetes, and sarcopenia.

Blended foods to try: Berrylicious Swiss Chard and Chia Smoothie (page 68); Tropical Kiwi, Coconut and Chia Seed Smoothie (page 101); Blueberry Chia Parfait (page 203).

Purchasing tips: Choose whole chia seeds that are either black (dark gray) or white (cream) in color to ensure the highest nutrient value. Brown or other colors can indicate immature chia seeds, or that there are other seeds mixed in.

FLAX SEEDS

Key nutrients: Protein, alpha-linolenic acid, fiber, vitamin E, manganese, potassium, enterolignans.

Health-promoting properties: The nutrients in flax seeds support the growth, maintenance and repair of muscles and other body tissues; promote satiety and slow digestion and stomach emptying; promote regularity; help one achieve and maintain a healthy body weight; lower blood sugar and insulin levels; lower cholesterol by binding bile; help the nerves and cells communicate via nerve impulses; lower blood pressure; reduce inflammation; prevent oxidation of the fats that make up cell membranes, myelin (the sheath that covers nerve tissues), proteins in the lens of the eye and lipoproteins (LDL and HDL cholesterol); help to inhibit damaging blood clotting, which

can interfere with healthy blood flow; have a potential role in maintaining peak bone health; and reduce the risk for cardiovascular disease (CVD) and hormone-associated cancers, such as breast, ovarian and prostate.

Health conditions that benefit: Age-related immune dysfunction, cataracts, CVD, dyslipidemia, essential fatty acid deficiencies, high blood pressure, metabolic syndrome, prediabetes and diabetes, and sarcopenia.

Blended foods to try: Protein Powerhouse with Blueberries and Flax Seeds (page 64); Apple, Blueberry and Kale with Flax Seeds (page 70); Pumpkin, Date and Flaxseed Smoothie (page 104).

Purchasing tips: Flax seeds can be purchased whole or ground (also called flaxseed meal). Smell flaxseed products before purchasing for rancidity, which will cause them to smell like oil-based paint. The nutrients in flax seeds are not accessible unless they are ground, but for the longest shelf life, you can purchase whole flax seeds and grind them in a coffee grinder or food processor just before use. Grind only as much as you need for a recipe. Whole flax seeds can be refrigerated in an airtight container for up to 1 year. Ground flax seeds can be stored in the freezer for up to 6 months.

GREEN PUMPKIN SEEDS (PEPITAS)

Key nutrients: Protein, fiber, vitamins B_3 and E, copper, iron, magnesium, manganese, phosphorus, potassium, zinc.

Health-promoting properties: The nutrients in green pumpkin seeds provide energy; support the growth, maintenance and repair of muscles and other body tissues; help to slow age-related muscle loss (sarcopenia); help repair damaged ligaments, cartilage and tendons; promote satiety and slow digestion and stomach emptying; promote regularity; may help with appetite and weight control; support the bowel's role in detoxification; lower blood sugar and insulin levels; lower cholesterol by binding bile; help the nerves and cells communicate via nerve impulses;

lower blood pressure; reduce inflammation; prevent oxidation of the fats that make up cell membranes, myelin (the sheath that covers nerve tissues), proteins in the lens of the eye and lipoproteins (LDL and HDL cholesterol); help to inhibit damaging blood clotting, which can interfere with healthy blood flow; promote healthy red blood cell formation, immune function and collagen production; support skin health and wound healing; are involved in neurotransmitter production and function; support mood and cognition; slow the progression of cataracts; and reduce the risk for cardiovascular disease, type 2 diabetes and dental caries.

Health conditions that benefit: Constipation, dyslipidemia, high blood pressure, low ferritin and risk of iron deficiency, metabolic syndrome, osteoporosis, prediabetes and diabetes, and sarcopenia.

Blended foods to try: Red and Green Smoothie with Pepitas (page 70); Roasted Pumpkin and Carrot Juice Soup (page 153); Nutty Date Truffles (page 209).

Purchasing tips: Choose shelled raw green pumpkin seeds that are completely green. Brown seeds are rancid. Green pumpkin seeds should have a light, nutty smell. Refrigerate seeds in an airtight container for up to 2 months.

HEMP SEEDS

Key nutrients: Protein, alpha-linolenic acid, fiber, vitamins B_1 and B_3, copper, iron, magnesium, manganese, phosphorus, potassium, zinc.

Health-promoting properties: The nutrients in hemp seeds support the growth, maintenance and repair of muscles and other body tissues; support the growth and maintenance of bone and teeth; help to slow age-related muscle loss (sarcopenia) and bone loss; support mood and cognition; help convert food into energy; promote satiety and slow the digestion of carbohydrate; may help with weight control; lower cholesterol and blood pressure; balance blood sugar; support red blood cell, collagen and cartilage formation; support skin health and wound healing; are involved in neurotransmitter production and function; and reduce the risk for cardiovascular disease, colon and breast cancer, and type 2 diabetes.

Health conditions that benefit: Constipation, diverticulosis, essential fatty acid deficiencies, hemorrhoids, high blood pressure, low ferritin stores and iron deficiency, prediabetes and diabetes, and sarcopenia.

Blended foods to try: Protein-Powered Kale, Berry, Hemp and Yogurt Smoothie (page 83); Pumpkin Cranberry Protein Smoothie (page 103); Spinach, Pineapple and Mint Smoothie (page 106)

Purchasing tips: For the best quality and taste, choose hemp seeds that are non-GMO and are certified organic. Hemp seeds should have a pleasing and slightly nutty taste. Canadian growers produce some of the highest-quality hemp seeds because of Canada's strict government regulations.

SUNFLOWER SEEDS

Key nutrients: Protein, fiber, vitamins B_3, B_5 and E, copper, iron, magnesium, manganese, phosphorus, potassium, zinc.

Health-promoting properties: The nutrients in sunflower seeds help convert food into energy; support the growth, maintenance and repair of muscles and other body tissues; help to slow age-related muscle loss (sarcopenia); help repair damaged ligaments, cartilage and tendons; slow digestion and stomach emptying; promote regularity; may help with appetite and weight control; support the bowel's role in detoxification; lower blood sugar and insulin levels; help the nerves and cells communicate via nerve impulses; lower blood pressure; reduce inflammation; support the adrenal glands; prevent oxidation of the fats that make up cell membranes, myelin (the sheath that covers nerve tissues), proteins in the lens of the eye and lipoproteins (LDL and HDL cholesterol); help to inhibit damaging blood clotting, which can interfere with healthy blood flow; promote healthy red blood cell formation, immune function and collagen production; support skin health and wound healing; are involved in neurotransmitter production and function; support mood and cognition; and reduce the risk for cardiovascular disease, type 2 diabetes and dental caries.

Health conditions that benefit: Cataracts, constipation, dyslipidemia, high blood pressure, low ferritin and risk of iron deficiency, metabolic syndrome, osteoporosis, prediabetes and diabetes, and sarcopenia.

Blended foods to try: Oats, Greens and Camu Camu Smoothie Bowl (page 86); Carrot Ginger Dressing (page 121); Gooey Almond Oat Balls (page 186).

Purchasing tips: Choose sunflower seeds that are raw, unflavored and additive-free. Use them raw or toast them at home to avoid the preservatives found in commercially processed roasted sunflower seeds.

NUTS AND NUT BUTTERS

ALMONDS AND ALMOND BUTTER

Key nutrients: Protein, fiber, vitamins B_2 and E, calcium, copper, magnesium, manganese, phosphorus, potassium.

Health-promoting properties: The nutrients in almonds help convert food into energy; support the growth, maintenance and repair of muscles and other body tissues; help to slow age-related muscle loss (sarcopenia); help repair damaged ligaments, cartilage and tendons; slow digestion and stomach emptying; promote regularity; may help with appetite and weight control; support the bowel's role in detoxification; lower blood sugar and insulin levels; play a role in lowering homocysteine levels; help the nerves and cells communicate via nerve impulses; lower blood pressure; reduce

inflammation; prevent oxidation of the fats that make up cell membranes, myelin (the sheath that covers nerve tissues), proteins in the lens of the eye and lipoproteins (LDL and HDL cholesterol); help to inhibit damaging blood clotting, which can interfere with healthy blood flow; promote healthy immune function and collagen production; support skin health and wound healing; are involved in neurotransmitter production and function; support mood and cognition; and reduce the risk for cardiovascular disease, type 2 diabetes and dental caries.

Health conditions that benefit: Cataracts, constipation, dyslipidemia, high blood pressure, low ferritin and risk of iron deficiency, metabolic syndrome, osteoporosis, prediabetes and diabetes, and sarcopenia.

Blended foods to try: Chai-Spiced Almond Cacao Smoothie (page 111); Greek-Inspired Almond "Feta" Vinaigrette (page 117); Sweet and Nutty Superfood Balls (page 208).

Purchasing tips: You can purchase almonds in the shell or shelled, with or without the skin. When you shake almonds in the shell, there should be no rattling sound, which indicates aging. Cut shelled almonds in half and check for solid white meat. Do not use if the center is yellowish or has a honeycomb texture. Store fresh almonds in an airtight container in the refrigerator or freezer for up to 2 years. Choose natural almond butter that is certified organic and is from a trusted source. Natural almond butter will most likely have been pasteurized, so it's not truly raw; nevertheless, this process is much better than roasting or treating with chemicals. Look carefully at the label to check for additional, and potentially undesirable, ingredients. A quality almond butter is brown, with some variations in coloring, and may have oils that have risen to the top of the jar.

CASHEWS AND CASHEW BUTTER

Key nutrients: Protein, copper, iron, magnesium, manganese, phosphorus, potassium, zinc.

Health-promoting properties: The nutrients in cashews promote satiety; provide amino acids for the growth and maintenance of muscle throughout the lifecycle; help prevent and slow age-related muscle loss (sarcopenia); help preserve bones and teeth; support age-related immune dysfunction; help lower blood pressure; support healthy blood sugar balance and insulin metabolism; provide structure to cell membranes and enable nerve impulses; promote red blood cell production and maintain iron stores in bone marrow; support healthy skin, collagen production and wound repair; support the repair of damaged ligaments, cartilage and tendons; and support neurotransmitter production and function.

Health conditions that benefit: Cardiovascular disease, dyslipidemia, high blood pressure, iron-deficiency anemia, metabolic disease, osteoporosis, prediabetes and diabetes, and sarcopenia.

Blended foods to try: Ayurveda-Inspired Chia Seed and Coconut Smoothie (page 100); Mint Cashew Cream Dip (page 132); Green Chocolate Milk (page 176).

Purchasing tips: Choose cashews that are raw, unflavored and additive-free. Cashews should be firm and slightly crunchy. They can be refrigerated up to 3 months and frozen for up to 6 months. Choose certified organic cashew butter that is made from raw cashews and is from a trusted source. Read the label to check for unwanted additives and preservatives. Cashew butter can be found in the condiments section or in the refrigerated area of your grocer and should be kept refrigerated once opened.

PEANUT BUTTER

Key nutrients: Protein, fiber, vitamins B_3 and E, magnesium, manganese, phosphorus, potassium.

Health-promoting properties: The nutrients in peanut butter help convert food into energy; support the growth, maintenance and repair of muscles and other body tissues; support the development of healthy bones and teeth; help to slow age-related muscle loss (sarcopenia); slow digestion and stomach emptying; promote regularity; support the bowel's role in detoxification; lower blood sugar and insulin levels; help the nerves and cells communicate via nerve impulses; lower blood pressure; prevent oxidation of the fats that make up cell membranes, myelin (the sheath that covers nerve tissues), proteins in the lens of the eye and lipoproteins (LDL and HDL cholesterol); help to inhibit damaging blood clotting, which can interfere with healthy blood flow; are involved in neurotransmitter production and function; help restore immune response in the elderly; may slow the progression of cardiovascular disease (CVD) and cataracts; and may help prevent dental caries.

Health conditions that benefit: Cataracts, CVD, high blood pressure, osteoporosis, prediabetes and diabetes, and sarcopenia.

Blended foods to try: Peanut Butter Chocolate Smoothie (page 108); Pineapple, Ginger and Peanut Butter Marinade (page 124); Sporty Peanut Butter Banana Smoothie (page 177).

Purchasing tips: Choose certified organic, natural peanut butter that is made from raw peanuts and is from a trusted source. Choose a butter without any added sugars or unwanted additives and preservatives.

CACAO, SPICES AND HERBS

CACAO POWDER AND NIBS

Key nutrients: Fiber, iron, magnesium, polyphenols.

Health-promoting properties: The nutrients in cacao products have antioxidant and anti-inflammatory properties; promote satiety and regularity; support gut health; support healthy blood sugar balance and insulin metabolism; lower and maintain blood pressure; positively influence gene expression and support communication between cells; and support healthy red blood cell production, helping to prevent fatigue and iron deficiency.

Health conditions that benefit:
Constipation, high blood pressure, iron-deficiency anemia, kidney disease, osteoporosis, prediabetes and diabetes, and stroke, as well as diseases with underlying inflammation and increased oxidation, such as arthritis, asthma, cardiovascular disease, depression, diabetes and lupus.

Blended foods to try: Chocolate and Almond Smoothie with Cacao Nibs (page 110); Chai-Spiced Almond Cacao Smoothie (page 111); Cacao Maple Oatmeal Malt (page 192).

CHICORY ROOT

Key nutrients: Vitamin K_1, beta-carotene, inulin and oligosaccharides, lutein and zeaxanthin, polyphenols.

Health-promoting properties: The nutrients in chicory root have antioxidant and anti-inflammatory properties; increase both the number and diversity of gut bacteria to improve overall digestive health; provide a source of energy for the cells of the colon; bind metal ions; enable appropriate coagulation of blood, to prevent excessive bleeding; organize mineral metabolism and support bone and tooth mineralization (including keeping calcium out of soft tissues, such as blood vessels and skin); maintain tooth enamel and support dental health; reduce the risk for, and may slow the progression of, atherosclerosis and advanced skin wrinkling; and reduce the risk for bone loss and osteoporosis.

Health conditions that benefit:
Atherosclerosis, inflammatory bowel disease (ulcerative colitis and Crohn's disease) when not in an active flare-up, irritable bowel syndrome, osteoporosis, as well as any condition in which significant inflammation and oxidative damage can occur, such as cardiovascular disease, cataracts, dementia, macular degeneration, prediabetes and diabetes and possibly autoimmune diseases like asthma and rheumatoid arthritis.

Blended foods to try: Iced Mocha Smoothie (page 85); Cold Beet Soup (page 147); Chocolate Pudding with Goji Berries (page 200).

CHILE PEPPERS

Key nutrients: Vitamin C, potassium, carotenoids, polyphenols.

Health-promoting properties: The nutrients in chile peppers have antioxidant and anti-inflammatory actions; enable collagen production, aiding repair of collagen-rich tissue, such as gums, teeth, bones, skin, ligaments, tendons and cartilage; support neurotransmitter production and function; improve and maintain blood vessel function; lower and maintain blood pressure; support immune function, the adrenal glands and appropriate stress responses; help the nerves and cells communicate via nerve impulses; help one manage acute and chronic stress; and reduce the risk for, and possibly the progression of, cataracts, heart disease, stroke, vascular dementia and some cancers (including stomach, lung and possibly breast).

Health conditions that benefit: Any disease with underlying inflammation and oxidation, such as cardiovascular disease, and prediabetes and diabetes.

Blended foods to try: Spicy Tomato Avocado Smoothie (page 105); Sweet Chile Dipping Sauce (page 127); Spicy Pumpkin Soup (page 149).

CILANTRO

Key nutrients: Beta-carotene, polyphenols.

Health-promoting properties: The nutrients in cilantro play a role in skin health and wound healing, including the maintenance of mucous membranes in the mouth, sinuses and digestive tract; have antioxidants and anti-inflammatory properties; support robust immune function; improve blood vessel function; are involved in the liver's normal detoxification pathways; support optimal vision; bind excess metals, such as copper and iron, reducing free radical production; support normal cell division and growth; support fetal development and a healthy pregnancy; and reduce the risk for cardiovascular disease, dementia, depression, diabetes and several cancers, including skin, breast, liver, colon and prostate.

Health conditions that benefit: Night blindness, wounds and any health condition with increased inflammation.

Blended foods to try: Cilantro Jalapeño Ranch Dressing (page 122); Creamy Beet, Ginger and Almond Dip (page 129); Guacamole with Tomatoes and Cilantro (page 141).

CINNAMON

Key nutrients: Polyphenols.

Health-promoting properties: The nutrients in cinnamon have antioxidant and anti-inflammatory properties; improve blood vessel function; bind excess metals, such as copper and iron, reducing free radical production; support normal cell division and growth; and are involved in the liver's normal detoxification pathways.

Health conditions that benefit: Any condition in which significant inflammation and oxidative damage can occur, such as cardiovascular disease, cataracts, dementia, macular degeneration, prediabetes and diabetes, and possibly autoimmune diseases like asthma and rheumatoid arthritis.

Blended foods to try: Blackberry Pear Smoothie (page 62); Berry Banana Smoothie Bowl (page 112); Mayan Chocolate Mango Maca Dessert (page 199).

GINGER

Key nutrients: Polyphenols.

Health-promoting properties: The nutrients in ginger have antioxidant and anti-inflammatory properties; improve blood vessel function; bind excess metals, such as copper and iron, reducing free radical production; support normal cell division and growth; and are involved in the liver's normal detoxification pathways.

Health conditions that benefit: Any condition in which significant inflammation and oxidative damage can occur, such as cardiovascular disease, cataracts, dementia, macular degeneration, prediabetes and diabetes, and possibly autoimmune diseases like asthma and rheumatoid arthritis.

Blended foods to try: Ginger, Lime and Arugula Pick-Me-Up (page 82); Chilled Avocado and Ginger Soup (page 144); Bountiful Berry Sorbet with Ginger and Mint (page 197).

MINT

Key nutrients: Potassium, beta-carotene, polyphenols.

Health-promoting properties: The nutrients in mint help the nerves and cells communicate via nerve impulses; improve blood vessel function and maintain healthy blood pressure and heartbeat; have antioxidant and anti-inflammatory properties; support the liver's normal detoxification pathways; and may reduce the risk for cardiovascular disease (CVD), kidney disease, kidney stones and possibly osteoporosis.

Health conditions that benefit: High blood pressure and associated conditions; any condition in which significant inflammation and oxidative damage can occur, such as cataracts, CVD, dementia, macular degeneration, and prediabetes and diabetes, and possibly autoimmune diseases like asthma and rheumatoid arthritis.

Blended foods to try: Spinach, Pineapple and Mint Smoothie (page 106); Mint Cashew Cream Dip (page 132); Pea Soup with Mushrooms, Watercress and Mint (page 155).

TURMERIC

Key nutrients: Iron, curcumin/curcuminoids.

Health-promoting properties: The nutrients in turmeric provide antioxidant power, both directly and indirectly by stimulating the production of other enzyme-based antioxidants, including glutathione; have potent anti-inflammatory abilities; support liver health and the liver's normal detoxification pathways; induce apoptosis, a programmed self-destruction of cells that helps prevent cells from growing out of control (a precursor to cancer); promote healthy blood vessel function and maintain healthy blood pressure; are involved in the production of red blood cells and maintain iron stores in the bone marrow; support cognition; may improve symptoms of depression; and may reduce the risk for and progression of colon cancer.

Health conditions that benefit: Iron-deficiency anemia; any disease with underlying inflammation, such as cardiovascular disease, diabetic kidney disease, lupus, prediabetes and diabetes and rheumatoid arthritis.

Blended foods to try: Ayurveda-Inspired Chia Seed and Coconut Smoothie (page 100); Spicy Spinach Cilantro Sauce (page 165); Exotic Mango, Banana and Avocado Pudding (page 199).

LIQUIDS

COCONUT WATER

Key nutrients: Vitamin C, potassium.

Health-promoting properties: The nutrients in coconut water help the nerves and cells communicate via nerve impulses; improve blood vessel function and maintain healthy blood pressure and heartbeat; protect proteins, fats and carbohydrates, as well as DNA and genes, from oxidation; reduce overall oxidative damage and inflammation; support the production and function of collagen and neurotransmitters; reduce the risk for kidney disease, kidney stones and possibly osteoporosis, as well as some cancers, including stomach, lung and possibly breast; and may help prevent cardiovascular disease (CVD) by inhibiting LDL cholesterol oxidation and lowering blood pressure.

Health conditions that benefit: High blood pressure and associated conditions; any condition with underlying inflammation, such as arthritis, CVD and diabetes.

Blended foods to try: Tropical Kiwi, Coconut and Chia Seed Smoothie (page 101); Strawberry Almond Dressing (page 120); Triple-Berry Sauce (page 166).

KEFIR

Key nutrients: Protein, carbohydrate, vitamins A, B_2, B_5 and D, calcium, magnesium, phosphorus, potassium, probiotic bacteria.

Health-promoting properties: The nutrients in kefir help convert food into energy; provide all of the essential amino acids needed for growth, repair and maintenance of body tissues; help to slow age-related muscle loss (sarcopenia) and preserve muscle during weight loss; can help one achieve and maintain a healthy body weight (with higher intakes); help to lower and maintain blood pressure and cholesterol; help one achieve and maintain healthy bone mass throughout life; can slow bone loss and support osteoporosis treatment when combined with extra vitamin D and magnesium; support healthy skin, mucous membranes and vision, especially night vision; enable the body to absorb calcium, phosphorus and magnesium; support mood, immune function and overall gut and digestive health; and can help prevent rickets and treat early rickets.

Health conditions that benefit: High blood pressure and associated conditions, osteoporosis, overweight and obesity, rickets and sarcopenia.

Blended foods to try: Red Grape, Peach and Raspberry Smoothie (page 69); Cold Beet Soup (page 147); Peppermint Patty Shake (page 190).

Nondairy milks

The nutrients in nondairy milks, such as almond, cashew, hazelnut, hemp or soy milk, vary with the product. Some are fortified with micronutrients such as zinc, calcium, vitamin D_2 and vitamin B_{12}. The fat profile varies among products. The only product with a reasonable amount of protein is soy milk. These milks are a good choice for vegans and people with a milk allergy or lactose intolerance.

MILK

Key nutrients: Protein, carbohydrate, vitamins A, B_2, B_5 and D, calcium, magnesium, phosphorus, potassium.

Health-promoting properties: The nutrients in milk help convert food into energy; provide all of the essential amino acids needed for growth, repair and maintenance of body tissues; help to slow age-related muscle loss (sarcopenia) and preserve muscle during weight loss; can help one achieve and maintain a healthy body weight (with higher intakes); help one achieve and maintain healthy blood pressure and bone mass throughout life; can slow bone loss and support osteoporosis treatment when combined with extra vitamin D and magnesium; and support healthy mucous membranes, healthy skin, the immune system and wound repair.

Health conditions that benefit: High blood pressure and associated conditions, osteoporosis, overweight and obesity, and sarcopenia.

Blended foods to try: Creamy Banana, Blueberry and Papaya Smoothie (page 74); Protein-Powered Kale, Berry, Hemp and Yogurt Smoothie (page 83); Triple-Threat Protein and Berry Smoothie (page 169).

TEA (BLACK, GREEN, OOLONG, WHITE)

Key nutrients: Fluoride, manganese, polyphenols.

Health-promoting properties: The nutrients in tea have antioxidant and anti-inflammatory properties; support liver health and disease management and the natural detoxification pathways in the liver; help bind excess metals, such as iron and copper, to reduce excessive oxidation and tissue damage; in combination with calcium and phosphorus, support optimal bone and tooth structure and enamel development; support numerous metabolic functions involved in energy metabolism, cartilage development and

wound repair; provide neuroprotection to help maintain cognitive function; positively modify genes to help fight cancer, cardiovascular disease (CVD) and diabetes; and may benefit blood sugar management in diabetes by supporting glucose metabolism.

Health conditions that benefit: Any condition with underlying inflammation, such as cancer, CVD and diabetes.

Blended foods to try: Strawberry, Camu Camu and Oolong Smoothie (page 93); Spicy White Bean Dip (page 135); Bountiful Berry Sorbet with Ginger and Mint (page 197).

PROTEIN FOODS

EGG WHITES (PASTEURIZED)

Key nutrient: Protein.

Health-promoting properties: The complete protein in egg whites provides all of the essential amino acids needed for growth, repair and maintenance of body tissues; helps to slow age-related muscle loss (sarcopenia) and preserve muscle during weight loss; promotes satiety; and (with higher intakes) can help one achieve and maintain a healthy weight.

Health conditions that benefit: Overweight and obesity, and sarcopenia.

Blended foods to try: Berry and Protein-Powered Greens (page 94); Cilantro Jalapeño Ranch Dressing (page 122); Blueberry Chia Parfait (page 203).

VEGAN PROTEIN POWDER (BROWN RICE, HEMP, PEA OR BLENDS)

Key nutrients: All have protein, carbohydrate, fiber, potassium; other nutrients vary.

Health-promoting properties: The nutrients in vegan protein powder help convert food into energy; provide all of the essential amino acids needed for growth, repair and maintenance of body tissues; help to slow age-related muscle loss (sarcopenia) and preserve muscle during weight loss; promote satiety and (with higher intakes) can help one achieve and maintain a healthy body weight; provide bulk to stool and support regularity; increase the number and diversity of gut bacteria, supporting gut health, immune function and mood; lower blood cholesterol and balance blood sugar by slowing the digestion of carbohydrate; lower and maintain blood pressure; and reduce the risk for cardiovascular disease, prediabetes and diabetes.

Health conditions that benefit: Constipation, diverticulosis, hemorrhoids, high blood pressure, overweight and obesity, and sarcopenia.

Blended foods to try: Kiwi, Goji Berry and Cacao Green Smoothie (page 78 with optional boost); Sporty Peanut Butter Banana Smoothie (page 177); Bountiful Berry, Spinach and Cashew Smoothie Bowl (page 178).

WHEY PROTEIN POWDER

Key nutrients: Protein, branched-chain amino acids, vitamins B_1, B_2 and B_5, calcium, magnesium, phosphorus, potassium, zinc.

Health-promoting properties: The nutrients in whey protein powder reduce inflammation and oxidative damage by increasing the body's production of glutathione; help convert food into energy; provide all of the essential amino acids needed for growth, repair and maintenance of body tissues; increase energy during exercise; help to slow age-related muscle loss (sarcopenia) and preserve muscle during weight loss; promote satiety and (with higher intakes) can help one achieve and maintain a healthy body weight; support bone development, health and density; lower blood pressure; support skin health and wound repair; support the adrenal glands; and

support the metabolism of cholesterol and several hormones.

Health conditions that benefit: High blood pressure, osteoporosis, overweight and obesity, and sarcopenia, as well as conditions with increased inflammation and oxidation, such as cardiovascular disease, diabetes, HIV and impaired immune function.

Blended foods to try: Blueberry and Coconut Protein Smoothie (page 63); Simply Satisfying Blueberry Mango Smoothie (page 91); Creamy Kale and Feta Dip (page 131 with optional boost).

YOGURT (REGULAR AND GREEK)

Key nutrients: Protein, carbohydrate, vitamins B_2 and B_5, calcium, magnesium, phosphorus, potassium; some may have probiotic bacteria.

Health-promoting properties: The nutrients in yogurt help convert food into energy; provide all of the essential amino acids needed for growth, repair and maintenance of body tissues; help to slow age-related muscle loss (sarcopenia) and preserve muscle during weight loss; promote satiety and (with higher intakes) can help one achieve and maintain a healthy body weight; lower and maintain blood pressure; support the development and maintenance of bones and teeth and slow bone loss; support and promote healthy gut bacteria if the yogurt contains "live bacteria cultures"; and support the adrenal glands.

Health conditions that benefit: High blood pressure and associated diseases, osteoporosis, overweight and obesity, sarcopenia.

Blended foods to try: Refreshing Mango, Strawberry and Carrot Smoothie (page 97); Tex-Mex Salad Dressing (page 123); Chilled Avocado and Ginger Soup (page 144).

Nutrition boosters

- **Açaí powder:** Açaí has an intense flavor that some describe as a blend of chocolate and blackberry. It is a source of linoleic acid (an omega-6 fat) and oleic acid (a monounsaturated fat) and is concentrated in omega-3s. It has a high concentration of flavonoids, which have been shown to reduce the risk for cardiovascular disease, lessen inflammation and protect blood vessels from damage. Improved blood vessel health and reduced inflammation may help support healthy moods and reduce the risk for depression. Protecting the blood vessels in the brain may help reduce the risk for dementia. *Key nutrients:* Omega-6 fatty acids, flavonoids.

- **Camu camu powder:** Camu camu contains beta-carotene and has a high concentration of vitamin C. Higher intakes of vitamin C from both food and supplements have been shown to reduce the risk for cardiovascular disease and cataracts, improve mood and reduce inflammation. Through its role in collagen production, vitamin C supports healthy skin and wound repair, and helps build and maintain healthy bones and teeth. *Key nutrients:* Vitamin C, beta-carotene.

- **Maca powder:** Maca has been called "Peruvian ginseng," and research supports a potentially similar adaptogenic role. (In herbal medicine, an adaptogen helps stabilize physiological processes by achieving and maintaining homeostasis, primarily with respect to the stress response.) Traditionally, maca has been used to treat fatigue and improve stamina, athletic performance, memory, libido and longevity, as well as to balance male and female hormone levels. While research is inconclusive, there is no doubt that maca is a nutritious food, containing several different types of fatty acids, amino acids, vitamins, minerals and numerous phytonutrients. *Key nutrients:* Fiber, folate, potassium, alpha- and beta-carotene, lutein/zeaxanthin, proanthocyanidins.

- **Matcha powder:** Matcha is a variety of high-quality green tea used in traditional South Asian tea ceremonies. Because it is so finely ground, the whole tea leaf is consumed, offering a concentrated source of antioxidants, including polyphenols. Research has shown that tea polyphenols play a beneficial role in the reduction and management of cardiovascular disease, type 2 diabetes, cancer and kidney stones, and help support mood, cognitive function, bone health and dental health. *Key nutrients:* Fluoride, carotenoids, polyphenols (flavonoids).

- **Pomegranate powder:** Pomegranate powder is high in the polyphenol proanthocyanidin, as well as the carotenoids alpha- and beta-carotene, lutein and zeaxanthin, which help to protect the eyes and blood vessels, reduce inflammation and support healthy skin. Its potassium helps reduce the risk for kidney stones and lowers blood pressure, which may reduce the risk for heart disease and stroke. Pomegranate powder is quite tart, so it's important not to overdo it if you add it as a booster. *Key nutrients:* Fiber, folate, potassium, alpha- and beta-carotene, lutein and zeaxanthin, proanthocyanidins.

- **Wheat germ:** Wheat germ is the most vitamin- and mineral-rich part of the wheat grain. It is rich in the minerals phosphorus and potassium and is a good source of vitamin E. Phosphorus is needed for healthy bones and teeth and is the main mineral used to make adenosine triphosphate (ATP), the most important energy-producing molecule in the body. Potassium helps lower blood pressure and is needed for neurotransmitter production. Vitamin E is an important fat-soluble antioxidant found in all cell membranes. *Key nutrients:* Vitamin E, phosphorus, potassium.

CHAPTER 3

The Health Benefits of Blended Foods

At its most fundamental level, the human body is a mass of elements that come together in complex molecules, compounds and structures to form cells, tissues and organs that work almost magically in concert to create our physical, psychological and emotional experience. In order for this to happen, the body needs a steady supply of nutrients, including protein, fat, carbohydrate, vitamins, minerals, water, electrolytes and phytonutrients — the building blocks of optimal structural and functional health.

Ensuring that the body gets the nutrition it needs helps to keep it healthy throughout life. Optimal nutrition has been shown to improve overall general health and energy levels, reduce the risk for degenerative chronic diseases, improve mood and other parameters of mental health, and help older adults maintain independence. In addition, diets based on minimally processed, nutrient-dense whole foods improve *quality* of life, helping people live not just longer, but also better — that is, they increase "health span," not just lifespan.

Adding blended foods to your diet is a great way to support your health goals, because you can squeeze a lot of high-quality foods into one great-tasting, nutritious and convenient meal or snack. Blended foods made from nutrient-dense whole foods can help you meet the recommended intakes of fruits, vegetables, grains, nuts and seeds consistently, day after day.

Are you ready to take your diet to the next level and experience the health benefits of blended foods?

General health benefits

Eating well for specific health goals is easy when you understand how to leverage certain foods and nutrients to your advantage. As part of a comprehensive approach to health, the recipes in this book, and the superfoods they're made with, can help you increase your health span and look and feel your best on a daily basis.

INCREASED ENERGY

When people talk about having energy, they are typically referring to a sense of "get-up-and-go": being able to be focused and think clearly, and being able to set out a task and have the oomph to see it through without feeling drained. When we feel like we don't have enough energy, it is really a symptom of poor energy output at the cellular level. Without a steady supply of the nutrients that are used to make energy — fat, carbohydrate and, to a lesser extent, protein — and the vitamins and minerals needed to support energy production, we start to feel sluggish, tired and moody, with a corresponding decrease in concentration.

A nutrient-dense diet

Research is clear that it is overall diet that influences nutritional health and well-being. In other words, it is the majority of your dietary choices that either moves you toward health or away from it; it's your nutritional bottom line that matters. While there is no one food that has it all when it comes to improving and maintaining health, reducing disease risk and managing disease, there are many foods that offer a lot of nutritional bang for the buck. These "superfoods" not only pack a lot nutrients into a serving, but also offer plenty of phytonutrients to help lessen the negative impact of chronic health conditions.

"Lack of energy" is a vague term and a nonspecific symptom, and to address it effectively we need to get to the root of the problem. A lack of energy may be caused by nutrient deficiencies. For example, insufficient iron, copper, vitamin B_{12}, vitamin B_6 and folate can lead to anemia; low vitamin D can cause muscle fatigue and aches; and inadequate intake of magnesium can decrease sleep quality. Lethargy or weariness can also be caused by a low mood, low motivation, boredom, apathy, depression, being overworked, stress, lack of exercise or inadequate sleep.

The key to lasting energy on all fronts is to make sure you are feeding your body the fuel and nutrients needed for energy production. A good rule of thumb is to try not to go longer than 4 hours or so in between meals and snacks, to help keep blood sugar balanced through the day. Meals and snacks that combine fat, protein and fiber-rich carbohydrates will help you feel full longer and provide lasting energy, but even fiber-rich foods on their own can do the trick.

Because the recipes in this book are made with whole foods, all of the fiber is retained, so they're a great choice for helping to fill those between-meal gaps. Most of them also provide protein and healthy fats, for the ultimate energy boost. Many of the smoothies and soups can even be considered meals on their own. And you get all this in a quickly prepared, easy-to-consume, portable package, to help you power through your day.

IMMUNE SUPPORT

The immune system includes the tonsils and adenoids, lymph nodes and vessels, thymus, spleen, bone marrow and several different types of white blood cells, which all work together in complex biological processes to protect us from disease and infections from viruses, bacteria, parasites, yeasts, molds and more. To function properly, the immune system relies on protein, carbohydrate and fat, as well as nearly every vitamin and mineral needed for human health.

Overreliance on caffeine and sugar

When we feel low in energy, we often reach for a cup of coffee or a piece of candy. Caffeine and sugar do help matters for a while: both can temporarily lift mood by increasing the production of feel-good neurotransmitters, such as dopamine and serotonin. Caffeine also lifts mood and increases energy by stimulating the release of endorphins, cortisol and norepinephrine (noradrenalin). There's nothing wrong with drinking a cup or two of coffee or eating a snack; in fact, maintaining a balanced blood sugar level is one of the best ways to sustain physical and mental energy. But you'll get better, longer-lasting results from a nutrient-rich smoothie, dip or soup than you will from overconsumption of caffeine or a sugar-laden snack. So don't rely too heavily on caffeine and sugar — they may give you a temporary lift, but they're no replacement for the energy provided by real, whole foods.

The overall quality of your daily diet has a direct impact on how well your immune system is able to respond to a potential pathogen or early cancer cells. Worldwide, malnutrition is the primary cause of immunodeficiency. And while we often think of malnutrition as being a problem only in the developing world, it is seen in varying degrees in industrialized countries, too. Certain subpopulations, in particular — people on a limited income, the elderly and hospitalized individuals — are at increased risk of malnutrition and, in turn, poor immune function. Marginal deficiencies are seen in those whose diets do not supply an adequate amount of the nutrients that support the immune system, leading to chronic infections or acute respiratory diseases (such as the common cold or influenza). In addition, recovery from illness or infection can be delayed and compromised by a blunted immune response. Illness often results in decreased appetite and reduced food intake, leading to further malnutrition.

Maintaining a robust immune system requires good-quality nutrition. Most people get enough protein and calories, two fundamental requirements for the immune system. But research shows that many of us miss the mark when it comes to getting the minimum recommended amount of several necessary vitamins and minerals, including vitamins A, B_6, C, D and E, folate and the minerals iron and zinc. Even marginal deficiencies can adversely affect immune health, increasing the risk for illness and infections.

Blended foods are, by definition, a blend of many different ingredients, and when you choose a variety of plant-based foods to create your smoothies, dips, soups and sauces, it becomes easy to ensure adequate intake of all of the essential nutrients.

INCREASED LONGEVITY

Human life expectancy has steadily increased over the past couple of centuries thanks to better nutrition, clean water, vaccines and better treatment of chronic conditions, and this trend is expected to continue. Study after study clearly shows that the key to living longer and living better is a diet based on a variety of nutrient-dense whole foods, including plenty of plant foods but also minimally processed animal foods. You don't need to eat a completely vegetarian diet; simply increasing the amount and variety of plant-based foods in your diet will allow you to experience their benefits.

A diet based on whole foods tends to be significantly lower in calories, refined sugars, industrial trans and other processed fats, artificial flavors and preservatives, and has a lot more fiber, vitamins, minerals and phytonutrients. This way of eating is consistently associated with lower rates of chronic degenerative diseases (the diseases of aging), such as cardiovascular disease, certain cancers, diabetes, respiratory disease, high blood pressure, dementia and Alzheimer's disease.

By increasing your consumption of nutritious foods, the recipes in this book will ensure that you're getting an abundance of the nutrients that have been shown to reduce the risk for chronic diseases that can lead to premature death or decreased quality of life.

Functional status

As we age, we want to extend not only our longevity but also our functional status: our ability to perform the normal daily activities required to meet our basic needs (such as bathing and shopping) and maintain our health and well-being. Good nutrition is the key to both longevity and prolonged functional status.

MOOD SUPPORT

Optimal mood depends on optimal brain cell structure and function. Brain cells use glucose, primarily from carbohydrate, as fuel. They also need a steady supply of the omega-3 fats EPA and DHA, amino acids (which are supplied by the digestion of protein) and a host of micronutrients that support neurotransmitter production and function, including the B complex vitamins, vitamins C and D, and the minerals iodine, iron, magnesium, selenium and zinc.

It's easy to pack blended foods with ingredients that are rich in these mood-supporting nutrients, ensuring that you're getting the nutrients your brain needs to maintain your mental health.

RADIANT SKIN

The skin is the largest organ in the body and, as with any organ, what we eat, drink and expose it to will influence its health — and, in this particular example, its appearance. But taking care of your skin isn't just about keeping it looking good; it's about keeping it healthy, so it can function optimally, providing you with protection from injury and a first line of defense against bacteria and viruses while regulating your temperature, helping you to sense your surroundings through your sense of touch, and producing vitamin D and cholesterol.

Many of us avoid excessive sun exposure and wear sunscreen to prevent burning and lower the risk for skin cancer, but we may not think of food as having a significant impact on skin health. Yet nutrition is a big player when it comes to skin that is healthy, radiant, supple and hydrated. In a process called cell turnover, new skin cells form in the lower layers of the epidermis and migrate to the surface. Underneath the epidermis is the dermis, a fibrous network of tissues where the supporting and structural proteins collagen and elastin are made. Both skin cells and the dermis need a steady supply of several different nutrients for optimal cell turnover and collagen and elastin production:

▸ **Vitamin A** helps newly forming skin cells differentiate into mature skin cells. A classic sign of poor vitamin A intake is scaly, rough and dry skin, so it's important to get a source of vitamin A in the diet.

▸ **Zinc** is involved in wound healing, including any kind of skin damage. In addition, it supports the immune system in fighting off skin infections and is needed for the synthesis of collagen and elastin. Working with vitamin A, zinc helps to support cell turnover and skin renewal. Zinc is also involved with the proteins that transport vitamin A in the blood and can help to maintain optimal blood levels of vitamin A.

▸ The **carotenoids** alpha- and beta-carotene, lutein, zeaxanthin and lycopene have all been shown to modestly protect the skin from UV damage. Because they are fat-soluble, these carotenoids accumulate in the fat layer underneath our dermis and, as powerful antioxidants, help to filter out UVA and UVB rays.

▸ **Vitamin C** wears a few hats when it comes to skin health: it is a versatile antioxidant, has anti-inflammatory properties and is crucial to collagen production. The hallmark of acute vitamin C deficiency (scurvy) is bruising, leaky blood vessels and capillaries, and swollen and bleeding gums, precisely because of insufficient collagen production.

▸ **Sulfur** is an often overlooked mineral, despite being the third most abundant mineral in the body. It is critical for collagen production and works with the mineral selenium to produce glutathione, one of the most important antioxidants in the body. Glutathione helps to neutralize free radicals in all cells, including skin cells, and is involved in tempering inflammation, which may improve symptoms of inflammatory skin conditions.

▸ **Polyphenols**, a broad category of phytonutrients found in fruits, vegetables, legumes, nuts, seeds, tea, herbs and spices, have been shown to benefit skin by offering protection against the incidental damaging effects of sunlight, such as collagen and elastin breakdown, UV-induced inflammation, skin cell proliferation, DNA damage that may increase the risk for skin cancer, and UV-induced suppression of the immune system.

The recipes in this book include a variety of foods that supply these nutrients, for skin that not only looks its best but is in the best shape to carry out all of its important functions.

Prevention and management of health conditions

In addition to their general health benefits, the recipes in this book can play an important role in reducing your risk for many common chronic diseases and managing any current health conditions. Our recipes are packed full of superfoods, which are likewise packed full of nutrients. Here's how our bodies use those nutrients to help us stay strong, ward off illnesses and recover from or manage disease.

ADDICTIONS

Alcohol and drug addiction take a toll on health. That's obvious. But many of us don't realize how significantly substance abuse contributes to malnutrition. Substance abuse can lead to a decrease in eating, sometimes for very long periods of time. It's not uncommon to hear people say they can go for several days with little to no food. Stimulant drugs can nearly eradicate appetite and hunger, while alcohol can displace food. Because alcohol has calories, people dealing with alcohol addiction can go several days without eating, or eating only one meal a day, and because they are getting some energy from the alcohol, they won't feel the fatigue caused by a lack of fuel.

People dealing with addictions actually need *more* nutrients to support the process of detoxification in the liver and to help repair damaged cells and tissues throughout the body. Unfortunately, alcohol and drugs impede nutrient absorption. Long-term use of these substances can cause inflammation in the digestive tract and damage the villi and microvilli (the absorptive structures of the small intestine). In turn, the decrease in food intake and absorption of nutrients impedes the day-to-day repair and maintenance of the very structures involved in absorption, leading to a vicious cycle. Substance abuse can also cause vomiting, diarrhea and increased urination, which exacerbate nutrient loss.

All of these complications of substance abuse lead to a widening gap between what the body needs to be at its best and what it's actually getting. But people recovering from addiction can take heart: once the substance is flushed from the body and quality nutrition is introduced, substantial healing and repair can, and do, occur.

Treatment, management and recovery

At every stage of addiction treatment, nutrition is an important contributor to successful physical, emotional and psychological recovery. Proper nutrition provides the body with the building blocks it needs for repair. Protein is needed to rebuild any muscle loss due to poor eating habits or prolonged periods of not eating, and protein also provides amino acids, which are the building blocks of neurotransmitters. Carbohydrate provides much-needed fuel for muscles, the nervous system and the brain, helping to improve and stabilize mood.

One of the more important roles of nutrition in addiction recovery is its impact on the health of the brain, both in terms of its structure and its function. The brain is very sensitive to what we eat and drink. Most of the dry weight of the brain is fat, with the remainder being water and protein. Ensuring that the diet has an appropriate amount of fat, with an emphasis on omega-3 fatty acids, will help to replenish the fatty acids that make up a significant part of the total fat in the brain.

Other key nutrients are the B vitamins. While all are important, when it comes to brain health and addiction recovery, thiamin (B_1), niacin (B_3), pyridoxine (B_6), folate (B_9), cobalamin (B_{12}) and choline stand out. The B vitamins, along with vitamin C, are water-soluble and need to be replaced daily, and are very sensitive to increased loss due to substance use. These and other nutrients, such as the minerals magnesium, copper, zinc, iron, selenium and iodine, are all needed for optimal neurotransmitter production and function, and therefore affect mood.

BONE AND TOOTH HEALTH

Bones and teeth are living tissues that are constantly being remodeled, with old tissue breaking down and being replaced by new tissue. This highly orchestrated process relies on a steady supply of bone- and tooth-building nutrients — not just calcium, but also phosphorus, magnesium, zinc, boron and vitamin D, as well as the supporting nutrients vitamins A, B_{12} and C, protein, potassium and lycopene. Sadly, many of us miss the mark when it comes to meeting the recommended minimum intake of these nutrients.

Bones and dentin (which lies under the enamel in teeth) are formed when strands of collagen are twisted together in a braid-like formation called a triple helix. This structure allows for bones' flexibility — they may seem like rigid structures, but they are capable of bending; if they didn't, they would snap under pressure and not allow us to move as we do. As the collagen framework forms, a specialized mineral cladding called hydroxyapatite, comprised of calcium and phosphorus, is laid down, helping to give bones and teeth their rigidity and strength. Thus, calcium and phosphorus are critical to healthy bones and teeth.

Magnesium plays a couple of roles in bone and tooth development. As a mineral, it becomes part of the structure of bones and teeth; as a cofactor in mineral metabolism, it works with zinc and boron to facilitate the physiological reactions of other nutrients needed for tissue development.

Vitamin A supports vitamin D, which enables the body to absorb dietary calcium, phosphorus and magnesium. Vitamin B_{12} can help lower and/or keep levels of homocysteine within a healthy range; elevated levels of homocysteine (an otherwise harmless amino acid produced as part of normal protein metabolism) are associated with increased bone loss. Vitamin C is essential for collagen production, without which the strength of bones and teeth will be compromised.

Protein is an essential source of the amino acids needed for collagen production. In fact, protein makes up about 50% of total bone volume, with minerals comprising the balance. Just like muscles, bones are a protein-based tissue.

Potassium and lycopene help prevent accelerated bone loss by tempering the rate of bone turnover. When the rate of bone breakdown is greater than the rate of new bone tissue formation, there is a net loss, and over time, bone mineral density suffers.

Osteopenia and osteoporosis

Osteopenia refers to bone density that is lower than the average peak bone density in the general public. Peak bone density is the amount of bone tissue a person has between the ages of 25 and 30, when bone density is at its highest. After the age of 30, everyone starts to lose bone tissue as a normal part of aging. The lower bone density seen in osteopenia is not low enough to be classified as osteoporosis, but osteopenia is a risk factor for osteoporosis.

Osteoporosis is characterized by deterioration of bone tissue, leading to low bone mass and increasing susceptibility to bone fractures because of increased bone fragility. Fractures associated with osteoporosis are more common than heart attacks, breast cancer and stroke combined. While osteoporosis is more prevalent in women, with one in three suffering an osteoporotic fracture in their lifetime, one in five men will also be affected.

BRAIN HEALTH

The human brain has about 84 billion neurons, or brain cells, and 100 trillion synapses, the part of neurons where neurotransmitters are produced. Neurotransmitters work to regulate mood, consolidate memory and more.

Although the brain makes up only about 2% of our body weight, it accounts for about 20% to 25% of our total metabolic demands; in this sense, it is a little greedy. While there's still lots to learn about the brain, we do know that what we eat and drink affects its structure and, in turn, its structure influences its function.

Dementia

Brain health largely depends on the health of the blood vessels that nourish it. Vascular dementia is a decline in cognitive skills caused by reductions in the flow of blood, and therefore oxygen and nutrients, to the neurons. Inadequate blood flow can lead to damaged tissues — in this case, neurons — and because the brain has a huge network of blood vessels, it's especially vulnerable. Alzheimer's disease is a form of dementia that causes problems with memory, thinking and behavior. It accounts for 60% to 80% of dementia cases. Alzheimer's is not considered a normal part of aging, but rather a combination of genetic susceptibility, lifestyle choices (including diet) and environmental factors. A hallmark of Alzheimer's is insulin resistance of the brain; it was this observation that lead to it being called "type 3 diabetes," a term coined in 2005.

A healthy diet can reduce the risk for dementia in several ways. First, it can help prevent overweight and obesity, or help with weight loss. Dementia, including Alzheimer's disease, is associated with overweight and obesity, insulin resistance, diabetes, high blood pressure and dyslipidemia (an imbalance of blood fats, such as triglycerides and HDL and LDL cholesterol). A nutrient-dense diet also provides brain-supportive nutrients such as omega-3 fatty acids, antioxidants, B vitamins (especially B_6, folate, B_{12} and choline), magnesium and selenium. It is estimated that a diet that includes plenty of fruits, vegetables, nuts, seeds, legumes, whole grains, fish and antioxidant-rich herbs and spices can reduce the risk for type 2 diabetes by 90% and Alzheimer's by 40% — something no medication can boast.

CANCER

According to the World Health Organization, the World Cancer Research Fund and the American Institute for Cancer Research, between 67% and 72% of cancer cases are preventable, and prevention offers the most cost-effective long-term strategy for the control of cancer.

Several of the risk factors for cancer — tobacco use, obesity, lack of activity, alcohol use, occupational exposures and UV exposure — are within our individual control, for the most part. However, there's no denying that some cancer risk is out of our control. Even with the best-laid plans for healthy living, you may still develop cancer. But you *can* significantly reduce your risk.

Prevention

The joint World Cancer Research Fund and American Institute for Cancer Research report *Food, Nutrition, Physical Activity and the Prevention of Cancer: A Global Perspective* is a comprehensive review of 7,000 rigorously designed scientific studies by 21 world-renowned scientists, who distilled the findings into nine general recommendations:

1. Be as lean as possible without becoming underweight.
2. Be physically active for at least 30 minutes every day. Limit sedentary behavior.
3. Avoid sugary drinks and limit consumption of calorie-rich foods.
4. Eat more of a variety of vegetables, fruits, legumes and 100% whole grains.
5. Limit consumption of red meats and processed meats.

6. Limit alcoholic drinks (if consumed at all) to two per day for men and one per day for women.
7. Limit consumption of high-sodium foods and highly processed foods.
8. Don't rely on supplements to protect against cancer.
9. Avoid tobacco use, including smoking and chewing.

At first glance, these recommendations may seem like common sense. Or perhaps they seem too good to be true: if reducing more than two-thirds of all cancers was really this simple, everybody would be doing it. But the fact of the matter is, most of us routinely miss the mark when it comes to actually following these recommendations. For example, the vast majority of us get less than half the recommended daily amount of fruits and vegetables.

Eating well and managing symptoms during treatment

Eating can be very challenging when you are dealing with cancer and its treatment, but a healthy diet is still important, as it can help you stay well before, during and after treatment. Cancer puts a strain on both your physical and psychological health, and your immune system needs lots of help to fight off infections.

Because surgery, radiation and chemotherapy can negatively affect your ability to eat, it is vital to find strategies to help you maintain your nutritional well-being and manage treatment-related symptoms.

Constipation and diarrhea are common side effects of cancer treatment, and each presents its own potential problems. Diarrhea carries the risk of dehydration and a loss of electrolytes, such as potassium, sodium and chloride. Maintaining optimal fluid intake is critical, and smoothies made with cooled tea, water, milk or nondairy milk can help. You may need to limit foods high in insoluble fiber during this time, but a dietitian can help you make the best choices for your situation. Soluble fiber, on the other hand, can help manage diarrhea, thanks to its ability to absorb excess fluids in the digestive tract. Ingredients such as oats, chia seeds, ground flax seeds and legumes are all good sources of soluble fiber. As for constipation, drinking plenty of fluids and increasing overall fiber intake is the best way to prevent and treat it.

Cancer treatment can also lead to oral health issues (such as mouth inflammation, dry mouth and thick saliva production) and challenges such as trouble swallowing, nausea and vomiting. These can all affect your ability or desire to eat and drink, increasing your risk of dehydration and malnutrition.

Maintaining and regaining weight

Getting enough protein and energy (calories) isn't easy when you're dealing with nausea, dry mouth and/or loss of appetite. Calorie-rich foods can help you maintain your weight, strength and sense of well-being. During cancer treatment, you may need to eat more higher-fat foods, such as nut and seed butters, avocado and full-fat milk, kefir and yogurt. Foods that are rich in carbohydrate, such as bananas, mangos, peaches, pears, dates and prunes, can also help to boost calories. Protein helps to preserve muscle and is needed almost everywhere in the body, including the cells and antibodies of the immune system. Smoothie-friendly proteins include pasteurized egg whites, yogurt, whey protein powder and vegetarian protein powders. Eating several smaller meals and snacks throughout the day can help you to meet your nutritional needs, and nutrient-dense smoothies, soups and spreads are easy to consume this way.

Each symptom needs to be managed on an individual basis, ideally with a dietitian, who can tailor the textures and temperatures of foods and liquids to ensure that you're meeting your needs. Blended foods have recognized value as part of a nutritional strategy during cancer treatment.

CARDIOVASCULAR HEALTH

Cardiovascular disease is the general term for diseases of the heart and blood vessels, including stroke, coronary artery disease (such as angina and myocardial infarction, or heart attack), issues with heart valves and the rhythms of one's heartbeat, peripheral artery disease and various other conditions. While nutrients play a role in all aspects of physical health, when it comes to cardiovascular disease, the focus tends to be on how the diet affects blood pressure and blood lipids (fats that circulate in the bloodstream).

Blood pressure

Many people believe that, to maintain healthy blood pressure, they simply need to reduce their sodium intake. But the reality is that only a small percentage of the population are "sodium responders." Other nutrients, including potassium, magnesium and calcium, also play a starring role in blood pressure management. Getting more of these nutrients, especially potassium, will not only help lower high blood pressure, but will also help prevent it from developing in the first place.

Potassium helps the kidneys excrete excess sodium from the blood and supports vasodilatation — the blood vessels' ability to relax and expand. Studies have shown that increasing the amount of potassium in the diet leads to lower blood pressure even without a reduction in sodium intake; thus, potassium can help to counter the effects of a high-sodium diet.

In addition, several phytonutrients have been shown to lower blood pressure, independent of potassium, magnesium and calcium — another reason to eat more plant foods.

Blood lipids

We have been led to believe that low-density lipoprotein (LDL, or "bad") cholesterol levels are the be-all and end-all when it comes to heart health. It's true that higher levels of LDL cholesterol are a risk factor for atherosclerosis (plaque development), which, over time, can lead to a narrowing of the blood vessels and possibly to a heart attack or ischemic stroke. But there's more to the picture: there are other blood lipids, including high-density lipoprotein (HDL, or "good") cholesterol, total cholesterol and triglycerides, and it's the ratio of these different lipids that influences cardiovascular disease risk, not simply LDL cholesterol levels alone.

Another consideration is the degree of LDL cholesterol oxidation. When damaged, LDL cholesterol increases inflammation of the blood vessels. This leads to free radical production, which, in turn, can lead to endothelial dysfunction — the inability of the blood vessels to expand and contract in a healthy manner. When LDL cholesterol is oxidized, it becomes prone to adhesion (it gets "sticky") and is more likely to penetrate into the walls of the blood vessels, leading to greater calcification, or plaque formation.

Dietary fiber helps balance blood lipids by keeping LDL cholesterol and triglycerides in a healthy range. Fiber binds to bile, which is made of cholesterol, and carries it out of the gut in the stool. The liver then recycles cholesterol from the blood to make new bile, keeping LDL levels within a healthy range. Fiber also slows the digestion and absorption of dietary carbohydrate, which can temper triglyceride production, ultimately leading to better blood lipid ratios.

The nutrient-dense foods in our recipes provide lots of fiber, as well as countless antioxidants and phytonutrients that not only help to prevent LDL cholesterol oxidation but also protect the lining of the blood vessels, lower inflammation and improve endothelial function.

ENDOCRINE HEALTH (INSULIN RESISTANCE, PREDIABETES AND TYPE 2 DIABETES)

Insulin resistance is a physical state in which the pancreas is producing insulin, the hormone that regulates blood sugar (glucose), but the insulin isn't used effectively by the body. The fat cells, muscles and liver no longer respond to insulin, and glucose gradually builds up in the blood. Insulin resistance is a slow burn: at first, the pancreas compensates by producing more insulin, which overcomes the resistance, keeping blood sugar in the healthy range. It can take 6 to 10 years for insulin resistance to progress to prediabetes and then to type 2 diabetes.

The *New England Journal of Medicine's* 2002 landmark study "Reduction in the Incidence of Type 2 diabetes with Lifestyle Intervention or Metformin" found that lifestyle, including achieving and maintaining a healthy weight, was more effective than the usual treatment — the medication metformin — in preventing the progression from prediabetes to type 2 diabetes. Smoothies and other blended foods are not, in and of themselves, a magic bullet for achieving a healthy body weight, but they can be an effective tool in your anti-diabetes toolbox, helping you get the nutrients you need for optimal insulin and glucose metabolism. These nutrients include magnesium, chromium, omega-3 fatty acids and vitamin D, as well as phytonutrients and antioxidants. Fruits, vegetables, nuts, seeds, whole grains, legumes and spices such as cinnamon and turmeric all contribute to an anti-diabetes dietary approach.

EYE HEALTH

As the organs of vision, the eyes are amazing structures that convert light energy into nerve impulses, via the optic nerve, which the brain interprets as images. It's no surprise that nutrition plays a large role in eye health, both keeping the eyes healthy for their day-to-day function and reducing the risk for eye disease. The heavy-hitting nutrients for eye health

Managing blood sugar with blended foods

As part of a comprehensive and integrative approach to healthy weight management, nutrient-dense blended foods can help people who would benefit from weight loss reduce their risk of developing type 2 diabetes, and can help those with diabetes better manage their blood sugar. They are a great way to pack in nutrition while keeping blood sugar balanced. A smoothie that incorporates the golden trio of fiber, fat and protein makes a quick and easy meal or snack to help you stay on target, particularly if it is consumed in place of a carbohydrate-dense coffee shop muffin or bagel — a grab-as-you-can choice that can result in a blood sugar rollercoaster.

include carotenoids (such as alpha- and beta-carotene, lutein and zeaxanthin), omega-3 fatty acids, vitamins A, C, D and E, and the minerals selenium and zinc.

Vitamin A is needed for the production of rhodopsin, a photosensitive chemical that is formed by specialized cells called rods, which are located in the retina at the back of the eye and help transmit light energy along the optic nerve to the brain. Rhodopsin is extremely sensitive to light and enables vision in low-light conditions, including night vision. (Night blindness is one of the classic vitamin A deficiency diseases.) Carotenoids that the body can convert to vitamin A — alpha-carotene, beta-carotene and beta-cryptoxanthin — can help fulfill our vitamin A needs.

Omega-3 fatty acids, especially DHA, are essential to eye structure, making up part of the fat in the cell membranes of eye tissue. Along with vitamin D, omega-3 fatty acids are also very effective at preventing and/or reducing inflammation, which can lead to eye irritation and dryness.

While there are various eye diseases, two of the more common ones that are strongly influenced by lifestyle are cataracts and macular degeneration.

Cataracts

Cataracts are insidious; they develop slowly and painlessly, without initial warning signs or symptoms, and are usually detected during routine eye exams. Over time, symptoms can include sensitivity to bright light or seeing halos around lights, double vision, poor night vision and a decreased ability to see details.

Cataracts are the leading cause of vision loss in people over 40. Lifestyle risk factors include smoking, alcohol consumption, excessive sun exposure and poorly managed diabetes.

The lenses of the eyes, composed of mostly water and proteins, are normally clear, and light passes through easily to reach the retina and macula, enabling vision. Cataracts interfere with this process. They form when proteins within the lens become damaged and clump together, leading to cloudiness. A simple analogy is that of egg whites: raw, the whites are transparent; as they cook, their protein structure changes and they become opaque. Over time, the cloudiness associated with cataracts becomes severe enough that it leads to blurred vision.

Bioflavonoids, the carotenoids lutein and zeaxanthin, and vitamins C and E have been shown to reduce the risk for cataract formation. By preventing the oxidation of the proteins in the lens, these antioxidant nutrients neutralize the free radicals produced as sunlight passes through, as well as the free radicals produced by lifestyle risk factors.

Age-related macular degeneration

Age-related macular degeneration (AMD), which is largely preventable, is the leading cause of blindness (the loss of sharp, detailed central vision) in people over 65. The greatest risk factors are smoking, increased pressure within the eyeball and poor diet.

The nutrients with the biggest impact on AMD prevention are lutein and zeaxanthin, yellow and reddish carotenoids that the eye preferentially concentrates in the macula, an area in the back of the eye, in the center of the retina. The macula is highly pigmented, appearing yellow to orange-reddish because of the presence of lutein and zeaxanthin. As antioxidants, these carotenoids help to protect the macula from the free radical damage that can occur when sunlight hits the back of the eye. Study after study demonstrates that those who consume lutein- and zeaxanthin-rich foods on a regular basis have a high concentration of these carotenoids in their maculae — they have a high macular density — and are at lower risk for AMD. Lutein- and zeaxanthin-rich foods include spinach, kale, turnips and collard greens.

Other nutrients that have been shown to reduce the risk for AMD include alpha- and beta-carotene, bioflavonoids, vitamins C, D and E, and zinc.

FALLS

Every year, millions of older people experience falls. The National Ageing Research Institute estimates that one out of every three people over the age of 65 falls each year. Older adults who live at home are estimated to have at least one fall per year, and about 10% have more than one fall. One-third of these falls result in serious injuries that require medical assistance, including head injuries and broken bones in the wrists, arms, ankles or hips. The most common reasons for fall-related hospitalizations are head injuries and hip fractures.

Falls have a significant impact on quality of life. Fall-related bruising and injuries lead to loss of independence and a reduced ability to perform the normal tasks of everyday living, such as shopping and cooking. Falls may even result in long hospital stays and subsequent placement in long-term care facilities.

While there are several different risk

factors for falls, including dehydration, diabetes, inactivity and taking multiple medications, nutrition plays a significant yet underappreciated role in both the prevention of falls and improved recovery after a fall.

Prevention

When it comes to reducing the risk of falls, it's all about keeping your muscles and bones strong. Muscles need a steady and ample supply of protein to maintain mass and prevent muscle loss (sarcopenia), carbohydrate for fuel and fluids for hydration. In addition, they require vitamin D_3, which helps maintain muscle mass and tone and improves neuromuscular and psychomotor function (the ability of the nerves to send impulses to the muscles). Better muscle tone improves balance and gait, and better nerve firing helps to maintain muscle tone and reaction time. Along with vitamin D_3, potassium, calcium and magnesium are also needed for optimal muscle contractions and movement.

While strong bones can't prevent someone from falling, strong bones are less likely to break in a fall. Bone health is reviewed on page 42.

Optimal nutrition also helps in the management of any comorbidities that might increase the risk for falls, such as diabetic neuropathy (nerve damage in diabetes).

Recovery

Good nutrition is critical for the best possible outcome during recovery from bruising, inflammation, wounds and fractures. Vitamins A and C and the mineral zinc are needed for wound repair. Antioxidants, such as vitamins C and E, and phytonutrients, such as alpha- and beta-carotene, lycopene, quercetin and lutein, help to temper inflammation so that healing can occur. Protein, calcium, phosphorus, magnesium, zinc and vitamins C, D_3 and K_2 are needed for optimal healing from fractures; studies have shown that without adequate amounts of these nutrients, healing time can be delayed and bone quality compromised.

GASTROINTESTINAL HEALTH

The human digestive tract is an impressive system. As it moves food along its length, it digests and absorbs nutrients and expels waste. It all starts in the mouth, where the act of chewing reduces larger pieces of food into smaller ones; saliva helps to moisten the food and also contains digestive enzymes that start the digestion process. From the mouth, food passes through the esophagus into the stomach, where stomach acid and digestive enzymes help to break down protein, and then into the small intestine, where most of the digestion and absorption of the macronutrients and micronutrients takes place. The last part of the digestive tract is the large intestine, or colon, which is responsible for reabsorbing water, sodium and other electrolytes into the body, and for the synthesis of vitamin K and biotin, a B-vitamin-like compound. No enzymatic digestion occurs here; whatever is left of the digested food mass moves on to be expelled via the rectum and anus.

Integral to the digestive process, and to our overall health, are the trillions of bacteria, or microbiota, that reside along the entire length of the digestive tract, from mouth to anus. We cannot survive without them and need an adequate amount and diversity of these "good" bacteria. Research is continually discovering new roles performed by these gut residents: they prevent overweight and obesity; reduce the risk for type 2 diabetes and colorectal cancer; contribute to better immune function and improved mood; prevent irritable bowel disease and inflammation of the gut lining; reduce the growth of pathogenic bacteria, viruses and yeasts that naturally reside in the gut; prevent allergies and more.

As many as 1,000 species of bacteria have been identified in humans, but the average person has 400 to 500 different species, in a mix unique to them. Your diversity of bacteria, while stable for the most part over your lifetime, can be altered by factors such as age, stress, the amount of fiber in your diet, whether your diet has a lot of added sugars, chronic alcohol use, recreational drug use and use of acid-reducing medications, certain pain medications and antibiotics. The best strategy to ensure the optimal health and well-being of your microbiota is to reduce anything that might be leading to an imbalance (dysbiosis) while giving the gut the dietary support it needs in the form of fiber, resistant starch, prebiotics and probiotics.

Resistant starch is the starch component of plant foods that enters the colon undigested. Bananas, oats, potatoes, lentils, white beans and green peas all provide resistant starch.

Sulfoquinovose

A recent discovery is an unusual type of sugar molecule called sulfoquinovose that's found abundantly in leafy green vegetables such as spinach, kale, collard greens and Swiss chard. Our microbiota love sulfoquinovose and use it as an energy source. Including leafy greens in your daily smoothie or soup will go a long way toward feeding your good gut bacteria.

Prebiotics are a type of fiber (inulins and oligosaccharides) that feeds the microbiota; they are found in high-fiber foods such as chicory root, garlic, onions, wheat bran and bananas. Probiotics are live bacteria found in fermented foods, such as kefir, some yogurts (if the container reads "contains live bacteria") and pickled foods like kimchi and sauerkraut.

But there's no need to overthink this; just remember that microbiota feed on fiber. When we consume a variety of plant foods, our microbiota ferment the various types of fiber and thus proliferate and maintain their diversity. Getting enough fiber and eating foods with probiotics ensures that our microbiota population remains robust.

Constipation

Constipation is a condition in which a person has difficulty emptying the bowels, usually with hardened feces and straining during a bowel movement. Although there is no consensus in the medical community on how often one should have a bowel movement, constipation is often defined as having fewer than three bowel movements per week. With chronic constipation, the difficulty passing stool can last for several weeks, or even longer.

The two simplest ways to prevent and/or treat constipation are to get enough fiber and fluids throughout the day. Including plant foods at each meal and snack will ensure that you'll meet your fiber goal of 25 grams per day for women and 38 grams per day for men. (Lower goals for those over 50 exist only because total food intake tends to decrease as we get older, not because more fiber is unhealthy at that age.)

Fiber helps prevent constipation in two ways: it stimulates peristalsis, the movement of food through the intestines; and it helps stool retain water, keeping it bulky and soft as it moves through the colon. Fiber's success however, depends on fluids, which give fiber the water it needs to bulk up. Without adequate fluids, increased fiber in your diet will backfire and lead to the very thing you're trying to prevent: more constipation.

Improved digestion

To improve overall gut health and digestion, you need to nurture your gut with food that supports the microbiota while making sure you get the vitamins and minerals that facilitate the act of digestion. Common digestive issues include bloating, cramping, gas, belching, acid reflux and irregular bowel movements (either too many or not enough). Today's food landscape offers countless options of poor nutritional quality: highly processed foods and food-like products that are devoid of fiber, vitamins and minerals, and loaded with industrial trans fat, sugar, sodium, artificial colors, flavorings and preservatives. These foods often cause digestive issues on their own, but they can also displace more wholesome foods that support digestive health.

Including nutrient-dense foods at every meal and snack can help to reset the gut. By providing bulk, whole foods help to reestablish normal peristalsis — intestinal contractions that move food along in a predictable pattern — and restore regular bowel movements. When things are moving along nicely, there's less chance of bloating, cramping or indigestion from a sluggish gut. Feeding the colon lots of fiber- and probiotic-rich foods ensures that our microbiota are at their best, so they can crowd out bad bacteria and yeasts and prevent them from colonizing.

INFLAMMATION

In simple terms, inflammation is the body's response to something that is harming it. The damaged tissue becomes inflamed to provoke the start of the healing process; in this sense, inflammation is a necessary part of self-preservation. When a harmful stimulus — whether it's a pathogenic bacterium, virus or fungus, a food allergy or sensitivity, or a physical irritant like a sliver — affects some part of the body, the immune system is alerted by the damaged tissue and responds with an attempt to fight off any potential infection and heal the affected area.

Acute inflammation starts rapidly (within seconds), increases in severity to help the healing process and then typically resolves within a few days to a couple of weeks. The warming, reddening and swelling of the skin after a bee sting is a classic example of localized acute inflammation. Other examples include a sore throat from a cold or flu, an inflamed scratch on the skin or a swollen sprained ankle. Tissue damage is usually mild and self-limited, with no long-term impairment.

Chronic inflammation is different. It can occur when an infection fails to resolve on its own; when there's a persistent irritant of low intensity; or as a response to an autoimmune disease, where the body's immune system attacks its own tissues. It has a slower onset, which can take days to ramp up, is less obvious and is more systemic (it is not isolated to one area of the body). Due to its progressive nature, chronic inflammation destroys tissues over the long term by causing oxidative damage and thickening and scarring of connective tissues, and by impairing cellular function and therefore tissue and organ function.

Chronic inflammation is often associated with cardiovascular disease, hepatitis and irritable bowel syndrome, as well as with

Cytokines

Chronic inflammation keeps the immune system running overtime, unceasingly stimulating the release of chemical signals called cytokines, whose job it is to orchestrate the inflammatory and healing response. Normally, when cytokines are released, they signal the body to fight infection, stimulate healing and repair and then degrade. When cytokines are constantly being released, as with chronic inflammation, it's like having slow-burning embers in the fireplace, just waiting for a flare-up.

autoimmune diseases such as asthma, celiac disease, lupus and rheumatoid arthritis. Lifestyle factors that can contribute to chronic inflammation include smoking, long-term alcohol use, long-term use of everyday medications, overweight or obesity, poor sleep quality, stress, eating trans fats and a high intake of added sugars. Chronic inflammation can last years, or decades, if the root cause isn't addressed.

The interplay between inflammation, free radical production and oxidation can become a vicious circle that if left unchecked can lead to, and aggravate, chronic degenerative diseases. When a stimulus triggers inflammation, free radical production and tissue oxidation, antioxidant reserves are depleted and the body becomes susceptible to further inflammation and oxidation, and produces even more free radicals, which use up more antioxidants. To stop this vicious circle in its tracks, we need to consume plenty of antioxidant nutrients, such as vitamins C and E, flavonoids, carotenoids, lycopene and polyphenols, as well as minerals, including zinc, selenium, copper and manganese, that the body uses to make the antioxidant enzymes glutathione peroxidase and superoxide dismutase.

Nutrient-packed foods can also help prevent and/or treat chronic degenerative diseases by bolstering the immune system, positively influencing cytokine production and activity, and providing the building blocks for tissue repair.

REPRODUCTIVE HEALTH

Historically, reproductive nutrition has focused on women's health — ensuring that a woman's body is as healthy as it can be before and during pregnancy. But current research shows that the quality of men's diets matters too. It turns out that the micronutrients in a man's diet are associated with sperm fitness and quality, particularly DNA quality. The more vitamins and minerals a male gets through his diet, the less damage to his sperm's DNA, the less chromosomal rearrangement and the less DNA fragmentation, especially in men who are middle-aged or older. Better sperm quality and improved ability to swim toward an ovum ensure the greatest likelihood of successful fertilization and pregnancy.

As for women, before they become pregnant (and ideally before they begin trying to conceive), they should be working toward optimizing their overall nutritional health by eating a variety of nutrient-dense foods with a focus on omega-3 fatty acids, iron and folate.

Pregnancy

Healthy eating during pregnancy is very important to ensure that your developing baby gets all the nutrients needed for growth and development. Research shows that maternal nutrition also influences her offspring's risk for chronic diseases, such as overweight and obesity, diabetes and asthma, later in life. Moreover, healthy eating lowers a pregnant woman's risk for her own health problems, such as gestational diabetes, high blood pressure, anemia, depression, pre-eclampsia, overweight and obesity, and micronutrient deficiencies.

Both mother and baby need an adequate supply of *all* the vitamins and minerals. Some nutrients, however, are of greater importance during pregnancy. Folate, for example, is needed to prevent the risk of certain birth defects of the brain and spinal cord, called neural tube defects. Getting more folate from leafy greens, legumes, sunflower seeds and peanuts, starting well before conception and continuing throughout the pregnancy, not only reduces the risk for these birth defects but also assists in the optimal development of red blood cells, thereby reducing the risk for anemia.

Iron is another pregnancy heavy hitter. It supports the large increase in the mother's red blood cell formation and ensures that the baby will have enough iron stores at birth. Doctors typically advise taking a prenatal multivitamin with minerals, as these formulas have more iron than regular multivitamins, but it is still important to focus on getting enough iron-rich foods in your diet. Most people know that meat is a high-iron food, but there are plenty of plant-based iron sources that can be included in a smoothie or a dip, such as oats, legumes, green leafy vegetables, nuts and seeds.

Calcium helps your growing baby build strong bones and teeth. It is also needed for a healthy heartbeat, to aid in nerve impulse transmission and for muscle tone and contractions. If you don't get enough calcium from your diet and don't get enough vitamin D to ensure optimal absorption of calcium from the gut, your body will pull calcium from your bones to meet its needs. Calcium-rich smoothie-friendly ingredients include milk, yogurt, kefir, calcium-fortified soy milk, almond milk or rice milk, soft tofu set with calcium salts, nuts and nut butters, seeds and seed butters, legumes and dark green leafy vegetables.

WEIGHT MANAGEMENT

Whether your goal is to lose weight, avoid weight gain or healthfully gain weight, weight management is all about calories. But it's not just the number of calories that matters, it's also the quality of those calories.

We get food energy, or calories, from food. How the body digests and extracts those calories is influenced by the nature of the food: 250 calories from gummy bears made with sugar, glucose syrup and starch is not equivalent to 250 calories from apples, which contain fiber, small amounts of protein and loads of phytonutrients. Minimally processed, nutrient-dense whole foods positively influence hormones that regulate appetite and promote satiety (a sense of fullness after eating) in a way that highly refined, highly processed foods can't. Whole foods are "self-limiting": it is harder to overeat calories from apples, bananas, broccoli and oatmeal than it is calories from candy or other refined foods.

Weight loss

Successful weight loss is not based on a simple dietary rule like "no eating after 7 p.m." or a special food or secret nutrient, nor is it about cutting out groups of food or a macronutrient like "carbs." Rather, healthy and successful weight loss requires a multipronged approach that reviews your attitudes and values about food and eating, does an inventory of the emotional aspects that influence your eating and food choices, explores possible emotional triggers for problematic eating, includes physical activity, works on improving your sleep quality, educates you on portion sizes and healthier options when dining out, and increases your knowledge about ingredients and cooking methods.

Healthy eating does require some effort. As the saying goes, "People don't plan to fail, but they often fail to plan." While there's no one-size-fits-all approach, structure helps

Portion Sizes

It is well understood that meals outside the home have more calories than meals at home, mostly because of larger portion sizes. Studies have proven that portion size influences how much we eat: we're inclined to finish whatever is served to us, even if we are no longer hungry. That's where a well-planned, nutritious recipe can help: the portion sizes are already figured out for you; all you need to do is prepare the recipe, divide it into the specified number of servings and enjoy! If you bring a smoothie or soup with you when you're at work or on the go, you'll avoid the temptations and large portions offered by the cafeteria, food court, restaurant or fast-food outlet.

people stay on track with goals of any kind. Meal planning helps us make healthier choices *and* eat less — the foundation of weight loss. Structure may also reduce the frequency and intensity of those sudden bouts of intense hunger that lead us to impulsively overindulge. You know the feeling: you're ravenous and want to stop that gnawing in your belly by grabbing the first thing you see. This is actually a normal, hardwired response, a defense mechanism that allowed the human race to survive when food was scarce. But it works against us when we're faced with an abundance of low-quality food choices.

The solution, again, is structure: planning what you're going to eat for the day — three main meals and one or two snacks is a typical pattern. If you have a nutritious complete meal in the morning, you'll be less tempted to eat a doughnut on your coffee break. If you have a healthy snack prepared and ready nearby when hunger strikes mid-afternoon, you won't go running to the vending machine for a bag of chips.

The recipes in this book fit into this structure perfectly because they're quick and easy to prepare and very portable. You might have a high-protein smoothie for breakfast, a hearty bean soup for lunch and a nutrient-rich dip with some sliced vegetables for your mid-afternoon snack. At dinner you might dress your salad with one of our tasty dressings, and after dinner, you might satisfy your sweet tooth by choosing one of our healthy desserts instead of a calorie- and sugar-laden option that offers no nutritional value to speak of. This is just an extreme example of how you can fit our recipes into a healthy pattern of eating — we don't expect that you will want to eat blended foods at every meal (though you certainly can)! The important thing to take away from this is the concept of meal planning: if you plan ahead and create your own nutrient-dense meals and snacks, in appropriate portion sizes for your weight-loss goals, you will be one step closer to meeting those goals.

Weight gain

Healthy weight gain relies on consuming more calories and protein. Ideally, the extra calories would come from wholesome foods and you would include some form of activity to build and maintain muscle in your weight-gain strategy. Eating more food can be a challenge for those who are trying to gain weight, especially if you don't feel hungry or find it difficult to make time to prepare extra snacks and/or meals. Smoothies can be a big help here: drinking a smoothie as part of one or more meals each day is an easy way to boost calories and protein — and vitamins and minerals to boot. Because it's in a drinkable form, a smoothie is easier to consume along with a meal than if you had to chew that same amount of food.

When weight gain is the goal, people are often advised to eat something every 3 hours or so, as they may not be able to consume enough calories in three meals a day, even if they are able to increase the size of those meals. Having a smoothie on hand makes snack time a breeze, helping to fill in the gaps between meals.

Five reasons we love smoothies

1. **They're a natural energy booster.** Our bodies need fuel if we want to feel our best. When we skip meals, our blood sugar dips, which can lead to decreased focus and a feeling of fatigue. The go-to in this situation is often a cup of coffee, because caffeine releases adrenaline, which gives us some pep, as well as dopamine, a neurotransmitter that helps us feel energized, alert and focused. While there's nothing wrong with small amounts of caffeine, coffee doesn't get to the bottom of our energy slump. A smoothie not only provides the body with fuel from carbohydrate and fat, but also has vitamins, minerals and phytonutrients for sustained energy.

2. **They're a healthy weight ally.** As part of an overall weight management approach, a nutritious smoothie can help you control your calorie intake, whether your goal is to lose weight, maintain weight or gain weight.

3. **They make it easy to stay healthy all year long.** Staying healthy year-round requires commitment and a strategic approach that includes getting enough rest, being active, participating in leisure activities, fostering healthy relationships and eating a nutritious diet. Easy-to-prepare meals and snacks that provide a variety of nutrient-dense foods are the foundation of healthy eating. Because smoothies can be made with a wide variety of nutrient-dense whole foods, you can enjoy them 365 days a year without ever feeling like you're stuck in a flavor rut.

4. **They're a nutritional powerhouse.** Packed with disease-fighting and health-promoting nutrients in a relatively small serving size, smoothies have a lot of bang for the nutritional buck without blowing the calorie budget. A smoothie made from whole foods stands head and shoulders above most of the other convenience-based food options out there.

5. **They're one of the best "fast foods."** It takes less than 10 minutes to make a smoothie (including cleanup!) — and even less if you prep ahead — and they're super-portable.

Increase fiber slowly

Just about everyone has heard the message to eat more fiber, and with good reason: it does a body good. Dietary fiber can be found in all plant foods and has many health-promoting properties. It supports and maintains bowel health, normalizes regularity, reduces the risk for cardiovascular disease and helps control blood sugar.

Fiber is a form of carbohydrate that our bodies cannot digest or absorb — but the healthy bacteria in our gastrointestinal tract love it! When they go to work digesting fiber, they produce some gas as a byproduct, so adding more fiber-rich foods to your diet too quickly can lead to excess gas production, which can cause bloating and cramps. The good news is, this can be easily managed by increasing the fiber in your diet gradually, over a few weeks, giving your friendly gut bacteria time to adjust. Many of the recipes in this book are fiber-rich, so be sure to account for this as you incorporate them into your diet!

MYTH-BUSTING

Myth: Smoothies have too much sugar

One of the major criticisms of blender drinks, smoothies and juices is that they contain too much sugar. Sugar causes a lot of confusion. Fruits, vegetables, whole grains, dairy products, legumes, nuts and seeds all contain carbohydrate, which is digested to provide (among other things) sugar, which the body uses for fuel. We need the sugar we get from these whole, unprocessed foods to survive. The concern about the sugar content of the modern diet is in regard to the added sugars (also called free or refined sugars) in processed foods. Added sugars also include sweeteners such as syrup, molasses and honey that we add when we prepare food from scratch. It is easy to overconsume refined sugars, as they are added liberally to processed foods and are easy to overuse in our everyday lives.

It is certainly possible to consume too much sugar if you drink a lot of fruit juice, but if a smoothie includes a variety of wholesome foods, it shouldn't contain a worrisome amount of sugar. Yes, a smoothie made with only fruit juice, fruit and honey would provide a concentrated source of food-based sugars, but that doesn't mean all smoothies are high in sugar. A smoothie with a balance of whole-food ingredients resembles a regular meal but in a blended form.

Myth: Smoothies reinforce abnormal or disordered eating

Some people suggest that smoothies promote disordered eating because they are meals in beverage form, and to promote them over solid meals moves people toward eating in a way that's new to human culture. This opinion is not supported by research. In fact, smoothies can normalize eating by helping people to appreciate the importance of good nutrition and eat a mix of different types of food that will increase satiety, promote overall health and increase fiber intake. They encourage people not to skip meals and increase a person's awareness of what they are putting into their body as they shop for wholesome ingredients, choose what foods to include, blend the recipe and drink it.

Myth: Liquid calories aren't satisfying

Liquid calories, such as alcohol, juice, soft drinks and other sweetened beverages, have been implicated in weight gain for a few reasons. One is that they are stealthy in nature, flying in under the radar so we lose track of how much we're consuming, which could lead to overconsumption of calories. Another potential problem is that they lack bulk and don't require chewing; consider how much longer it takes to eat 2 medium apples than to drink an 8-ounce (250 mL) glass of unsweetened apple juice, yet both provide the same amount of calories and sugar. In this sense, whole foods are more self-limiting: they take time to chew and to get to our stomachs. Liquid calories also affect our sense of satiety; research shows that when people drink juice or soft drinks, they don't automatically eat less at the next meal as they might if they ate a snack based on solid foods.

But smoothies and blended soups are different. Made with whole foods, they contain all of the food components of solid food, including nutrients that are satiating — the golden trio of protein, fat and fiber. Smoothies can also be thickened as desired to promote satiety.

Myth: Smoothies are no different than juices

Smoothies are very different from juices that have been extracted from whole foods. While they contain similar vitamin, mineral and phytonutrient content, juices lack the fiber of the whole fruits and vegetables they were made from. Smoothies contain all the components of whole foods, most notably the fiber, and can also contain ingredients that provide fat and protein, which juices don't. Smoothies truly are a meal in a glass, mug or bowl.

Myth: Blending breaks down fiber

Studies have shown that some fiber is broken down during the blending process, but that has not been proven to have any negative nutritional impact. Fiber content and quality are not negatively affected in any meaningful way in blended foods. High-fiber blended foods still promote satiety and can help balance blood sugar, lower cholesterol, promote digestive health and prevent and treat constipation.

Myth: Blending destroys nutrients

Some argue that blending foods increases the exposure of delicate nutrients to oxygen, resulting in nutrient losses via oxidation or oxidative damage. Food preparation of any kind — cooking, freezing, canning, food processing — always leads to some amount of nutrient loss; this isn't new or controversial. But any loss is nutritionally inconsequential in the long run when a variety of whole foods are eaten and when those foods make up the vast majority of food we eat.

Myth: Smoothies cause weight gain

Consuming excess calories over the long term can lead to weight gain, but no one food is "fattening" in and of itself. Smoothies would only contribute to weight gain if they were consumed above and beyond the amount of food needed to maintain a given body weight.

PART TWO

Superfood Recipes for Your NutriBullet

Blending and NutriBullet Basics

If you are looking for a quick and easy way to boost your daily consumption of healthy foods, blending superfoods into an array of smoothies, dips, sauces and soups is the ideal solution. The beauty of using a NutriBullet is that you can have a tasty, healthy, portable meal, snack or dessert in under a minute.

Blending is perfect for busy people who want to add healthy foods to their diet with little effort and minimal cleanup. The NutriBullet offers many benefits, but three in particular stand out:

1. You can make blended foods with no added sugars, chemicals or preservatives.
2. You can make a fresh smoothie-to-go in less time than it takes to stop and pick one up, and at a much lower cost.
3. You can make healthy snacks to take with you for a quick pick-me-up during the day instead of grabbing a much less healthy treat.

The recipes in this book are written for the NutriBullet, but you can easily adapt them to work in a larger high-performance blender.

About the NutriBullet

The NutriBullet is a high-powered cyclonic blender that breaks down ingredients so completely that our bodies are able to gain the maximum benefits from the nutrients they contain. The base of this amazing blender is only 5½ inches (13.5 cm) wide by 8 inches (20 cm) tall, so it fits easily into any size kitchen, dorm room or work space, and can even be packed for traveling.

There are a number of models of the NutriBullet available. You may also see various models of the less powerful Magic Bullet, made by the same company. Whichever one you choose, the primary features you should look for are wattage and capacity. The NutriBullet motors range from 600 watts to 1,700 watts of power, while the Magic Bullet motors have 250 watts. The capacities range from 24 to 45 oz (750 mL to 1.3 L). For our recipes, we primarily used the 900-watt, 24-oz (750 mL) NutriBullet. Other power levels and sizes will also work well, but you may need to increase or decrease the blending time slightly.

For each recipe, we specify the size of cup to use. The standard cup for most NutriBullets is the tall cup, which holds 24 oz (750 mL). This is the size used in most of our recipes. The small cup, which holds 16 oz (500 mL), is useful for some dips, dressings and smaller smoothies. The extra-tall cup (also called the colossal cup), which holds 32 oz (1 L), is used to make big-batch recipes, for more servings.

If using a high-performance blender

If you want to try adapting our recipes to a larger blender, you will want to make sure to use a high-performance blender (such as a Vitamix) so that you can be sure you are extracting the most nutrients from fruits and vegetables and are completely blending skins, stems, seeds, nuts and some spices and herbs. Conventional blenders are good for some fruit smoothies, milkshakes and protein drinks but cannot handle the tougher ingredients and may leave your recipes a bit chunky instead of silky smooth.

If you're using a blender that has its extracting blade on the bottom of the blending container, you will want to add the ingredients in the recipe in reverse order.

Whichever size cup you are using, never add ingredients above the "Max Line."

To make the recipes in this book in your NutriBullet, just add the ingredients in the order instructed, screw the extractor blade onto the cup, and push and turn the cup into the base unit for the recommended time. In under a minute, you will have a delicious superfood-powered smoothie — it really is that simple.

Recommended accessories

Aside from your NutriBullet and some standard kitchen utensils, there are a few other gadgets that you will need (or will find handy) when preparing the recipes in this book.

- **Chef's knife:** A chef's knife is the best tool for cutting fruits and vegetables to fit into your cup.
- **Zester or grater:** If making a recipe that calls for citrus zest, you will need a zester or a rasp grater, such as a Microplane, to zest the fruit.
- **Kitchen gloves:** These are useful when you're handling hot peppers, certain spices and fruits or vegetables that can stain your hands.
- **Baking sheets:** You will use these to roast or freeze some ingredients before use.
- **Airtight containers:** You will want to have several of these on hand for freezing or refrigerating ingredients and completed recipes. Make sure to label and date your containers; it's surprisingly easy to forget what you put in there, and when.

The NutriBullet pantry

The superfoods used in our recipes were outlined in detail in chapter 2. In addition to these nutrient-dense powerhouses, there are certain staples used in a large number of recipes that you will want to make sure to have on hand.

OILS

We use a variety of oils in our recipes. Many are oils made from superfood seeds and nuts, including flaxseed oil, hempseed oil, pumpkin seed oil, sunflower oil, cashew oil and peanut oil. We also use virgin olive oil and coconut oil, which are also considered healthy options, when they are best for the overall flavor of the recipe. Using the type of oil specified in the recipe will give you the best balance of flavors in the finished dish.

VINEGARS

Vinegar can impact the texture, color, flavor and thickness of recipes, adding acidity and sourness that can increase our enjoyment of our food. There are many types of vinegar, each of which has its own unique flavor. The vinegars used in this book include balsamic vinegar, apple cider vinegar, red wine vinegar, white wine vinegar and unseasoned rice vinegar. If you are unsure which vinegars to have on hand, start with whichever one is used in a recipe you want to make, then expand your pantry provisions from there.

CITRUS ZEST AND JUICE

Many recipes include lemon, lime and orange juice and/or zest. Citrus adds flavor and acidity that will brighten the flavors of the final product. Use freshly squeezed juice whenever possible, or use a pure juice without any added sugar or other added ingredients.

HERBS, SEASONINGS AND FLAVORINGS

When adding herbs, seasonings and flavorings, remember that a little goes a long way. For the best flavor and consistency, always use the amount specified in the recipe.

VANILLA

We favor pure vanilla extract because it is processed from the vanilla bean, not from alternate sources. Pure vanilla has no added ingredients and is more intense and complex in flavor.

Substitutions

Not a fan of kefir? Peaches aren't in season? You've run out of sunflower seeds? Not to worry: these simple substitutions will save the day. The flavor and/or texture of the finished recipe might be somewhat different, but it will still be delicious and nutritious.

Note that the substitutions go both ways: foods in the left-hand column can be replaced with foods from the right-hand column, and vice versa.

Instead of	Try
Almond butter	Cashew butter, sunflower seed butter
Arugula	Dandelion greens, dark lettuces, kale, spinach, watercress
Beans	Any other type of bean, lentil or pea
Blackberries	Blueberries, cherries, raspberries, strawberries
Bok choy	Arugula, dandelion greens, dark lettuces, kale, spinach
Carrots	Butternut or acorn squash, pumpkin purée, sweet potato
Coconut water	Water
Dates	Prunes or soaked dried figs
Goji berries	Dried cranberries, dried currants or raisins
Greek yogurt	Yogurt
Kale	Arugula, bok choy, dark lettuces, spinach, Swiss chard
Kefir	Milk, nondairy milk
Kiwifruit	Mangos, oranges, tangerines
Mangos	Apricots, nectarines, peaches
Peaches	Apricots, mangos, nectarines
Pears	Apples, peaches, plums
Pineapple	Oranges
Pumpkin purée	Butternut or acorn squash, carrots, sweet potato
Rolled oats	Quinoa flakes
Spinach	Bok choy, dark lettuces, kale, Swiss chard
Sunflower seeds	Any other seeds or chopped nuts
Tea	Water
Tomatoes	Red bell peppers
Whey protein powder	Skim milk powder

Let's get blending!

Once you've decided on a recipe you want to prepare, read through the entire recipe and review the equipment and ingredient lists to make sure you have everything you need on hand. For best results, purchase fresh fruits, vegetables and herbs just before you want to use them, or at the most 2 to 3 days ahead.

You will have the most success if you have all of the ingredients prepped and ready to go before you start following the recipe steps (unless otherwise directed in the method).

Here are some more quick tips for the best results:

- Use the manual included with your NutriBullet for a complete description of how to assemble and use it. The manufacturer is the expert on how to safely use its equipment for best results.
- Measure ingredients carefully.
- Always add ingredients in the order listed and according to the recipe directions.
- Follow the recipe steps exactly and in the order listed.
- Wipe down the blender base and housing after each use, and clean the cup, extractor and any covers. Be careful when cleaning and storing the extractor blades, as they are very sharp.

Breakfast Smoothies

Blackberry Pear Smoothie 62

Blueberry Muffin Smoothie.............62

Blueberry and Coconut Protein
   Smoothie 63

Protein Powerhouse with
   Blueberries and Flax Seeds...........64

Blueberry, Pineapple and
   Spinach Boost.................................65

Raspberry, Beet and Mint
   Protein Smoothie 65

Strawberry Grape Smoothie............66

Dreamy Berry and Kale
   Smoothie 66

Berry-Berry-Berry Smoothie............67

Berry and Almond Smoothie...........67

Berrylicious Swiss Chard
   and Chia Smoothie.........................68

Red Grape, Peach and
   Raspberry Smoothie.......................69

Grape, Carrot and Peach
   Smoothie 69

Red and Green Smoothie
   with Pepitas....................................70

Apple, Blueberry and Kale
   with Flax Seeds 70

Pear, Kiwi and Key Lime
   Smoothie 71

Pear, Camu Camu and Arugula
   Smoothie 72

Oatmeal, Peach and Yogurt
   Smoothie 72

Apricot Berry Green Smoothie........73

Banana, Blueberry and Orange
   Smoothie 74

Creamy Banana, Blueberry
   and Papaya Smoothie....................74

Banana, Peach, Citrus and
   Goji Berry Smoothie 75

Banana and Mango Green
   Smoothie 75

Pineapple, Grape and Spinach
   Smoothie 76

Pineapple, Avocado and
   Watercress Smoothie 76

Pineapple, Mango and
   Goji Berry Smoothie 77

Kiwi, Goji Berry and Cacao
   Green Smoothie 78

Beet, Banana and Oat Smoothie.....79

Beet, Citrus and Açaí Berry
   Smoothie 80

Carrot, Raspberry and Oatmeal
   Breakfast...80

Carrot, Mango, Citrus and Ginger
   Smoothie with Hemp Seeds 81

Cucumber Pineapple Green
   Smoothie 82

Ginger, Lime and Arugula
   Pick-Me-Up.....................................82

Protein-Powered Kale, Berry,
   Hemp and Yogurt Smoothie 83

Fiber-Powered Kale, Apple and
   Ginger Smoothie 84

Rejuvenating Spinach, Cucumber
   and Avocado Smoothie 85

Iced Mocha Smoothie 85

Oats, Greens and Camu Camu
   Smoothie Bowl 86

Oats, Greens and Matcha
   Smoothie Bowl 87

Pumped-Up Fall Harvest
   Pumpkin Breakfast Bowl...............88

Blackberry Pear Smoothie

Sweet and juicy pears combined with tart blackberries make this smoothie divine and give your day a boost. By reducing LDL cholesterol oxidation and promoting blood vessel health, this smoothie supports healthy blood pressure and may help reduce the risk for cardiovascular disease and dementia.

MAKES 1 SERVING

- **Tall cup**

1	pear (such as Bartlett or Taylor's Gold), cored and halved	1
1	banana, halved	1
1 cup	blackberries	250 mL
1 tsp	ground cinnamon	5 mL
Pinch	ground cloves	Pinch
2 tsp	liquid honey	10 mL
	Unsweetened almond milk	
1 tbsp	cacao nibs	15 mL

1. Add pear, banana, blackberries, cinnamon, cloves and honey to the tall cup. Add almond milk to the "Max Line." Twist the extractor blade onto the cup to seal. Blend for 30 seconds or until smooth. Sprinkle with cacao nibs.

TIPS

Pears are often sold not quite ripe so they don't become damaged before you get them home. Plan to ripen them at home for a few days before blending them. You can store them in a paper bag to speed up the ripening process.

You can substitute a frozen banana for the fresh. Your smoothie will be much thicker.

Blueberry Muffin Smoothie

If you love blueberry muffins, then you are certainly going to want to add this smoothie to your morning routine. Full of fiber and protein, this smoothie helps to keep your appetite in check while providing anticancer phytonutrients and gut-friendly prebiotics.

MAKES 1 SERVING

- **Tall cup**

1	frozen banana, halved	1
1 cup	frozen blueberries	250 mL
⅔ cup	plain Greek yogurt	150 mL
½ cup	large-flake (old-fashioned) rolled oats	125 mL
1 tbsp	ground flax seeds (flaxseed meal)	15 mL
2 tsp	lemon juice	10 mL
1 tsp	pure vanilla extract	5 mL
	Unsweetened almond milk	

1. Add banana, blueberries, yogurt, oats, flax seeds, lemon juice and vanilla to the tall cup. Add almond milk to the "Max Line." Twist the extractor blade onto the cup to seal. Blend for 30 seconds or until smooth.

> **Optional Nutrition Boost**
> Add 1 tbsp (15 mL) wheat germ after the flax seeds.

Blueberry and Coconut Protein Smoothie

Start your day with this refreshing, energizing smoothie with plump, sweet blueberries and creamy coconut. With antioxidants, protein, calcium and phosphorus, this is a delicious bone-building smoothie.

MAKES 1 SERVING

- **Tall cup**

1	peach, halved and pitted	1
1½ cups	frozen blueberries	375 mL
¼ cup	whey protein powder	60 mL
1 tbsp	pure maple syrup	15 mL
1 tsp	pure vanilla extract	5 mL
	Coconut milk	

Optional Nutrition Boost

Add 1 to 1½ tsp (5 to 7 mL) pomegranate powder after the protein powder.

1. Add peach, blueberries, protein powder, maple syrup and vanilla to the tall cup. Add coconut milk to the "Max Line." Twist the extractor blade onto the cup to seal. Blend for 30 seconds or until smooth.

TIP

Fresh blueberries can be used in place of frozen. You may want to add 1 to 2 ice cubes to make the smoothie colder, but it is still wonderful without them.

Protein Powerhouse with Blueberries and Flax Seeds

Start your day with a protein boost in this sweet, creamy banana and blueberry smoothie. The protein in this smoothie helps to preserve muscle while the lignans may help to reduce the risk for certain cancers, such as breast, prostate and ovarian.

MAKES 1 SERVING		
• **Tall cup**		
½	frozen or fresh banana	½
¾ cup	frozen blueberries	175 mL
3 tbsp	whey protein powder	45 mL
1 tbsp	ground flax seeds (flaxseed meal)	15 mL
2 tsp	liquid honey	10 mL
	Unsweetened almond milk	

1. Add banana, blueberries, protein powder, flax seeds and honey to the tall cup. Add almond milk to the "Max Line." Twist the extractor blade onto the cup to seal. Blend for 30 seconds or until smooth.

TIP

To freeze bananas, peel and cut in half. Place on a baking sheet lined with parchment paper, without overlapping, and cover with plastic wrap. Freeze for 2 hours or until solid. Remove from freezer and transfer bananas to a storage bag or an airtight container and freeze for up to 3 months.

Blueberry, Pineapple and Spinach Boost

Why not give your health a boost with spinach and vitamin C–rich fruits and berries? With magnesium to support insulin metabolism, prebiotics to support digestive health, and B vitamins and antioxidants to support cardiovascular and brain health, this refreshing pick-me-up has a little bit of everything.

MAKES 1 SERVING

- **Tall cup**

1 cup	lightly packed trimmed spinach	250 mL
1	banana, halved	1
1 cup	fresh pineapple chunks	250 mL
1 cup	blueberries	250 mL
2 tbsp	orange juice	30 mL
	Water	

Optional Nutrition Boost
Add 1 tbsp (15 mL) chia seeds after the blueberries.

1. Add spinach, banana, pineapple, blueberries and orange juice to the tall cup. Add water to the "Max Line." Twist the extractor blade onto the cup to seal. Blend for 30 seconds or until smooth.

TIPS

Add 2 to 3 ice cubes to the cup before adding water for a thicker and colder smoothie.

You can substitute frozen banana, pineapple chunks or blueberries for the fresh. Do not add any ice cubes.

Raspberry, Beet and Mint Protein Smoothie

This rockin' red smoothie is loaded with beets, berries and protein for a great way to start your day on a high note. With protein, calcium, flavonoids, fiber, magnesium, betaine and carotenoids, this smoothie promotes healthy bones, heart and gut health and weight management.

MAKES 1 SERVING

- **Tall cup**

1	small beet, peeled and halved	1
1 cup	raspberries	250 mL
¾ cup	plain Greek yogurt	175 mL
3 tbsp	goji berries	45 mL
3	mint leaves	3
	Unsweetened hemp milk	

1. Add beet, raspberries, yogurt, goji berries and mint leaves to the tall cup. Add hemp milk to the "Max Line." Twist the extractor blade onto the cup to seal. Blend for 30 seconds or until smooth.

TIPS

Wear kitchen gloves when peeling and cutting the beet to avoid staining your hands.

You can substitute another type of milk, such as almond or cashew, for the hemp milk.

Strawberry Grape Smoothie

Strawberries pair well with sweet-tart grapes and a hint of ancho chile pepper to give this smoothie a bright taste. Rich in flavonoids and vitamin C, it can help to reduce the risk for cancer and diabetes and may help to preserve cognitive function.

MAKES 1 SERVING

- **Tall cup**

1 cup	halved strawberries	250 mL
1 cup	halved seedless red grapes	250 mL
2 tbsp	almonds	30 mL
½ tsp	ancho chile powder	2 mL
1 tbsp	lemon juice	15 mL
½ tsp	pure vanilla extract	2 mL
	Unsweetened almond milk	
	Sliced strawberries (optional)	
	Mint leaves (optional)	

Optional Nutrition Boost
Add 1½ tsp (7 mL) maca powder after the almonds.

1. Add strawberries, grapes, almonds, chile powder, lemon juice and vanilla to the tall cup. Add almond milk to the "Max Line." Twist the extractor blade onto the cup to seal. Blend for 30 seconds or until smooth.

2. If desired, garnish with sliced strawberries and mint leaves.

VARIATION

Strawberry Rhubarb Smoothie: In step 1, add ½ cup (125 mL) fresh or frozen sliced rhubarb and 1½ tsp (7 mL) sugar or agave syrup, and reduce the grapes to ½ cup (125 mL).

Dreamy Berry and Kale Smoothie

Green and glorious kale is combined with banana, berries, chia seeds and lemon juice for a sweet and citrusy flavor punch. This smoothie delivers a good dose of minerals, protein, vitamin B_3 (niacin) and omega-3 fatty acids. The high fiber content will keep you feeling full and satisfied.

MAKES 1 SERVING

- **Tall cup**

1 cup	lightly packed trimmed kale leaves	250 mL
½	banana	½
1 cup	blueberries	250 mL
½ cup	strawberries	125 mL
2 tbsp	chia seeds	30 mL
3	ice cubes (optional)	3
2 tbsp	lemon juice	30 mL
	Water	

1. Add kale, banana, blueberries, strawberries, chia seeds, ice cubes (if using) and lemon juice to the tall cup. Add water to the "Max Line." Twist the extractor blade onto the cup to seal. Blend for 30 seconds or until smooth.

TIP

To hull strawberries, use a sharp paring knife and cut in a circular motion, pointing toward the center, around the leaves and stem and into the whiter flesh part beneath. Remove the hull and discard.

Berry-Berry-Berry Smoothie

This smoothie is the berry lover's dream. The trio of berries gets an added boost with red grapes and almond milk. The fiber, magnesium, potassium, flavonoids and vitamin C in this smoothie help protect the cardiovascular system from diabetes, inflammation and high blood pressure.

MAKES 1 SERVING

- **Tall cup**

½ cup	frozen raspberries	125 mL
½ cup	frozen blueberries	125 mL
½ cup	frozen halved strawberries	125 mL
½ cup	frozen halved seedless red grapes	125 mL
2 tbsp	almond butter	30 mL
1 tbsp	lemon juice	15 mL
½ tsp	pure vanilla extract	2 mL
	Unsweetened almond milk	

Optional Nutrition Boost
Add 2 tbsp (30 mL) goji berries after the grapes.

1. Add raspberries, blueberries, strawberries, grapes, almond butter, lemon juice and vanilla to the tall cup. Add almond milk to the "Max Line." Twist the extractor blade onto the cup to seal. Blend for 30 seconds or until smooth.

TIPS

You can use fresh berries in place of frozen. Add 2 to 3 ice cubes before adding the almond milk for a thicker and colder smoothie.

To easily cut your grapes in half before freezing, place the grapes in between two flat plates or plastic container lids. Using a sharp knife, cut with a horizontal motion between the two plates, cutting through the grapes.

Berry and Almond Smoothie

This royal blue smoothie is packed with three types of berries, banana and fiber-rich almond butter to give your body the royal treatment. With lots of minerals, vitamin B_2 (riboflavin) and vitamin E, this smoothie supports the immune system and neurotransmitter production and helps to prevent anemia.

MAKES 1 SERVING

- **Tall cup**

½	frozen banana	½
½ cup	frozen strawberries	125 mL
½ cup	frozen raspberries	125 mL
½ cup	frozen blackberries	125 mL
2 tbsp	almond butter	30 mL
2 tsp	lemon juice	10 mL
	Unsweetened almond milk	

1. Add banana, strawberries, raspberries, blackberries, almond butter and lemon juice to the tall cup. Add almond milk to the "Max Line." Twist the extractor blade onto the cup to seal. Blend for 40 seconds or until smooth.

TIPS

If you prefer, you can substitute 3 tbsp (45 mL) almonds in place of the almond butter. There may be some small bits of almonds in your smoothie, which adds a unique consistency.

You can use fresh berries in place of frozen. Add 2 to 3 ice cubes before adding the almond milk for a thicker and colder smoothie.

Berrylicious Swiss Chard and Chia Smoothie

If you don't fall in love with the deep blue color of this smoothie, you will certainly love the vibrant taste and the nutritional boost it supplies. Impressively packed with antioxidants, fiber, omega-3 fatty acids and minerals (including potassium), this smoothie almost does it all.

MAKES 1 SERVING

- **Tall cup**

2 cups	packed torn Swiss chard leaves (about 2 large)	500 mL
½ cup	blueberries	125 mL
½ cup	blackberries	125 mL
¼ cup	goji berries	60 mL
2 tbsp	chia seeds	30 mL
1 tbsp	liquid honey	15 mL
	Coconut milk	

1. Add Swiss chard, blueberries, blackberries, goji berries, chia seeds and honey to the tall cup. Add coconut milk to the "Max Line." Twist the extractor blade onto the cup to seal. Blend for 30 seconds or until smooth.

TIP

Swiss chard stems can be used in several ways. One of my favorites is to pickle them. Cut the stems into about 3-inch (7.5 cm) lengths and arrange vertically in a large-mouth canning jar. Combine ½ cup (125 mL) granulated sugar, 1 tbsp (15 mL) celery seeds, 1 cup (250 mL) white vinegar, and 2 tbsp (30 mL) Thai chile sauce (such as Sriracha) in a measuring cup. Pour into jar, doubling pickling liquid recipe as needed to cover the stems. Cover and refrigerate for at least 2 days or for up to 1 week. Serve alongside your favorite sandwich or burger.

Red Grape, Peach and Raspberry Smoothie

Chin-drippingly juicy peaches go magically with the tartness of grapes and the sweet and tangy essence of raspberries and orange. This smoothie is loaded with healthy probiotic bacteria, fiber, calcium, potassium and anti-inflammatory phytonutrients.

MAKES 1 SERVING

- **Tall cup**

1	peach, halved and pitted	1
1 cup	seedless red grapes	250 mL
1 cup	raspberries	250 mL
1 tsp	ground ginger	5 mL
2 tbsp	orange juice	30 mL
2 tsp	pure maple syrup	10 mL
	Plain kefir	

1. Add peach, grapes, raspberries, ginger, orange juice and maple syrup to the tall cup. Add kefir to the "Max Line." Twist the extractor blade onto the cup to seal. Blend for 30 seconds or until smooth.

TIP

Yellow peaches have a yellow peel with a red blush. If you plan to use them the same day, choose peaches that are soft when lightly pressed with your finger. If the flesh is still firm, let the peaches stand 2 days at room temperature. Select peaches of varying ripeness to use over a few days.

Grape, Carrot and Peach Smoothie

Sweet and juicy peaches get a super boost from carrots, red grapes and chia seeds. The phytonutrients in the form of falcarinol, flavonoids and carotenoids in this smoothie may help reduce the risk for cancer and cardiovascular disease, while the prebiotics support healthy mood.

MAKES 1 SERVING

- **Tall cup**

1	banana, halved	1
1	peach, halved and pitted	1
1	carrot, cut into 2-inch (5 cm) chunks (see tip)	1
1 cup	seedless red grapes	250 mL
1 tbsp	chia seeds	15 mL
2 tbsp	orange juice	30 mL
	Water	

1. Add banana, peach, carrot, grapes, chia seeds and orange juice to the tall cup. Add water to the "Max Line." Twist the extractor blade onto the cup to seal. Blend for 40 seconds or until smooth.

TIP

You may peel the carrots, if you like; however, the peel contains many beneficial nutrients and leaving the peel on makes your smoothie preparation faster. Just be sure to scrub it well under running water before cutting.

Red and Green Smoothie with Pepitas

Grapes add a slightly sweet and sour influence to this creamy smoothie that is packed with greens, seeds and green tea. Rich in antioxidants, vitamin B_3 (niacin), vitamin E and several minerals, this smoothie lowers inflammation and supports eye health and mood.

MAKES 1 SERVING

- **Tall cup**

1 cup	lightly packed torn Swiss chard leaves	250 mL
1	banana, halved	1
1	pitted prune (dried plum)	1
1 cup	red grapes	250 mL
2 tbsp	raw green pumpkin seeds (pepitas)	30 mL
	Brewed green tea (about 1 cup/ 250 mL), cooled	

Optional Nutrition Boost
Add 1 to 1½ tsp (5 to 7 mL) wheatgrass powder after the pumpkin seeds.

1. Add Swiss chard, banana, prune, grapes and pumpkin seeds to the tall cup. Add green tea to the "Max Line." Twist the extractor blade onto the cup to seal. Blend for 30 seconds or until smooth.

Apple, Blueberry and Kale with Flax Seeds

Tart, sweet, citrusy and green all rolled up into a delicious smoothie. Full of pectin and soluble fiber, this smoothie can help to lower cholesterol and support digestive health.

MAKES 1 SERVING

- **Tall cup**

1 cup	lightly packed trimmed kale leaves	250 mL
1	tart apple (such as Granny Smith, Braeburn or Jonathan), quartered	1
½	frozen banana	½
1 cup	frozen blueberries	250 mL
1 tbsp	ground flax seeds (flaxseed meal)	15 mL
2 tbsp	lemon juice	30 mL
	Coconut water	

1. Add kale, apple, banana, blueberries, flax seeds and lemon juice to the tall cup. Add coconut water to the "Max Line." Twist the extractor blade onto the cup to seal. Blend for 30 seconds or until smooth.

TIP

You can replace the kale with arugula, spinach or watercress.

Optional Nutrition Boost
Add 1 to 1½ tsp (5 to 7 mL) camu camu powder after the flax seeds.

Pear, Kiwi and Key Lime Smoothie

Succulent pear comes together with kiwi, mango and tart key lime for a refreshing smoothie. Vitamin C supports collagen production and healthy skin, fiber helps to promote digestive health and lower cholesterol, and potassium and magnesium lower blood pressure. This smoothie does a body good.

MAKES 1 SERVING

- **Tall cup**

2	small kiwifruits, peeled and halved	2
1	pear, halved	1
1	key lime, peeled	1
⅔ cup	frozen mango chunks	150 mL
3	ice cubes	3
1 tbsp	liquid honey	15 mL
	Coconut water	
1 tbsp	cacao nibs	15 mL
	Unsweetened shredded coconut (optional)	

Optional Nutrition Boost
Add 2 tsp (10 mL) cacao powder after the mango.

1. Add kiwis, pear, key lime, mango, ice cubes and honey to the tall cup. Add coconut water to the "Max Line." Twist the extractor blade onto the cup to seal. Blend for 30 seconds or until smooth.

2. Garnish with cacao nibs and shredded coconut (if using).

TIP

Choose kiwis that are firm, yet ripe and unblemished for this smoothie. A ripe kiwi will give to slight pressure when pressed with your thumb.

Pear, Camu Camu and Arugula Smoothie

This sweet and tangy smoothie is a satisfying and fabulous way to get your greens in early. It supports detoxification processes in the liver and healthy skin and bones, and the vitamin C helps reduce the risk for cardiovascular disease and cancer.

MAKES 1 SERVING		

- **Tall cup**

2 cups	packed arugula	500 mL
1	pear, halved	1
½	avocado	½
⅔ cup	frozen seedless red grapes	150 mL
2 tsp	camu camu powder	10 mL
1 tbsp	lime juice	15 mL
	Coconut water	

Optional Nutrition Boost
Add ⅛ tsp (0.5 mL) spirulina powder after the camu camu powder.

1. Add arugula, pear, avocado, grapes, camu camu powder and lime juice to the tall cup. Add coconut water to the "Max Line." Twist the extractor blade onto the cup to seal. Blend for 30 seconds or until smooth.

TIP

To choose a ripe avocado, place it in the palm of your hand and squeeze gently. It should be firm but give slightly. Color does not indicate ripeness, as some varieties turn dark green or black and others have a lighter green skin. Avoid avocados with dark blemishes.

Oatmeal, Peach and Yogurt Smoothie

Get your morning off to a great start with this creamy batch of rolled oats, peaches and yogurt with a hint of nuts and butterscotch from the maca powder. The unique compounds in maca, along with potassium, magnesium and prebiotics, all help to normalize the body's stress response. The smoothie is packed with muscle-loving protein, too.

MAKES 1 SERVING		

- **Tall cup**

1	banana, halved	1
1	peach, halved and pitted	1
1 cup	plain yogurt	250 mL
3 tbsp	large-flake (old-fashioned) rolled oats	45 mL
2 tsp	maca powder	10 mL
2 tsp	liquid honey	10 mL
	Milk	

Optional Nutrition Boost
Add 2 tbsp (30 mL) wheat germ after the oats.

1. Add banana, peach, yogurt, oats, maca powder and honey to the tall cup. Add milk to the "Max Line." Twist the extractor blade onto the cup to seal. Blend for 30 seconds or until smooth.

TIPS

Look for yogurt that contains live active yogurt cultures, as this type contains the most desirable health properties.

Maca powder can be found online or in specialty health-food stores.

Apricot Berry Green Smoothie

Eating your greens doesn't have to be boring — and this smoothie is anything but that. We've topped it off with creamy banana, a powerhouse of berries and sweet dried apricots for an antioxidant-rich morning smoothie. It contains nutrients that support the liver's natural detoxification process.

- **Tall cup**

½ cup	lightly packed trimmed spinach	125 mL
½ cup	lightly packed trimmed kale leaves	125 mL
2	dried apricots	2
1	banana, halved	1
½ cup	frozen mixed berries (such as blackberries, raspberries and strawberries)	125 mL
	Unsweetened almond milk	

Optional Nutrition Boost
Add 1 to 1½ tsp (5 to 7 mL) pomegranate powder after the berries.

1. Add spinach, kale, apricots, banana and berries to the tall cup. Add almond milk to the "Max Line." Twist the extractor blade onto the cup to seal. Blend for 30 seconds or until smooth.

TIP

You can use fresh berries in place of the frozen. You may want to add 2 to 3 ice cubes to make it cooler and thicker.

Banana, Blueberry and Orange Smoothie

Simple and incredibly refreshing are the hallmarks of this healthy purple smoothie. Brimming with potassium, vitamin C and several types of polyphenols, this smoothie supports a healthy nervous system, wound repair and skin health, and may help reduce the risk for cancer.

MAKES 1 SERVING		

- **Small cup**

1	frozen banana, halved	1
1	orange, peeled and seeded	1
½ cup	frozen blueberries	125 mL
	Water	

Optional Nutrition Boost
Add 1 to 1½ tsp (5 to 7 mL) açaí powder after the blueberries.

1. Add banana, orange and blueberries to the small cup. Add water to the "Max Line." Twist the extractor blade onto the cup to seal. Blend for 30 seconds or until smooth.

TIP

You can double this recipe and prepare it in the extra-tall cup. Enjoy one now and keep one cool for later in the day.

Creamy Banana, Blueberry and Papaya Smoothie

Kick off your day with an energy-boosting blend of banana and blueberries. Papaya and yogurt make this a creamy mood-lifting smoothie. Rich in vitamin C, potassium and prebiotics, this smoothie supports digestive and cardiovascular health.

MAKES 1 SERVING		

- **Tall cup**

1	banana, halved	1
1 cup	cubed papaya	250 mL
½ cup	blueberries	125 mL
¼ cup	plain Greek yogurt	60 mL
3	ice cubes	3
1 tsp	pure vanilla extract	5 mL
	Milk	

Optional Nutrition Boost
Add 1 to 1½ tsp (5 to 7 mL) açaí powder after the yogurt.

1. Add banana, papaya, blueberries, yogurt, ice cubes and vanilla to the tall cup. Add milk to the "Max Line." Twist the extractor blade onto the cup to seal. Blend for 30 seconds or until smooth.

TIPS

If you use frozen fruit, you can eliminate the ice cubes.

You can substitute unsweetened almond milk or soy milk for the milk in this recipe.

Banana, Peach, Citrus and Goji Berry Smoothie

The goji berry has been touted for its medicinal properties dating back to ancient China. The bright red and sweet berries add a delicious and nutritious punch to this smoothie. Because it is potassium-rich, it helps to move nutrients into and waste out of cells and lowers blood pressure. Antioxidants protect blood vessels from damage.

- **Tall cup**

1	banana	1
½	large red grapefruit, peeled and seeded	½
½ cup	frozen sliced peaches	125 mL
¼ cup	goji berries	60 mL
	Water	

1. Add banana, grapefruit, peaches and goji berries to the tall cup. Add water to the "Max Line." Twist the extractor blade onto the cup to seal. Blend for 30 seconds or until smooth.

TIP

Any large grapefruit will work. I particularly like red grapefruits because they are just a bit sweeter but still deliver a punch of citrus.

Banana and Mango Green Smoothie

When you want a serious smoothie to start your day, this power-packed combination of spinach, mango, banana and protein is the perfect choice. Blend it up with some cinnamon, honey and rice milk and you will be more than ready to tackle the world. Loaded with potassium, lutein, zeaxanthin and beta-carotene, it supports both brain and skin health.

- **Tall cup**

1 cup	lightly packed trimmed spinach	250 mL
1	small mango, peeled and halved	1
1	banana, halved	1
2½ tbsp	whey protein powder	37 mL
1 tsp	ground cinnamon	5 mL
1 tbsp	liquid honey	15 mL
	Unsweetened rice milk	

Optional Nutrition Boost
Add 1 tbsp (15 mL) chia seeds after the protein powder.

1. Add spinach, mango, banana, protein powder, cinnamon and honey to the tall cup. Add rice milk to the "Max Line." Twist the extractor blade onto the cup to seal. Blend for 20 seconds or until smooth.

TIP

If using frozen mango chunks, use 1 cup (250 mL).

Pineapple, Grape and Spinach Smoothie

Pineapple and red grapes combine with coconut water to give the spinach smoothie a slightly tropical twist. The smoothie's fiber, folate, vitamin K, magnesium and vitamin C make it a bone- and brain-loving treat.

MAKES 1 SERVING		

• **Tall cup**

1 cup	lightly packed trimmed spinach	250 mL
½	banana, halved	½
½ cup	pineapple chunks	125 mL
½ cup	red grapes	125 mL
2	ice cubes	2
	Coconut water	

Optional Nutrition Boost
Add 1 to 1½ tsp (5 to 7 mL) camu camu powder after the grapes.

1. Add spinach, banana, pineapple, grapes and ice cubes to the tall cup. Add coconut water to the "Max Line." Twist the extractor blade onto the cup to seal. Blend for 30 seconds or until smooth.

TIPS

You can use the whole banana to make your smoothie a bit creamier or just snack on the leftover half while enjoying your smoothie.

For a slightly thicker smoothie, use 3 ice cubes.

Pineapple, Avocado and Watercress Smoothie

Going green gets even better with the creamy combination of avocado, watercress and sweet, tart pineapple and pomegranate. This smoothie is packed with anticancer and anti-inflammatory polyphenols and a lot of blood pressure–lowering potassium. The carotenoids help to preserve eye health.

MAKES 1 SERVING		

• **Tall cup**

1 cup	lightly packed trimmed watercress	250 mL
1	avocado, halved	1
1 cup	pineapple chunks, fresh or canned, in juice	250 mL
1½ tsp	pomegranate powder	7 mL
3	ice cubes	3
1 tbsp	lime juice	15 mL
	Water	

1. Add watercress, avocado, pineapple, pomegranate powder, ice cubes and lime juice to the tall cup. Add water to the "Max Line." Twist the extractor blade onto the cup to seal. Blend for 30 seconds or until smooth.

TIP

To choose a ripe avocado, place it in the palm of your hand and squeeze gently. It should be firm but give slightly. Color does not indicate ripeness, as some varieties turn dark green or black and others have a lighter green skin. Avoid avocados with dark blemishes.

Pineapple, Mango and Goji Berry Smoothie

Get the mojo of the tropics with the bright taste of pineapple, mango and goji berries blended with coconut, green tea and chia seeds. This drink is rich in anti-inflammatory compounds, fiber and potassium.

MAKES 1 SERVING

- **Tall cup**

1	mango, cut into chunks	1
½ cup	pineapple chunks	125 mL
¼ cup	unsweetened shredded coconut	60 mL
2 tbsp	goji berries	30 mL
1 tsp	chia seeds	5 mL
½ tsp	ground turmeric	2 mL
1 cup	brewed green tea, cooled	250 mL
	Coconut water	
	Additional goji berries (optional)	
	Additional unsweetened shredded coconut (optional)	
	Pineapple wedge (optional)	

1. Add mango, pineapple, coconut, goji berries, chia seeds, turmeric and green tea to the tall cup. Add coconut water to the "Max Line." Twist the extractor blade onto the cup to seal. Blend for 30 seconds or until smooth.

2. Garnish with goji berries, shredded coconut and a pineapple wedge, if desired.

TIPS

To choose a perfectly ripened mango, squeeze it gently to check if it gives slightly. Do not choose a mango by color, as some varieties display a spectrum of red to yellow colors. The base of the stem will have a fruity aroma when ripe.

You can use frozen pineapple or canned pineapple in juice if fresh is not readily available.

Kiwi, Goji Berry and Cacao Green Smoothie

Sweet and tangy kiwi and goji berries add a light and refreshing taste to baby spinach. This smoothie contains ample prebiotics and fiber and is an antioxidant and anti-inflammatory powerhouse with carotenoids, vitamin C and polyphenols.

MAKES 1 SERVING

- **Tall cup**

1 cup	lightly packed baby spinach	250 mL
1	banana, halved	1
1	kiwifruit, peeled	1
3 tbsp	goji berries	45 mL
2 tbsp	packed fresh mint	30 mL
1 tbsp	cacao powder	15 mL
3	ice cubes	3
	Coconut water	
2 tsp	cacao nibs (optional)	10 mL

Optional Nutrition Boost
Add 1 tbsp (15 mL) brown rice protein powder after the cacao powder.

1. Add spinach, banana, kiwi, goji berries, mint, cacao powder and ice cubes to the tall cup. Add coconut water to the "Max Line." Twist the extractor blade onto the cup to seal. Blend for 30 seconds or until smooth.

2. If desired, garnish with cacao nibs.

TIP

Use a frozen banana and kiwi in place of the fresh and eliminate 1 or all of the ice cubes.

Beet, Banana and Oat Smoothie

If you don't like beets but want to take advantage of their powerful nutritional benefits, then this smoothie is for you. The beet adds the bright red color to this smoothie, but its flavor is camouflaged by the other ingredients. Beets have unique phytonutrients that support liver health.

MAKES 1 SERVING

- **Tall cup**

1	small beet, peeled and halved	1
1	frozen or fresh banana, halved	1
2 tbsp	large-flake (old-fashioned) rolled oats	30 mL
1 tbsp	chia seeds	15 mL
2	ice cubes (optional)	2
2 tsp	liquid honey	10 mL
½ tsp	orange extract or pure vanilla extract	2 mL
	Unsweetened almond milk	

> **Optional Nutrition Boost**
> Add 1 tbsp (15 mL) wheat germ after the chia seeds.

1. Add beet, banana, oats, chia seeds, ice cubes (if using), honey and extract to the tall cup. Add almond milk to the "Max Line." Twist the extractor blade onto the cup to seal. Blend for 30 seconds or until smooth.

TIPS

Wear kitchen gloves when peeling and halving the beet to avoid staining your hands.

Add ice cubes to the cup before adding the almond milk to make a thicker and colder smoothie.

You can substitute another type of milk, such as soy or dairy, for the almond milk.

Beet, Citrus and Açaí Berry Smoothie

Oranges and lemons coalesce with colorful beets in this divine, flavorful smoothie with liver-loving phytonutrients.

MAKES 2 SERVINGS		
• **Tall cup**		
2	small beets, peeled and halved	2
1	orange, peeled and halved	1
1	lemon, peeled and halved	1
1	pitted soft date, preferably Medjool	1
2 tbsp	chopped fresh mint	30 mL
1 tsp	açaí powder	5 mL
3	ice cubes	3
	Unsweetened almond milk	

Optional Nutrition Boost
Add 1 tbsp (15 mL) chia seeds after the mint.

1. Add beets, orange, lemon, date, mint, açaí powder and ice cubes to the tall cup. Add almond milk to the "Max Line." Twist the extractor blade onto the cup to seal. Blend for 30 seconds or until smooth.

TIPS

Wear kitchen gloves when peeling and cutting beets to avoid staining your hands.

While a variety of fresh dates will work in this recipe, Medjool dates are softer and sweeter than many other varieties.

Choose dates that are plump, soft and have shiny skin. They should not have any evidence of crystalizing sugar on their skin.

Carrot, Raspberry and Oatmeal Breakfast

Why not start your day with a dose of vegetables, fruits, grains and protein and feel like you did your body a favor? Carrots contain a phytonutrient called falcarinol, which has been shown to have promising anticancer properties. In addition, this smoothie provides beta- and alpha-carotene, flavonoids and vitamin C, making it a great source of anticancer compounds.

MAKES 1 SERVING		
• **Tall cup**		
1	carrot, cut into chunks	1
1	banana, halved	1
½	orange, peeled and seeded	½
½ cup	raspberries	125 mL
½ cup	plain yogurt	125 mL
¼ cup	large-flake (old-fashioned) rolled oats	60 mL
	Unsweetened almond milk	

1. Add carrot, banana, orange, raspberries, yogurt and oats to the tall cup. Add almond milk to the "Max Line." Twist the extractor blade onto the cup to seal. Blend for 30 seconds or until smooth.

Optional Nutrition Boost
Add 1 to 1½ tsp (5 to 7 mL) açaí powder after the oats.

Carrot, Mango, Citrus and Ginger Smoothie with Hemp Seeds

Loaded with fruits, vegetables, a bit of spice and everything nice, this smoothie delivers great things to your body. This smoothie benefits any health condition with underlying inflammation and supports liver health and cognition.

MAKES 1 SERVING

- **Tall cup**

1	small carrot, cut into chunks	1
1	orange, peeled and seeded	1
1	½- by ½-inch (1 by 1 cm) piece gingerroot	1
½ cup	frozen mango chunks	125 mL
½ cup	frozen pineapple chunks	125 mL
1 tbsp	hemp seeds	15 mL
¾ tsp	ground turmeric	3 mL
1½ tbsp	lemon juice	22 mL
	Water	

Optional Nutrition Boost
Add 1 to 1½ tsp (5 to 7 mL) açaí powder after the hemp seeds.

1. Add carrot, orange, ginger, mango, pineapple, hemp seeds, turmeric and lemon juice to the tall cup. Add water to the "Max Line." Twist the extractor blade onto the cup to seal. Blend for 40 seconds or until smooth.

TIP

You can substitute a ¼- by ¼-inch (0.5 by 0.5 cm) piece of fresh turmeric for the ground turmeric.

Cucumber Pineapple Green Smoothie

Crisp, bright cucumbers and vitamin-rich bok choy unite with the sweet and tart flavors of pineapple and goji berries for a morning smoothie that is cool and refreshing. The phytonutrients found in cruciferous vegetables like bok choy are tough anticancer compounds and support liver detoxification.

MAKES 1 SERVING

- **Tall cup**

1 cup	lightly packed torn bok choy	250 mL
1	small cucumber, cut into chunks	1
1 cup	pineapple chunks, fresh or canned, in juice	250 mL
2 tbsp	goji berries	30 mL
3	ice cubes	3
	Water	

Optional Nutrition Boost
Add 1 tsp (5 mL) açaí powder after the goji berries.

1. Add bok choy, cucumber, pineapple, goji berries and ice cubes to the tall cup. Add water to the "Max Line." Twist the extractor blade onto the cup to seal. Blend for 30 seconds or until smooth.

TIPS

You can substitute trimmed kale leaves or spinach, or a combination, for the bok choy.

Canned pineapple can be purchased in 8-to 20-oz (227 to 567 g) cans. You can use a whole 8-oz (227 mL) can for this recipe. If using a larger can, refrigerate the remaining pineapple in an airtight container for up to 1 week or freeze for up to 3 months.

Ginger, Lime and Arugula Pick-Me-Up

Apple, banana, ginger and lime give the peppery arugula a slightly sweet and tangy balance of flavors. Offering bioflavonoids such as like quercetin, glucosinolates and fiber, this smoothie helps the liver and digestive tract with detoxification. Rich in potassium, it also helps to lower blood pressure and the risk of stroke.

MAKES 1 SERVING

- **Tall cup**

1 cup	lightly packed arugula	250 mL
1	tart apple (such as Granny Smith, Braeburn or Jonathan), quartered	1
1	½- by ½-inch (1 by 1 cm) piece gingerroot	1
½	banana	½
3	ice cubes	3
3 tbsp	lime juice	45 mL
	Coconut water	

Optional Nutrition Boost
Add 1 tbsp (15 mL) wheat germ after the banana.

1. Add arugula, apple, ginger, banana, ice cubes and lime juice to the tall cup. Add coconut water to the "Max Line." Twist the extractor blade onto the cup to seal. Blend for 30 seconds or until smooth.

TIP

A ½- by ½-inch (1 by 1 cm) piece of gingerroot yields about 1½ tsp (7 mL) grated gingerroot. You can find grated gingerroot in jars in well-stocked grocery stores and can use it in place of the fresh. Refrigerate after opening.

Protein-Powered Kale, Berry, Hemp and Yogurt Smoothie

Power-start your day with this creamy combination of kale, blueberries and nutty hemp seeds swirling in Greek yogurt. Full of protein, this smoothie can help preserve muscle. Packed with antioxidants, B vitamins and bone-building minerals, it's like a multivitamin in a glass.

MAKES 1 SERVING

- **Tall cup**

1 cup	lightly packed trimmed kale leaves	250 mL
1	banana, halved	1
¾ cup	strawberries, hulled	175 mL
¾ cup	blueberries	175 mL
1 cup	plain Greek yogurt	250 mL
2 tbsp	hemp seeds	30 mL
	Milk	

1. Add kale, banana, strawberries, blueberries, yogurt and hemp seeds to the tall cup. Add milk to the "Max Line." Twist the extractor blade onto the cup to seal. Blend for 30 seconds or until smooth.

TIPS

Look for yogurt that contains live and active yogurt cultures since this type of cultured yogurt contains the most desirable health properties.

Hemp seeds can be found online or in the nuts and seeds section of well-stocked grocery stores and natural foods stores.

Fiber-Powered Kale, Apple and Ginger Smoothie

Kale, apple and banana get Moroccan-inspired treatment with date, ginger and coconut flakes. Rich in prebiotics, this smoothie supports healthy gut bacteria. Phytonutrients and fiber promote detoxification via the digestive tract and liver.

MAKES 1 SERVING

- **Tall cup**

1 cup	lightly packed trimmed kale leaves	250 mL
1	pitted soft date, preferably Medjool	1
1	½- by ½-inch (1 by 1 cm) piece gingerroot	1
½	apple	½
½	banana	½
2 tbsp	unsweetened flaked coconut	30 mL
2 tsp	roasted chicory root granules	10 mL
	Coconut water	

1. Add kale, date, ginger, apple, banana, coconut and chicory to the tall cup. Add coconut water to the "Max Line." Twist the extractor blade onto the cup to seal. Blend for 30 seconds or until smooth.

TIPS

While a variety of fresh dates will work in this recipe, Medjool dates are softer and sweeter than many other varieties.

Choose dates that are plump, soft and have shiny skin. They should not have any evidence of crystalizing sugar on their skin.

A ½- by ½-inch (1 by 1 cm) piece of gingerroot yields about 1½ tsp (7 mL) grated gingerroot. You can find grated gingerroot in jars in well-stocked grocery stores and you can use it in place of the fresh. Refrigerate after opening.

Rejuvenating Spinach, Cucumber and Avocado Smoothie

This refreshing combination of spinach, cucumber and avocado has hints of ginger and almonds for a perfect kick start to your day. Packed with potassium and the antioxidants lutein and beta-carotene, this smoothie supports healthy blood pressure and heart and eye health.

MAKES 1 SERVING

- **Tall cup**

1 cup	lightly packed spinach	250 mL
1	$\frac{1}{4}$- by $\frac{1}{4}$-inch (0.5 by 0.5 cm) piece gingerroot	1
$\frac{1}{4}$	cucumber	$\frac{1}{4}$
$\frac{1}{4}$	avocado	$\frac{1}{4}$
1 tbsp	liquid honey	15 mL
	Unsweetened almond milk	

Optional Nutrition Boost
Add 1 tbsp (15 mL) ground flax seeds (flaxseed meal) after the avocado.

1. Add spinach, ginger, cucumber, avocado and honey to the tall cup. Add almond milk to the "Max Line." Twist the extractor blade onto the cup to seal. Blend for 20 seconds or until smooth.

TIP

A $\frac{1}{4}$- by $\frac{1}{4}$-inch (0.5 by 0.5 cm) piece of gingerroot yields about $\frac{3}{4}$ tsp (3 mL) grated gingerroot. You can find grated gingerroot in jars in well-stocked grocery stores and you can use it in place of fresh. Refrigerate after opening.

Iced Mocha Smoothie

Chocolate meets chicory root for a sweet, creamy coffee-flavored smoothie to get you energized. Rich in cacao polyphenols, this smoothie reduces blood pressure and promotes healthy blood vessels. The magnesium supports insulin metabolism, and the prebiotics in the cacao powder and nibs benefit healthy gut flora.

MAKES 1 SERVING

- **Tall cup**

2	pitted soft dates, preferably Medjool	2
1$\frac{1}{2}$ tbsp	cacao powder	22 mL
1 tbsp	whey protein powder	15 mL
Pinch	sea salt	Pinch
5	ice cubes	5
1 cup	brewed New Orleans–style coffee (see tip), cooled	250 mL
	Unsweetened almond milk	
2 tsp	cacao nibs	10 mL

1. Add dates, cacao powder, protein powder, salt, ice cubes and coffee to the tall cup. Add almond milk to the "Max Line." Twist the extractor blade onto the cup to seal. Blend for 30 seconds or until smooth.

2. Garnish with cacao nibs.

TIPS

Brew 1 tbsp (15 mL) ground coffee and 2 tsp (10 mL) roasted chicory root granules with 1 cup (250 mL) water.

While a variety of fresh dates will work in this recipe, Medjool dates are softer and sweeter than many other varieties.

Choose dates that are plump, soft and have shiny skin. They should not have any evidence of crystalizing sugar on their skin.

Oats, Greens and Camu Camu Smoothie Bowl

Start your day with a healthy serving of oatmeal, kale and tangy camu camu powder for a breakfast that is filled with fiber, healthy greens and energy-boosting vitamins and minerals. This smoothie helps to preserve both vision and cognitive function by nourishing the brain and eyes.

MAKES 1 SERVING

- **Tall cup**

Smoothie

1 cup	lightly packed baby kale	250 mL
1	frozen banana, halved	1
¼ cup	large-flake (old-fashioned) rolled oats	60 mL
1	¼- by ¼-inch (0.5 by 0.5 cm) piece gingerroot	1
2 tsp	camu camu powder	10 mL
4 to 6 tbsp	unsweetened almond milk	60 to 90 mL

Topping

1	kiwifruit, peeled and cut into chunks	1
¼ cup	blueberries	60 mL
¼ cup	chopped pitted soft dates, preferably Medjool (see tips, page 84)	60 mL
3 tbsp	sunflower seeds	45 mL
3 tbsp	cashews	45 mL

Optional Nutrition Boost
Add 2 tbsp (30 mL) chia seeds to the topping.

1. *Smoothie:* Add kale, banana, oats, ginger, camu camu powder and 4 tbsp (60 mL) almond milk to the tall cup. Twist the extractor blade onto the cup to seal. Blend for 30 seconds or until thick and smooth. If smoothie is too thick, blend in more almond milk, 1 tbsp (15 mL) at a time, for 10 seconds or until the desired consistency is reached. Using a silicone spatula, transfer smoothie to a bowl.

2. *Topping:* Arrange kiwi, blueberries, dates, sunflower seeds and cashews on top of smoothie.

TIPS

The base smoothie portion of a smoothie bowl is meant to be thick, almost pudding-like, in order to support the toppings. If it looks like it's not blending well, you may need to remove the cup from the base and shake or tap it to encourage the ingredients to resettle in the cup before blending again.

Smoothie bowls are meant to have a colorful and festive patterned top. So enjoy yourself while making pretty patterns of your choosing.

Oats, Greens and Matcha Smoothie Bowl

Smoothies are not just for drinking; you can also make them thicker and creamier and eat them with a spoon. The toppings make this blend very inviting, so have fun decorating the top of your smoothie bowl. If you want to get the kids excited about breakfast, just introduce them to smoothie bowls.

MAKES 1 SERVING

- **Tall cup**

Smoothie

1 cup	lightly packed trimmed watercress	250 mL
1	frozen banana, halved	1
1	1- by 1-inch (2.5 by 2.5 cm) piece gingerroot	1
¼ cup	large-flake (old-fashioned) rolled oats	60 mL
1 tsp	matcha powder	5 mL
¼ cup to ½ cup	unsweetened almond milk	60 to 125 mL

Topping

1	peach, sliced	1
¼ cup	blueberries	60 mL
¼ cup	chopped pitted soft dates, preferably Medjool (see tips, page 84)	60 mL
3 tbsp	goji berries	45 mL
3 tbsp	sunflower seeds	45 mL

Optional Nutrition Boost
Add 1 tbsp (15 mL) chia seeds to the topping.

1. *Smoothie:* Add watercress, banana, ginger, oats, matcha powder and ¼ cup (60 mL) almond milk to the tall cup. Twist the extractor blade onto the cup to seal. Blend for 30 seconds or until thick and smooth. If smoothie is too thick, blend in more almond milk, 1 tbsp (15 mL) at a time, for 10 seconds or until the desired consistency is reached. Using a silicone spatula, transfer smoothie to a bowl.

2. *Topping:* Arrange peach, blueberries, dates, goji berries and sunflower seeds on top of smoothie.

TIPS

The base smoothie portion of a smoothie bowl is meant to be thick, almost pudding-like, in order to support the toppings. If it looks like it's not blending well, you may need to remove the cup from the base and shake or tap it to encourage the ingredients to resettle in the cup before blending again.

A 1- by 1-inch (2.5 by 2.5 cm) piece of gingerroot yields about 1 tbsp (15 mL) grated gingerroot. You can find grated gingerroot in jars in well-stocked grocery stores. Refrigerate after opening.

Pumped-Up Fall Harvest Pumpkin Breakfast Bowl

Nab some fresh pumpkins from roadside stands, farmers' markets and grocery stores when they are abounding with these orange gems. This nutritional smoothie supports overall health by providing fiber, loads of antioxidants, vitamin B_3 (niacin), lignans and several minerals.

MAKES 2 SERVINGS

- **Tall cup**

Smoothie

2	frozen bananas, halved	2
1 cup	puréed pumpkin (see tip, page 104) or canned pumpkin purée (not pie filling)	250 mL
3	pitted soft dates, preferably Medjool (see tips, page 84)	3
Pinch	ground allspice	Pinch
Pinch	ground cloves	Pinch
Pinch	ground nutmeg	Pinch
1/4 to 1/2 cup	unsweetened almond milk	60 to 125 mL

Topping

1	fresh banana, sliced	1
1/2 cup	dried cranberries	125 mL
1/4 cup	unsweetened shredded coconut	60 mL
3 tbsp	chopped pecans	45 mL
3 tbsp	sunflower seeds	45 mL
	Chia seeds	
	Ground flax seeds (flaxseed meal)	

1. *Smoothie:* Add frozen bananas, pumpkin, dates, allspice, cloves, nutmeg and 1/4 cup (60 mL) almond milk to the tall cup. Twist the extractor blade onto the cup to seal. Blend for 30 seconds or until thick and smooth. If smoothie is too thick, blend in more almond milk, 1 tbsp (15 mL) at a time, for 10 seconds or until the desired consistency is reached. Using a silicone spatula, transfer smoothie to 2 bowls, dividing equally.

2. *Topping:* Arrange sliced bananas, cranberries, coconut, pecans, sunflower seeds, chia seeds and flax seeds on top of the smoothie.

TIPS

The base smoothie portion of a smoothie bowl is meant to be thick, almost pudding-like, in order to support the toppings. If it looks like it's not blending well, you may need to remove the cup from the base and shake or tap it to encourage the ingredients to resettle in the cup before blending again.

To freeze bananas, peel and halve bananas. Place on a baking sheet lined with parchment paper, without overlapping, and cover with plastic wrap. Freeze for 2 hours or until solid. Remove from freezer and transfer bananas to a storage bag or an airtight container and freeze for up to 3 months.

Anytime Smoothies

Blackberry, Beet and Chia Seed Smoothie 90

Raspberry, Peach and Chia Seed Smoothie 90

Simply Satisfying Blueberry Mango Smoothie 91

Cranberry, Blueberry and Kale Smoothie 92

Strawberry, Camu Camu and Oolong Smoothie 93

Berry and Protein-Powered Greens 94

Black Forest Berry Blast 94

Pear, Cranberry and Bok Choy Smoothie 95

Mango Agua Fresca 96

Refreshing Mango, Strawberry and Carrot Smoothie 97

Sparkling Pineapple Mango Refresher 98

Pineapple, Mango and Bok Choy Smoothie 99

Ayurveda-Inspired Chia Seed and Coconut Smoothie 100

Tropical Kiwi, Coconut and Chia Seed Smoothie 101

Cooling Avocado, Cucumber and Grapefruit Smoothie 102

Pumpkin Cranberry Protein Smoothie 103

Pumpkin, Date and Flaxseed Smoothie 104

Spicy Tomato Avocado Smoothie 105

Hydrating Spinach, Berry and Orange Smoothie 106

Spinach, Pineapple and Mint Smoothie 106

Land and Sea Green Smoothie with Chocolate and Berries 107

Peanut Butter Chocolate Smoothie 108

Creamy Almond Chocolate Smoothie 109

Chocolaty Almond and Date Smoothie 109

Chocolate and Almond Smoothie with Cacao Nibs 110

Chai-Spiced Almond Cacao Smoothie 111

Berry Banana Smoothie Bowl 112

Chocolate, Blackberry, Banana Superfood Smoothie Bowl 113

Pumpkin, Oat and Pomegranate Smoothie Bowl 114

Blackberry, Beet and Chia Seed Smoothie

Give your body and mind the royal treatment with this royal-blue sweet and savory smoothie. Sometimes underappreciated, beets boast a lot of potassium, carotenoids, folate and phytonutrients that support liver health.

MAKES 1 SERVING		
• Tall cup		
1	small beet, peeled and halved	1
1	pitted soft date	1
¾ cup	frozen blackberries	175 mL
¼ cup	lightly packed mint leaves	60 mL
1 tbsp	chia seeds	15 mL
3	ice cubes	3
2 tbsp	lemon juice	30 mL
	Unsweetened almond milk	

Optional Nutrition Boost
Add 1 tbsp (15 mL) wheat germ after the chia seeds.

1. Add beet, date, blackberries, mint, chia seeds, ice cubes and lemon juice to the tall cup. Add almond milk to the "Max Line." Twist the extractor blade onto the cup to seal. Blend for 35 seconds or until smooth.

TIPS

Wear kitchen gloves when peeling and halving beet to avoid staining your hands.

You can substitute another type of milk, such as soy or dairy, for the almond milk.

Raspberry, Peach and Chia Seed Smoothie

Packed with disease-fighting ingredients such as carotenoids, polyphenols and vitamin C, this smoothie also has a fresh and inviting taste.

MAKES 1 SERVING		
1	banana, halved	1
1	peach, halved and pitted	1
1	pear, cored and halved	1
⅔ cup	raspberries	150 mL
1 tbsp	chia seeds	15 mL
	Unsweetened almond milk	

Optional Nutrition Boost
Add 1 tsp (5 mL) açaí powder after the chia seeds.

1. Add banana, peach, pear, raspberries and chia seeds to the tall cup. Add almond milk to the "Max Line." Twist the extractor blade onto the cup to seal. Blend for 20 seconds or until smooth.

TIP

Choose a banana that is firm and free of bruises. The stem and tip should be intact. A completely yellow banana or a yellow banana with some spots is fully ripened. When purchasing bananas, select ones that are at varying stages of ripeness if you want to use them over several days. A banana typically moves from one stage of ripeness to the next daily.

Simply Satisfying Blueberry Mango Smoothie

Great for a quick pick-me-up, this sweet, protein-packed smoothie will give your body a midday boost. Potassium to lower blood pressure, carotenoids and phytonutrients to lower inflammation and risk for cancer — healthy never tasted so good.

MAKES 1 SERVING

- **Tall cup**

1	small mango, cut into chunks	1
1 cup	frozen blueberries	250 mL
½ cup	plain yogurt	125 mL
2 tbsp	vanilla or chocolate whey protein powder	30 mL
1 tbsp	liquid honey	15 mL
1 tsp	pure vanilla extract	5 mL
	Coconut water	
2 tsp	cacao nibs	10 mL
	Unsweetened shredded coconut (optional)	

Optional Nutrition Boost

Add 1 tsp (5 mL) maca powder after the protein powder.

1. Add mango, blueberries, yogurt, protein powder, honey and vanilla to the tall cup. Add coconut water to the "Max Line." Twist the extractor blade onto the cup to seal. Blend for for 30 seconds or until smooth. Garnish with cacao nibs and shredded coconut (if using).

TIP

To choose a perfectly ripened mango, squeeze it gently to check if it gives slightly. Do not choose a mango by color, as some varieties display a spectrum of red to yellow colors. Occasionally, the base of the stem will have a fruity aroma.

Cranberry, Blueberry and Kale Smoothie

This lush berry-packed smoothie is bursting with all-around taste and whole body goodness. With antioxidant polyphenols and compounds that support the liver's natural detoxification process, this is a great nutrition boost any time of the day.

MAKES 1 SERVING

- **Tall cup**

1 cup	lightly packed baby kale	250 mL
1	banana, halved	1
¾ cup	fresh or frozen cranberries	175 mL
¾ cup	blueberries	175 mL
3	ice cubes (optional)	3
	Coconut water	

Optional Nutrition Boost
Add 1½ tsp (7 mL) pomegranate powder after the blueberries.

1. Add kale, banana, cranberries, blueberries and ice cubes (if using) to the tall cup. Add coconut water to the "Max Line." Twist the extractor blade onto the cup to seal. Blend for 20 to 30 seconds or until smooth.

TIPS

Choose kale with smaller leaves that are moist, crisp and free of tiny holes. The leaves should be a rich green color with no yellow or brown spots.

To store fresh kale, wrap unwashed leaves in damp paper towels and refrigerate for up to 3 days. Your kale may stay fresh longer, but it will develop a stronger taste the longer it is stored.

You may want to add 2 tsp (10 mL) liquid honey, stevia or agave nectar for sweetness if your kale has a stronger taste than you desire.

If using fresh cranberries, you may want to add the ice cubes for a thicker consistency.

Strawberry, Camu Camu and Oolong Smoothie

Full of flavor and loaded with vitamin C, magnesium, potassium, and vitamin K, this smoothie is high on our list of favorites.

<table>
<tr><td colspan="3">MAKES 1 SERVING</td></tr>
</table>

- **Tall cup**

1	banana, halved	1
1	peach, halved and pitted	1
1	kiwifruit, peeled	1
1 cup	strawberries	250 mL
1 tsp	camu camu powder	5 mL
	Brewed oolong tea (about 1 cup/250 mL), cooled	

1. Add banana, peach, kiwi, strawberries and camu camu powder to the tall cup. Add oolong tea to the "Max Line." Twist the extractor blade onto the cup to seal. Blend for 20 seconds or until smooth.

TIPS

Choose a peach that has a sweet fragrance. The base color should be soft gold to yellow. The blush top color indicates variety of peach, not ripeness. Peaches should be soft, but not mushy; do not squeeze peaches as they bruise easily.

If you are using peaches over a number of days, select peaches at varying degrees of ripeness. Firm peaches can be stored at room temperature and ripen in up to 3 days. Refrigerate ripe peaches for up to 1 week.

Berry and Protein-Powered Greens

Grab this smoothie for a midday snack to pump up your immune system. The triple dose of strawberries, raspberries and blueberries gives this spinach smoothie a delightful fruity taste.

MAKES 1 SERVING

- **Tall cup**

1 cup	baby spinach	250 mL
½ cup	halved strawberries	125 mL
½ cup	raspberries	125 mL
½ cup	blueberries	125 mL
3 tbsp	packed fresh mint	45 mL
1 tbsp	almonds	15 mL
¼ cup	pasteurized egg whites	60 mL
	Coconut water	

Optional Nutrition Boost
Add 1 tsp (5 mL) green powder (such as spirulina, wheatgrass or chlorella) after the almonds.

1. Add spinach, strawberries, raspberries, blueberries, mint, almonds and egg whites to the tall cup. Add coconut water to the "Max Line." Twist the extractor blade onto the cup to seal. Blend for 30 seconds or until smooth.

TIPS

Smoothies made with egg whites should be refrigerated or consumed within 2 hours.

Fresh or frozen berries can be used in this recipe. Use whatever is in season or you have on hand. The frozen berries will give the smoothie a thicker consistency. If you are using fresh, you can add 1 to 2 ice cubes to the cup before adding the coconut water, if you desire.

Black Forest Berry Blast

If you have ever experienced the sheer delight of indulging in a Black Forest cake, you will surely enjoy our smoothie version. This smoothie has muscle-loving protein, carotenoids for eye health and anti-inflammatory phytonutrients.

MAKES 1 SERVING

- **Tall cup**

1 cup	lightly packed baby spinach	250 mL
½ cup	frozen raspberries	125 mL
½ cup	pitted cherries	125 mL
3 tbsp	cacao powder	45 mL
3 tbsp	whey protein powder	45 mL
1 tbsp	chia seeds	15 mL
	Unsweetened almond or hazelnut milk	

1. Add spinach, raspberries, cherries, cacao powder, protein powder and chia seeds to the tall cup. Add almond milk to the "Max Line." Twist the extractor blade onto the cup to seal. Blend for 30 seconds or until smooth.

TIPS

When pitting cherries, wear kitchen gloves to avoid staining your hands. Pit them over a bowl in the deepest part of your sink, if possible, as the cherry juice can spurt all over.

To pit cherries without a store-bought cherry pitter, insert a pastry tip, chopstick or heavy straw into the stem end of the cherry and push the stone through.

Pear, Cranberry and Bok Choy Smoothie

The slightly peppery, tender leaves and stems of bok choy enhance the sweet and savory flavors of pear, cranberry, peanut butter and ginger in this delightfully unique smoothie. With antioxidants, potassium and anti-inflammatory ginger, this smoothie covers many health-promoting bases.

MAKES 1 SERVING

- **Tall cup**

1½ cups	coarsely chopped baby bok choy	375 mL
1	pear, cored and halved	1
½	frozen or fresh banana	½
½ cup	frozen or fresh cranberries	125 mL
1	½- by ½-inch (1 by 1 cm) piece gingerroot	1
1 tbsp	natural smooth peanut butter	15 mL
2 tsp	lemon juice	10 mL
	Coconut milk	

1. Add bok choy, pear, banana, cranberries, ginger, peanut butter and lemon juice to the tall cup. Add coconut milk to the "Max Line." Twist the extractor blade onto the cup to seal. Blend for 30 seconds or until smooth.

TIPS

Choose bok choy with rigid, firm, spot-free leaves and stems. The leaves can be dark green or yellow-green, depending on the variety. The stalks can also be yellow-green or off-white.

If using fresh banana or cranberries, you can add up to 3 ice cubes before adding the coconut milk to make the smoothie colder and firmer.

A ½- by ½-inch (1 by 1 cm) piece of gingerroot yields about 1½ tsp (7 mL) grated gingerroot. You can find grated gingerroot in jars in well-stocked grocery stores and can use it in place of the fresh. Refrigerate after opening.

Mango Agua Fresca

This refreshing Central American favorite is an ideal thirst quencher. Our version is a cross between a traditional agua fresca, which strains out all the pulp, and a smoothie, which is thicker. This smoothie provides a good dose of vitamin C, alpha-carotene and potassium to boot.

MAKES 1 SERVING

- **Tall cup**

1	mango, peeled and quartered	1
1	kiwifruit, peeled	1
2 tbsp	packed fresh mint	30 mL
3	ice cubes	3
1 tsp	lime juice	5 mL
1 tsp	liquid honey	5 mL
	Water	
1	lime wedge (optional)	1
2	sprigs mint (optional)	2

1. Add mango, kiwi, chopped mint, ice cubes, lime juice and honey to the tall cup. Add water to the "Max Line." Twist the extractor blade onto the cup to seal. Blend for 20 seconds or until smooth. If desired, garnish with lime wedge and sprigs of mint.

TIPS

To choose a perfectly ripened mango, squeeze it gently to check if it gives slightly. Do not choose a mango by color, as some varieties display a spectrum of red to yellow colors. Occasionally, the base of the stem will have a fruity aroma.

Choose a kiwi that is firm and unblemished. The kiwi should give to slight pressure when pressed with your thumb. The size of the kiwi does not indicate ripeness or flavor, so choose any size that looks best to you.

Blueberry Muffin Smoothie (page 62)

Raspberry, Beet and Mint Protein Smoothie (page 65)

Pumped-Up Fall
Harvest Pumpkin
Breakfast Bowl (page 88)

Sparkling Pineapple Mango Refresher (page 98)

Spicy Tomato Avocado Smoothie (page 105)

Chocolate, Blackberry, Banana Superfood Smoothie Bowl (page 113)

African-Inspired Lentil Dip (page 133)

Pineapple, Cashew and Chile Pepper Spread (page 142)

Refreshing Mango, Strawberry and Carrot Smoothie

This revitalizing smoothie is fresh, tasty and abounding with mango, orange, berries and veggies. This smoothie gets its unique antioxidant falcarinol, a potent carotenoid that helps to reduce the risk of cancer, from raw carrot.

MAKES 1 SERVING

- **Tall cup**

1	carrot, cut into chunks	1
½	orange, peeled and seeded	½
½ cup	frozen mango chunks	125 mL
½ cup	frozen strawberries	125 mL
½ cup	plain yogurt	125 mL
2 tbsp	packed fresh mint	30 mL
½ tsp	pure vanilla extract	2 mL
	Coconut water	

Optional Nutrition Boost
Add 1 tsp (5 mL) açaí powder after the mint.

1. Add carrot, orange, mango, strawberries, yogurt, mint and vanilla to the tall cup. Add coconut water to the "Max Line." Twist the extractor blade onto the cup to seal. Blend for 30 seconds or until smooth.

TIP

Choose mint that has crisp and bright green leaves. A bunch of freshly cut mint can be stored with its stems in a glass of water at room temperature for up to 1 week. If purchasing packaged mint leaves, store in a sealable bag or airtight container in your refrigerator.

Sparkling Pineapple Mango Refresher

Serve as a virgin cocktail before dinner or enjoy this refreshing drink any time of the day. Packed with anti-inflammatory compounds, vitamin C and potassium, this smoothie does a body good.

MAKES 2 SERVINGS

- **Tall cup**

1	lime	1
1 cup	frozen mango chunks	250 mL
5	ice cubes	5
1 cup	unsweetened pineapple juice	250 mL
	Sparkling water	

Optional Nutrition Boost
Add 1½ tsp (7 mL) açaí powder after the mango.

1. Using a paring knife, cut 2 to 4 thin strips of zest from the lime. Set aside (discard the remaining zest or reserve for another use).

2. Squeeze lime juice into the tall cup and add mango, ice cubes and pineapple juice. Twist the extractor blade onto the cup to seal. Blend for 45 seconds or until smooth.

3. Pour into individual glasses and top with sparkling water. Garnish with lime peel.

VARIATION

Pour smoothie into ice pop molds and freeze until solid.

TIP

You can grate zest from the remaining lime peel for later use before juicing. Place measured amounts of the zest in ice cube trays, cover with water and freeze until solid and for up to 3 months.

Pineapple, Mango and Bok Choy Smoothie

We love the tropical flavors of the pineapple and mango in this smoothie. Bok choy, kelp, banana and cilantro contribute to the healthful properties of this rich and nutritious smoothie.

MAKES 1 SERVING

- **Tall cup**

1½ cups	coarsely chopped baby bok choy	375 mL
1	fresh or frozen banana, halved	1
1 cup	canned or fresh pineapple chunks, with juice	250 mL
¾ cup	fresh or frozen mango chunks	175 mL
2 tbsp	lightly packed fresh cilantro	30 mL
1 tsp	kelp granules	5 mL
	Coconut water	

1. Add bok choy, banana, pineapple, mango, cilantro and kelp to the tall cup. Add coconut water to the "Max Line." Twist the extractor blade onto the cup to seal. Blend for 30 seconds or until smooth.

TIPS

Choose bok choy with rigid, firm, spot-free leaves and stems. The leaves can be dark green or yellow-green, depending on the variety. The stalks can also be yellow-green or off-white.

To choose a perfectly ripened mango, squeeze it gently to check if it gives slightly. Do not choose a mango by color, as some varieties display a spectrum of red to yellow colors. Occasionally, the base of the stem will have a fruity aroma.

Kelp granules can be purchased online or at specialty food markets.

Ayurveda-Inspired Chia Seed and Coconut Smoothie

This smoothie introduces a plethora of healthy ingredients to your diet. The spices and flavorings are inspired by the ancient Hindu art of medicine. With fiber for optimal digestive health, potassium for a healthy heartbeat and anti-inflammatory turmeric, this smoothie is a triple threat.

MAKES 1 SERVING

- **Tall cup**

2	pitted soft dates, preferably Medjool (see tips, page 102)	2
1	banana, halved	1
¼ cup	unsalted raw cashews	60 mL
2 tbsp	chia seeds	30 mL
1	½- by ½-inch (1 by 1 cm) piece gingerroot	1
1 tsp	ground turmeric	5 mL
1 tsp	grated lemon zest	5 mL
¼ tsp	freshly ground black pepper	1 mL
½ tsp	pure vanilla extract	2 mL
	Coconut water	

1. Add dates, banana, cashews, chia seeds, ginger, turmeric, lemon zest, pepper and vanilla to the tall cup. Add coconut water to the "Max Line." Twist the extractor blade onto the cup to seal. Blend for 30 seconds or until smooth.

TIPS

Unsalted raw cashews can be found in the bulk section of well-stocked grocery stores.

Choose a banana that is firm and free of bruises. The stem and tip should be intact. A completely yellow banana or a yellow banana with some spots is fully ripened. When purchasing bananas, select ones that are at varying stages of ripeness if you want to use them over several days. A banana typically moves from one stage of ripeness to the next daily.

To ripen a banana, place it in a brown paper bag at room temperature.

A ½- by ½-inch (1 by 1 cm) piece of gingerroot yields about 1½ tsp (7 mL) grated gingerroot. You can find grated gingerroot in jars in well-stocked grocery stores and can use it in place of the fresh. Refrigerate after opening.

Tropical Kiwi, Coconut and Chia Seed Smoothie

Bring on the kiwi and coconut for a soothing smoothie that will transport you to the South Pacific. As a cruciferous vegetable, kale has phytonutrients that support the liver's natural detoxification process. This smoothie also delivers a good dose of magnesium, potassium, and vitamins K and C.

MAKES 1 SERVING

- **Tall cup**

1 cup	lightly packed trimmed kale leaves	250 mL
1	frozen banana, halved	1
1	kiwifruit, peeled	1
¼ cup	unsweetened flaked coconut	60 mL
2 tbsp	chia seeds	30 mL
1 tbsp	agave nectar	15 mL
2 tsp	lime juice	10 mL
	Coconut water	

Optional Nutrition Boost
Add 2 tbsp (30 mL) whey protein powder after the chia seeds.

1. Add kale, banana, kiwi, coconut, chia seeds, agave nectar and lime juice to the tall cup. Add coconut water to the "Max Line." Twist the extractor blade onto the cup to seal. Blend for 30 seconds or until smooth.

TIPS

You can make this smoothie ahead, substituting a fresh banana for the frozen, if desired. Place the blended smoothie in the refrigerator for 6 hours or overnight to give the chia seeds time to gel and create a pudding-like consistency. Stir before eating.

Choose a kiwi that is firm and unblemished. The kiwi should give to slight pressure when pressed with your thumb. The size of the kiwi does not indicate ripeness or flavor, so choose any size that looks best to you.

Cooling Avocado, Cucumber and Grapefruit Smoothie

Refreshing and rehydrating are the trademarks of this smoothie — perfect for hot days or after a workout. Packed with potassium, carotenoids and unique phytonutrients, this smoothie will help to maintain a healthy blood pressure, promote eye health and support liver detoxification.

MAKES 1 SERVING

- **Tall cup**

1 cup	lightly packed trimmed watercress	250 mL
3	pitted soft dates, preferably Medjool	3
½	grapefruit, peeled and seeded	½
¼	cucumber	¼
¼	avocado	¼
1 tbsp	lime juice	15 mL
	Water	

Optional Nutrition Boost

Add 2 tbsp (30 mL) plain, vanilla or chocolate whey protein powder after the avocado.

1. Add watercress, dates, grapefruit, cucumber, avocado and lime juice to the tall cup. Add water to the "Max Line." Twist the extractor blade onto the cup to seal. Blend for 20 seconds or until smooth.

TIPS

Half of a lime will yield about 1 tbsp (15 mL) lime juice.

Substitute coconut water for the plain water, if you prefer.

While a variety of fresh dates will work in this recipe, Medjool dates are softer and sweeter than many other varieties.

Choose dates that are plump, soft and have shiny skin. They should not have any evidence of crystalizing sugar on their skin.

Pumpkin Cranberry Protein Smoothie

This savory and sweet protein smoothie makes a wonderfully filling midday meal. Rich in nutrients such as omega-3 fatty acids, zinc, copper, potassium, and vitamins B_1 and B_3, this smoothie supports brain and heart health.

MAKES 1 SERVING

- **Tall cup**

1 cup	puréed pumpkin (see tip, page 104) or canned pumpkin purée (not pie filling)	250 mL
½ cup	frozen cranberries	125 mL
½ cup	plain Greek yogurt	125 mL
2 tbsp	hemp seeds	30 mL
1	1- by 1-inch (2.5 by 2.5 cm) piece gingerroot	1
½ tsp	ground allspice	2 mL
3	ice cubes	3
2 tbsp	pure maple syrup	30 mL
	Unsweetened soy milk	

1. Add pumpkin, cranberries, yogurt, hemp seeds, ginger, allspice, ice cubes and maple syrup to the tall cup. Add soy milk to the "Max Line." Twist the extractor blade onto the cup to seal. Blend for 30 seconds or until smooth.

TIPS

Choose cranberries that are firm, plump and deep red. They should not be shriveled, soft or discolored. Fresh cranberries can be refrigerated for up to 7 months or frozen for up to 1 year.

You can substitute ¼ cup (60 mL) dried cranberries for the fresh cranberries.

A 1- by 1-inch (2.5 by 2.5 cm) piece of gingerroot yields about 1 tbsp (15 mL) grated gingerroot. You can find grated gingerroot in jars in well-stocked grocery stores. Refrigerate after opening.

Pumpkin, Date and Flaxseed Smoothie

We should have called this pumpkin pie in a glass. While you already have an idea how great this smoothie tastes, just wait until you find out how good it is for you. Packed with several types of carotenoids, monounsaturated fat, folate, zinc, copper, and vitamins B_3 and E, this smoothie supports the immune system and brain health.

MAKES 1 SERVING

• Tall cup

1 cup	lightly packed trimmed spinach	250 mL
4	pitted soft dates, preferably Medjool (see tips, page 102)	4
½	avocado	½
¾ cup	puréed pumpkin (see tip) or canned pumpkin purée (not pie filling)	175 mL
2 tbsp	ground flax seeds (flaxseed meal)	30 mL
¼ tsp	ground ginger	1 mL
¼ tsp	ground nutmeg	1 mL
⅛ tsp	ground allspice	0.5 mL
⅛ tsp	ground cloves	0.5 mL
½ tsp	pure vanilla extract	2 mL
	White or green tea	

1. Add spinach, dates, avocado, pumpkin, flax seeds, ginger, nutmeg, allspice, cloves and vanilla to the tall cup. Add white tea to the "Max Line." Twist the extractor blade onto the cup to seal. Blend for 20 seconds or until smooth.

TIP

Puréed Pumpkin: Preheat oven to 350°F (180°C). Cut 1 pie pumpkin in half and remove seeds. Arrange, cut side down, on rimmed baking sheet lined with foil. Bake for 45 minutes to 1 hour or until pumpkin is soft when pressed and juices are beginning to caramelize. Let cool. Scoop out pumpkin flesh and drain in a fine-mesh sieve. Add to the "Max Line" of the extra-tall cup, in batches as necessary. Blend for 30 seconds or until smooth. Repeat with remaining pumpkin. Measure pumpkin into 1-cup (250 mL) batches and store in individual airtight containers in the refrigerator for up to 1 week or in the freezer for up to 3 months.

Spicy Tomato Avocado Smoothie

A deliciously intoxicating version of a Virgin Bloody Mary with tomatoes, green goodies and a little spicy kick. As a source of lycopene and other compounds found in tomatoes, this smoothie promotes cardiovascular, skin and prostate health. The iodine in dulse supports the thyroid for healthy metabolism.

MAKES 1 SERVING

- **Tall cup**

1 cup	packed arugula	250 mL
2	small heirloom or beefsteak tomatoes, halved and cored	2
½	avocado	½
2½ tsp	hot pepper flakes	12 mL
1 tsp	dulse flakes	5 mL
1 tsp	ground ginger	5 mL
3 to 4	ice cubes	3 to 4
1 tbsp	Worcestershire sauce	15 mL
	Brewed green tea (about 1 cup/ 250 mL), cooled	

> **Optional Nutrition Boost**
> Add 3 tbsp (45 mL) whey protein powder after the avocado.

1. Add arugula, tomatoes, avocado, hot pepper flakes, dulse flakes, ginger, ice cubes and Worcestershire sauce to the tall cup. Add green tea to the "Max Line." Twist the extractor blade onto the cup to seal. Blend for 20 seconds or until smooth.

TIPS

Choose tomatoes that have rich colors and smell sweet. Tomatoes vary in color but all contain nutrients. They should have smooth skins with no cracks, bruises or soft spots.

If you're feeling adventurous and love spiciness, add a pinch of cayenne pepper or a peeled clove of garlic with the tomatoes.

Hydrating Spinach, Berry and Orange Smoothie

Keeping your body hydrated, especially during a workout, can be challenging. But this refreshing smoothie makes your job easier. The healthy bacteria in your gut will love the prebiotics and other fibers found in this smoothie; a healthy gut is associated with better mood, digestion and immunity.

MAKES 1 SERVING

- **Tall cup**

½ cup	lightly packed trimmed spinach	125 mL
1	small orange, peeled and seeded	1
½	banana	½
½ cup	raspberries	125 mL
½ cup	red seedless grapes	125 mL
2 tbsp	açaí powder	30 mL
2 tsp	chicory root powder	10 mL
2 tsp	liquid honey or agave nectar	10 mL
	Water	

1. Add spinach, orange, banana, raspberries, grapes, açaí powder, chicory root and honey to the tall cup. Add water to the "Max Line." Twist the extractor blade onto the cup to seal. Blend for 30 seconds or until smooth.

TIP

You can substitute blackberries or blueberries for the raspberries in this smoothie.

Optional Nutrition Boost
Add ½ to 2 tsp (2 to 10 mL) pomegranate powder after the chicory root.

Spinach, Pineapple and Mint Smoothie

Fresh spinach, mint and pineapple unite for a refreshing and nutritionally powerful smoothie packed with potassium, beta-carotene, alpha-carotene, lutein and prebiotics, supporting gut health and the nervous system while promoting eye and skin health.

MAKES 1 SERVING

- **Tall cup**

1 cup	lightly packed trimmed spinach	250 mL
2	fresh or frozen bananas, halved	2
1 cup	fresh or canned pineapple chunks, with juice	250 mL
¼ cup	lightly packed fresh mint leaves	60 mL
2 tbsp	hemp seeds	30 mL
	Coconut water	

Optional Nutrition Boost
Add 1 tsp (5 mL) açaí powder after the hemp seeds.

1. Add spinach, bananas, pineapple, mint and hemp seeds to the tall cup. Add coconut water to the "Max Line." Twist the extractor blade onto the cup to seal. Blend for 30 seconds or until smooth.

TIP

Choose fresh pineapples that are yellow-orange in color and have bright skin. A ripe pineapple will smell very fragrant and the leaves will pull out easily when tugged. Do not choose even a slightly green or unripe pineapple since they do not ripen well after being picked.

Land and Sea Green Smoothie with Chocolate and Berries

Going green gets even more interesting with this combination of land- and sea-grown vegetables with berries and chocolate. Iodine-rich dulse helps support the thyroid gland and therefore energy levels and a sense of well-being. A good source of vitamins, minerals and phytonutrients, this smoothie is a heavy hitter.

MAKES 1 SERVING

- **Tall cup**

1 cup	firmly packed trimmed watercress	250 mL
2	pitted soft dates, preferably Medjool (see tips, page 102)	2
1	small carrot, halved	1
1 cup	frozen raspberries	250 mL
1 tbsp	cacao powder	15 mL
1 tsp	dulse flakes	5 mL
	Unsweetened almond milk	

Optional Nutrition Boost
Add 1 tbsp (15 mL) natural almond butter after the dulse.

1. Add watercress, dates, carrot, raspberries, cacao powder and dulse to the tall cup. Add almond milk to the "Max Line." Twist the extractor blade onto the cup to seal. Blend for 30 seconds or until smooth.

TIP

Choose watercress that has crisp and bright green leaves with no yellowing. Watercress is delicate and, as such, is best eaten within 1 day of purchase. Both the leaves and stems are edible, but the stems tend to get tougher later in the season.

Peanut Butter Chocolate Smoothie

This smoothie reminds me of those famous chocolate-covered peanut butter cups but with a healthy twist and without the guilt. With too many nutrients to list, this smoothie adds to your nutritional defenses against cancer, supports bone and cardiovascular health and helps to maintain muscle.

MAKES 1 SERVING		

- **Tall cup**

½	banana	½
1 cup	raspberries	250 mL
⅔ cup	plain Greek yogurt	150 mL
1½ tbsp	cacao powder	22 mL
3 tbsp	natural smooth peanut butter	45 mL
	Unsweetened almond milk	
	Cacao nibs (optional)	

Optional Nutrition Boost

Add 1 to 1½ tsp (5 to 7 mL) maca powder after the cacao powder.

1. Add banana, raspberries, yogurt, cacao powder and peanut butter to the tall cup. Add almond milk to the "Max Line." Twist the extractor blade onto the cup to seal. Blend for 30 seconds or until smooth. If desired, sprinkle with cacao nibs.

TIP

Choose raspberries that are plump, evenly colored and have a soft, glossy appearance. They should be free of bruises and discoloration. Refrigerate fresh raspberries for up to 2 days. Handle raspberries carefully and rinse gently before using.

Creamy Almond Chocolate Smoothie

If you are craving a chocolate malt, then this fusion of flavor will satisfy your taste buds and give you a nutritious boost — a very tasty way to get some protein, calcium, phosphorus, and vitamins B_2 and B_5.

MAKES 1 SERVING

- **Tall cup**

1	frozen banana, halved	1
2/3 cup	plain yogurt	150 mL
1 tbsp	cacao powder	15 mL
1 tbsp	ground flax seeds (flaxseed meal)	15 mL
1 tbsp	vanilla or chocolate whey protein powder	15 mL
2 tbsp	natural almond butter	30 mL
1 tbsp	pure maple syrup	15 mL
	Unsweetened almond milk	

Optional Nutrition Boost
Add 1 tsp (5 mL) maca powder after the protein powder.

1. Add banana, yogurt, cacao powder, flax seeds, protein powder, almond butter and maple syrup to the tall cup. Add almond milk to the "Max Line." Twist the extractor blade onto the cup to seal. Blend for 30 seconds or until smooth.

TIP

Look for yogurt that contains live active yogurt cultures, as this type has the most desirable health properties.

Chocolaty Almond and Date Smoothie

This creamy chocolate and almond-infused smoothie sweetened with fresh dates will put a dreamy smile on your face. B vitamins, vitamin E, potassium and prebiotics — this smoothie covers a lot of bases, from healthy mood support to digestive health and more.

MAKES 1 SERVING

- **Tall cup**

4	pitted soft dates, preferably Medjool	4
1 1/2	frozen bananas, halved	1 1/2
3 tbsp	whey protein powder	45 mL
1 tbsp	cacao powder	15 mL
1 tbsp	natural almond butter	15 mL
	Unsweetened almond milk	

1. Add dates, bananas, protein powder, cacao powder and almond butter to the tall cup. Add almond milk to the "Max Line." Twist the extractor blade onto the cup to seal. Blend for 30 seconds or until smooth.

TIPS

While a variety of fresh dates will work in this recipe, Medjool dates are softer and sweeter than many other varieties.

Choose dates that are plump, soft and have shiny skin. They should not have any evidence of crystalizing sugar on their skin.

Chocolate and Almond Smoothie with Cacao Nibs

The combination of chocolate and almonds is like eating your favorite candy bar in a good-for-your-body smoothie. The antioxidants in this creamy, chocolaty smoothie help to keep your skin healthy and healthy-looking. It is also rich in lutein and zeaxanthin, which help reduce the risk of macular degeneration.

MAKES 1 SERVING

- **Tall cup**

1 cup	lightly packed trimmed spinach	250 mL
1	frozen banana, halved	1
3 tbsp	almonds	45 mL
1 tbsp	cacao powder	15 mL
3	ice cubes	3
1 tbsp	liquid honey (optional)	15 mL
	Unsweetened almond milk	
1 tbsp	cacao nibs	15 mL
1 tbsp	unsweetened shredded coconut	15 mL

Optional Nutrition Boost
Add 1 tsp (5 mL) maca powder after the cacao powder.

1. Add spinach, banana, almonds, cacao powder, ice cubes and honey (if using) to the tall cup. Add almond milk to the "Max Line." Twist the extractor blade onto the cup to seal. Blend for 40 seconds or until smooth. Garnish with cacao nibs and shredded coconut.

TIPS

Choose spinach with thin, flexible leaves, indicating a younger and more tender plant.

Buy loose-leaf spinach, if possible, so you can select individual younger, green and unbruised leaves.

Chai-Spiced Almond Cacao Smoothie

In this sweet and savory smoothie, cacao, almond butter and dates are blended with an exotic mix of spices. The cacao polyphenols promote healthy blood vessels and lower blood pressure, and almond butter boosts your daily quota of copper, manganese, vitamin E and vitamin B_2.

MAKES 1 SERVING

- **Tall cup**

5	pitted soft dates, preferably Medjool	5
¼ cup	natural almond butter	50 mL
½	frozen banana	½
1 tbsp	cacao powder	15 mL
1 tsp	ground ginger	5 mL
½ tsp	ground cinnamon	2 mL
¼ tsp	ground cardamom	1 mL
¼ tsp	ground allspice	1 mL
¼ tsp	ground cloves	1 mL
½ tsp	pure vanilla extract	2 mL
	Unsweetened almond milk	

Optional Nutrition Boost
Add 1 tsp (5 mL) maca powder after the ginger.

1. Add dates, almond butter, cacao powder, ginger, cinnamon, cardamom, allspice, cloves and vanilla to the tall cup. Add almond milk to the "Max Line." Twist the extractor blade onto the cup to seal. Blend for 40 seconds or until smooth.

TIPS

While a variety of fresh dates will work in this recipe, Medjool dates are softer and sweeter than many other varieties.

Choose dates that are plump, soft and have shiny skin. They should not have any evidence of crystalizing sugar on their skin.

If using a different variety of dates that are more wrinkled and semi-tender, soak them in warm water for at least 1 hour and up to 6 hours. Drain before using.

Berry Banana Smoothie Bowl

Oh, smoothie bowls, where have you been all my life? Delicious, healthy and absolutely inviting, these bowls are a winning combination. Full of fiber and prebiotics, this smoothie supports gut and digestive health, and the ample potassium promotes communication throughout the nervous system.

MAKES 2 SERVINGS

- **Extra-tall cup**

Smoothie

5	large pitted soft dates, preferably Medjool, divided (see tips, page 102)	5
2	frozen bananas, halved	2
1	fresh banana, halved, divided	1
½ cup	frozen blueberries	125 mL
½ cup	frozen raspberries	125 mL
1 tsp	ground cinnamon	5 mL
¼ cup	natural smooth peanut butter	60 mL
¼ to ½ cup	unsweetened almond milk	60 to 125 mL

Topping

¼ cup	fresh blueberries	60 mL
3 tbsp	unsweetened flaked coconut	45 mL
2 tbsp	goji berries	30 mL
1 tbsp	ground flax seeds (flaxseed meal)	15 mL
1 tbsp	chia seeds	15 mL
2 tsp	raw green pumpkin seeds (pepitas)	10 mL

1. *Smoothie:* Add 3 dates, frozen bananas, half the fresh banana, frozen blueberries, raspberries, cinnamon, peanut butter and ¼ cup (60 mL) almond milk to the extra-tall cup. Twist the extractor blade onto the cup to seal. Blend for 30 seconds or until thick and smooth. If smoothie is too thick, blend in more almond milk, 1 tbsp (15 mL) at a time, for 10 seconds or until the desired consistency is reached. Using a silicone spatula, transfer smoothie to 2 bowls, dividing equally.

2. *Topping:* Slice remaining half fresh banana. Chop remaining dates. Arrange banana, dates, fresh blueberries, coconut, goji berries, flax seeds, chia seeds and pumpkin seeds on top of smoothie.

TIPS

The base smoothie portion of a smoothie bowl is meant to be thick, almost pudding-like, in order to support the toppings. If it looks like it's not blending well, you may need to remove the cup from the base and shake or tap it to encourage the ingredients to resettle in the cup before blending again.

Smoothie bowls are meant to have a colorful and festive patterned top. So enjoy yourself while making any pretty or mouthwatering pattern of your choosing.

Chocolate, Blackberry, Banana Superfood Smoothie Bowl

For all of you chocolate lovers, here is a healthy, mouthwatering smoothie bowl with berries, banana, greens and, of course, chocolate. This smoothie has bone-loving nutrients like calcium, magnesium, vitamin K and potassium. Your cardiovascular system will benefit from the carotenoids, too.

MAKES 1 SERVING

- **Tall cup**

Smoothie

1 cup	lightly packed trimmed spinach	250 mL
1	frozen banana, halved	1
⅔ cup	frozen blackberries	150 mL
2 tbsp	chocolate whey protein powder	30 mL
2 tsp	cacao powder	10 mL
2 tsp	roasted chicory root granules	10 mL
2 tsp	granulated sugar or coconut sugar	10 mL
4 to 6 tbsp	unsweetened almond milk	60 to 90 mL

Topping

½	fresh banana	½
¼ cup	fresh or drained canned pineapple chunks	60 mL
2 tbsp	cacao nibs	30 mL
2 tbsp	slivered almonds	30 mL
2 tbsp	unsweetened flaked coconut	30 mL
1 tbsp	goji berries	15 mL
1 tbsp	chia seeds	15 mL

1. *Smoothie:* Add spinach, frozen banana, blackberries, protein powder, cacao powder, chicory root, sugar and 4 tbsp (60 mL) almond milk to the tall cup. Twist the extractor blade onto the cup to seal. Blend for 30 seconds or until thick and smooth. If smoothie is too thick, blend in more almond milk, 1 tbsp (15 mL) at a time, for 10 seconds or until the desired consistency is reached. Using a silicone spatula, transfer smoothie to a bowl.

2. *Topping:* Cut fresh banana into slices. Arrange banana, pineapple, cacao nibs, almonds, coconut, goji berries and chia seeds on top of smoothie.

TIPS

The base smoothie portion of a smoothie bowl is meant to be thick, almost pudding-like, in order to support the toppings. If it looks like it's not blending well, you may need to remove the cup from the base and shake or tap it to encourage the ingredients to resettle in the cup before blending again.

Smoothie bowls are meant to have a colorful and festive patterned top. So enjoy yourself while making any pretty or mouthwatering pattern of your choosing.

Pumpkin, Oat and Pomegranate Smoothie Bowl

This hearty, sweet and slightly tart smoothie bowl showcases a wealth of superfoods that not only taste amazing, but also deliver a payload of nutrients too numerous to list but that benefit the whole body.

- **Tall cup**

Smoothie

1	frozen banana, halved	1
1 cup	puréed pumpkin (see tip, page 104) or canned pumpkin purée (not pie filling)	250 mL
¼ cup	large-flake (old-fashioned) rolled oats	60 mL
2 tsp	pomegranate powder	10 mL
½ tsp	ground cinnamon	2 mL
3	ice cubes	3
1 tbsp	light (fancy) molasses	15 mL
4 to 6 tbsp	unsweetened almond milk	60 to 90 mL

Topping

½	fresh banana, sliced	½
¼ cup	blueberries	60 mL
¼ cup	pomegranate seeds	60 mL
3 tbsp	raw green pumpkin seeds (pepitas)	45 mL

1. *Smoothie:* Add frozen banana, pumpkin, rolled oats, pomegranate powder, cinnamon, ice cubes, molasses and 4 tbsp (60 mL) almond milk to the tall cup. Twist the extractor blade onto the cup to seal. Blend for 30 seconds or until thick and smooth. If smoothie is too thick, blend in more almond milk, 1 tbsp (15 mL) at a time, for 10 seconds or until the desired consistency is reached. Using a silicone spatula, transfer smoothie to a bowl.

2. *Topping:* Arrange sliced banana, blueberries, pomegranate seeds and pumpkin seeds on top of smoothie.

TIPS

To remove the seeds from a pomegranate, cut the pomegranate in half, hold the pomegranate cut side down over a bowl and use a wooden spoon to firmly tap the outside of the pomegranate. The seeds will drop into the bowl.

The base smoothie portion of a smoothie bowl is meant to be thick, almost pudding-like, in order to support the toppings. If it looks like it's not blending well, you may need to remove the cup from the base and shake or tap it to encourage the ingredients to resettle in the cup before blending again.

Smoothie bowls are meant to have a colorful and festive patterned top. So enjoy yourself while making any pretty or mouthwatering pattern of your choosing.

Dressings, Dips and Spreads

Tomato Vinaigrette.........................116

Greek-Inspired Almond
    "Feta" Vinaigrette 117

Blueberry Sesame Dressing...........118

Raspberry Poppy Seed Dressing....119

Strawberry Almond Dressing........120

Carrot Ginger Dressing 121

Cilantro Jalapeño Ranch
    Dressing..122

Tex-Mex Salad Dressing 123

Pineapple, Ginger and
    Peanut Butter Marinade..............124

Cranberry, Pineapple and
    Almond Relish 125

Avocado and Pineapple Salsa........126

Sweet Chile Dipping Sauce............127

Romesco Dipping Sauce with
    Tomatoes and Almonds 128

Creamy Beet, Ginger and
    Almond Dip 129

Spicy Moroccan-Inspired
    Tomato Dip....................................130

Creamy Kale and Feta Dip............131

Mint Cashew Cream Dip................132

African-Inspired Lentil Dip 133

Time-Out Black Bean Dip 134

Spicy White Bean Dip 135

Chickpea and Yogurt Dip..............136

Traditional Creamy Hummus 137

Pesto Almond Hummus.................138

Spinach, Hot Pepper and Yogurt
    Hummus...139

Mango Guacamole 140

Guacamole with Tomatoes
    and Cilantro 141

Pineapple, Cashew and
    Chile Pepper Spread 142

Tomato Vinaigrette

This zesty vinaigrette combines lush red tomatoes, pear and spicy turmeric notes for a tasty topping or marinade. This vinaigrette is an anti-inflammatory superstar with tomatoes, turmeric, and basil.

MAKES 2 CUPS (500 ML)

- **Tall cup**

1 cup	packed fresh basil leaves	250 mL
3	plum (Roma) tomatoes, cored, halved and seeded	3
1	pear (such as Bartlett or Taylor's gold), halved	1
1 tbsp	ground turmeric	15 mL
2 tsp	dry mustard	10 mL
1 tsp	hot pepper flakes (optional)	5 mL
2	cloves garlic	2
¾ cup	sunflower oil	175 mL
¼ cup	red wine vinegar or apple cider vinegar	60 mL

1. Add basil, tomatoes, pear, turmeric, mustard, hot pepper flakes (if using), garlic, oil and vinegar to the tall cup. Twist the extractor blade onto the cup to seal. Blend for 30 seconds or until smooth.

2. Serve immediately or store in an airtight container in the refrigerator for up to 3 days.

TIP

Choose tomatoes that have a deep, rich color. They should be firm with no cracks, wrinkles or bruises. They should smell sweet and slightly woody. Store ripe tomatoes, uncovered, at room temperature. To speed up ripening, place them in a pierced paper bag with an apple or kiwi. Ripe tomatoes will last up to 3 days.

Greek-Inspired Almond "Feta" Vinaigrette

This zesty faux-feta vinaigrette is perfect for drizzling over tomatoes, greens or chickpeas. As a good source of vitamins B_2 and E, copper and manganese, this dressing supports healthy mood and cognition and is a source of antioxidants.

MAKES 1 CUP (250 ML)

- Small cup
- Strainer, lined with 3 layers of cheesecloth
- Kitchen string
- Tall cup

Almond Feta

½ cup	raw almonds, blanched (see tip)	125 mL
¾ tsp	kosher salt	3 mL
1	clove garlic	1
2 tbsp	lemon juice	30 mL
1½ tbsp	sunflower oil	22 mL
¼ cup	cold water	60 mL

Vinaigrette

4	fresh basil leaves	4
2 tsp	fresh thyme leaves	10 mL
2 tsp	fresh oregano leaves	10 mL
1 tsp	fresh rosemary leaves	5 mL
3	cloves garlic	3
	Juice of 2 lemons	
½ cup	sunflower oil	125 mL
¼ cup	red wine vinegar	60 mL
	Kosher salt and freshly ground black pepper	

> **Optional Nutrition Boost**
> Add 2 tsp (10 mL) chia seeds as a garnish to any salad where you use this vinaigrette.

1. *Almond Feta:* Add almonds, salt, garlic, lemon juice, oil and cold water to the small cup. Twist the extractor blade onto the cup to seal. Blend for 30 seconds or until smooth.

2. Remove the cup from the power base and twist off the extractor blade. Spoon mixture into prepared strainer set over a bowl. Pull edges of cheesecloth up and twist around cheese to form a ball, squeezing gently to remove moisture, and tie with string. Return ball to strainer and refrigerate for 12 hours. Discard liquids.

3. *Vinaigrette:* Remove feta from cheesecloth and add to the tall cup. Add basil, thyme, oregano, rosemary, garlic, lemon juice, oil and vinegar on top of feta. Season with salt and pepper. Twist the extractor blade onto the cup to seal. Blend for 20 seconds or until well combined.

4. Serve immediately or store in an airtight container in the refrigerator for up to 3 days.

TIPS

To blanch almonds, place them in a small bowl and cover with 3 inches (7.5 cm) cold water. Let stand at room temperature for 24 hours. Drain and discard liquid. Rinse almonds under cold water and drain again.

You can double the feta recipe: use half in the vinaigrette and use the remaining half as crumbles. To make the feta slightly crumbly, after step 2, preheat oven to 200°F (100°C). Spread cheese into a ¾-inch (2 cm) thick sphere on a baking sheet lined with parchment paper. Bake for 40 minutes or until slightly firm. Let cool. Use immediately or store the cooled feta in an airtight container in the refrigerator for up to 2 days.

Blueberry Sesame Dressing

This refreshing dressing, full of polyphenols and carotenoids, adds both nutritional value and a bright and creamy nuance to any of your favorite salad greens. Try a combination of arugula, kale and/or spinach for maximum benefit.

MAKES 1½ CUPS (375 ML)

- **Tall cup**

1 cup	blueberries	250 mL
1	¼- by ¼-inch (0.5 by 0.5 cm) piece gingerroot	1
4 to 6 tbsp	unsweetened almond milk	60 to 90 mL
2 tbsp	tahini	30 mL
1 tbsp	lemon juice	15 mL
2 tsp	pure maple syrup (optional)	10 mL

Optional Nutrition Boost

Add 1 tsp (5 mL) pomegranate powder after the ginger.

1. Add blueberries, ginger, 4 tbsp (60 mL) almond milk, tahini, lemon juice and maple syrup (if using) to the tall cup. Twist the extractor blade onto the cup to seal. Blend for 20 seconds or until smooth.

2. If the dressing is too thick, blend in more almond milk, 1 tbsp (15 mL) at a time, for 10 seconds or until the desired consistency is reached.

3. Serve immediately or store in an airtight container in the refrigerator for up to 1 week.

TIPS

Serve over salad greens, top with additional blueberries and garnish with slivered almonds or sunflower seeds.

A ¼- by ¼-inch (0.5 by 0.5 cm) piece of gingerroot yields about 1 tsp (5 mL) grated gingerroot. You can find grated gingerroot in jars in well-stocked grocery stores and can use it in place of the fresh. Refrigerate after opening.

Raspberry Poppy Seed Dressing

Sweet, ruby raspberries are the cornerstone of this refreshing dressing. It is garden-party-worthy served over a crisp summer salad. Rich in polyphenols like flavonoids, this dressing helps to lower inflammation while protecting the blood vessels of the cardiovascular system and helping to preserve eye health.

MAKES 1¼ CUPS (300 ML)

- **Tall cup**

⅓ cup	raspberries	75 mL
1½ tsp	pomegranate powder	7 mL
1	small shallot	1
⅓ cup	sunflower oil	75 mL
¼ cup	raspberry vinegar (see tip) or red wine vinegar	60 mL
¼ cup	water	60 mL
2 tbsp	pomegranate molasses or liquid honey	30 mL
1 tbsp	poppy seeds	15 mL
	Kosher salt	

1. Add raspberries, pomegranate powder, shallot, oil, vinegar, water and pomegranate molasses to the tall cup. Twist the extractor blade onto the cup to seal. Blend for 20 seconds or until combined.

2. Add poppy seeds and season to taste with salt. Cover the tall cup with the twist-on cover and shake gently to combine.

3. Serve immediately or store in an airtight container in the refrigerator for up to 3 days.

TIP

To make raspberry vinegar, pack 2 cups (500 mL) raspberries into a 1-pint (500 mL) jar with a tight-fitting lid. Pour 1 cup (250 mL) red wine vinegar overtop. Cover jar and let stand at room temperature for 1 week. Pour raspberry vinegar into a strainer lined with 2 layers of cheesecloth set over a bowl. Let drain. Discard solids. Pour raspberry vinegar into a clean glass container and refrigerate for up to 6 months.

Strawberry Almond Dressing

For a strawberry dressing that will brighten up greens, yogurt or fresh fruit salads, this combination of almonds and strawberries will grab your attention. Strawberries boast some of the highest amounts of vitamin C (a versatile antioxidant and essential nutrient for the production of collagen, a structurally supportive protein found in skin, teeth, bones and blood vessels).

MAKES 1 CUP (250 ML)

- **Tall cup**

1 cup	strawberries	250 mL
1 tbsp	coconut sugar or granulated sugar	15 mL
¼ tsp	kosher salt	1 mL
2 tbsp	sunflower oil	30 mL
1 tbsp	balsamic vinegar	15 mL
1 tbsp	natural almond butter	15 mL
¼ cup	coconut water	60 mL

Optional Nutrition Boost
Add 1½ tsp (7 mL) pomegranate powder before the salt.

1. Add strawberries to the tall cup and sprinkle with coconut sugar. Let stand for 30 minutes. Add salt, oil, vinegar, almond butter and coconut water to the tall cup. Twist the extractor blade onto the cup to seal. Blend for 20 seconds or until combined.

2. Serve immediately or store in an airtight container in the refrigerator for up to 1 week.

TIP

Strawberries don't ripen further after they're picked. Choose berries that are bright red and have a natural sheen and fresh green leaves and stems. Store strawberries in the refrigerator. Just before serving, rinse berries in cold water, with stems intact, and blot dry with paper towel. Remove hulls just before using. Strawberries taste best at room temperature.

Carrot Ginger Dressing

Colorful and bursting with pizzazz, this dressing is the perfect accompaniment to salad greens or as a dip for vegetables. If you need a quick pick-me-up, this superfood dressing will become one of your go-to dressings. As a good source of vitamins B_3, B_5 and E, as well as several minerals and fiber, this dressing supports healthy red blood cell production, immune function and collagen production.

MAKES 1 CUP (250 ML)

- **Medium cup**

¾ cup	sliced carrots	175 mL
¼ cup	chopped sweet onion (such as Vidalia)	60 mL
1	¼- by ¼-inch (0.5 by 0.5 cm) piece gingerroot	1
¼ cup	unseasoned rice vinegar	60 mL
2 tbsp	tahini	30 mL
¼ cup	sunflower oil	60 mL
2 tbsp	unsalted raw sunflower seeds, toasted (see tip)	30 mL

Optional Nutrition Boost
Add 2 tsp (10 mL) chia seeds after the ginger.

1. Add carrots, onion, ginger, vinegar and tahini to the medium cup. Twist the extractor blade onto the cup to seal. Blend for 20 seconds or until smooth.

2. Remove the cup from the power base and twist off the extractor blade. Add oil. Twist the extractor blade onto the cup to seal. Blend for 10 seconds or until emulsified.

3. Serve immediately or store in an airtight container in the refrigerator for up to 1 week. Garnish with sunflower seeds just before serving.

TIPS

To toast sunflower seeds, heat a small dry skillet over medium-high heat, add raw sunflower seeds and cook, stirring constantly, for 2 to 3 minutes or until fragrant and lightly browned. Immediately transfer to a bowl and let cool before adding as garnish.

This dressing is ideal for a base green salad topped with chicken, tofu or pork.

Cilantro Jalapeño Ranch Dressing

This creamy, all-natural dressing packs a bit of a wallop and is ideal to spice up a Tex-Mex salad or any other favorite salad combinations. It's not every day you find a higher-protein dressing like this one, thanks to the yogurt and egg whites versus a classic ranch dressing's sour cream and mayonnaise.

MAKES 1½ CUPS (375 ML)

- **Tall cup**

½ cup	lightly packed fresh cilantro leaves and tender stems	125 mL
1 tsp	dry mustard	5 mL
1 tsp	kosher salt	5 mL
¼ tsp	freshly ground black or white pepper	1 mL
1	clove garlic	1
1	jalapeño pepper, seeded	1
1 cup	plain yogurt	250 mL
¼ cup	plain Greek yogurt	60 mL
2 tbsp	sunflower oil	30 mL
1 tbsp	pasteurized egg whites	15 mL
1 tbsp	lime juice	15 mL

1. Add cilantro, mustard, salt, pepper, garlic, jalapeño, plain yogurt, Greek yogurt, oil, egg whites and lime juice to the tall cup. Twist the extractor blade onto the cup to seal. Blend for 30 seconds or until smooth.

2. Serve immediately or store in an airtight container in the refrigerator for up to 3 days.

TIPS

Choose cilantro that has bright green leaves with no yellowing or signs of wilting. If using stems, make sure they are tender. Cilantro should smell slightly pungent with a hint of anise.

Store cilantro loosely wrapped in paper towel in the crisper drawer of your refrigerator.

Use kitchen gloves when handling jalapeño peppers and avoid touching your skin and eyes.

For a super-powered salad, add this dressing to sliced avocado, sliced tomatoes, raw green pumpkin seeds (pepitas) and greens (such as kale, spinach or watercress).

Tex-Mex Salad Dressing

This simple, creamy cilantro and lime dressing dazzles on any green leafy salad or vegetable side dish and shines as a marinade for chicken and pork. Many might not think of cilantro as a good source of beta-carotene and polyphenols, but it is; cilantro helps reduce inflammation and the risk for cardiovascular disease.

MAKES ABOUT 1¼ CUPS (300 ML)

- **Tall cup**

	Grated zest and juice of 4 limes	
½ cup	lightly packed fresh cilantro leaves and tender stems	125 mL
½ cup	pumpkin seed oil	125 mL
1 tbsp	agave nectar (optional)	15 mL
1 tbsp	plain Greek yogurt	15 mL
	Kosher salt and freshly ground black pepper	

1. Add lime zest, lime juice, cilantro, oil, agave nectar (if using) and yogurt to the tall cup. Season with salt and pepper. Twist the extractor blade onto the cup to seal. Blend for 20 seconds or until smooth.

2. Serve immediately or store in an airtight container in the refrigerator for up to 1 week.

TIPS

To use as a marinade, add 1 lb (500 g) chicken breasts or pork shoulder steaks to a large sealable plastic bag and pour ¼ cup (60 mL) dressing over top. Seal bag and refrigerate for 2 hours. Drain and discard marinade.

Look for Greek yogurt that contains live active yogurt cultures, as this type has the most desirable health properties.

You can use liquid honey, stevia or coconut sugar in place of the agave nectar.

Pineapple, Ginger and Peanut Butter Marinade

This sweet and tangy marinade adds a flavor punch to skewered chicken and pork. While dulse or kelp flakes are an unlikely ingredient, they're a wonderful alternative to salt and make this marinade a good source of iodine, a mineral many are not getting enough of.

MAKES 1½ CUPS (375 ML)

- **Tall cup**

1	orange, peeled and seeded	1
¼ cup	canned or fresh pineapple chunks, with juice	60 mL
2 tbsp	packed brown sugar	30 mL
1 tsp	dulse or kelp flakes	5 mL
½ tsp	grated gingerroot	2 mL
1	clove garlic	1
¼ cup	natural smooth peanut butter	60 mL
¼ cup	coconut amino acids	60 mL
2 tbsp	unseasoned rice vinegar	30 mL
2 tsp	agave nectar or liquid honey	10 mL
2 tsp	peanut oil	10 mL

1. Add orange, pineapple, brown sugar, dulse, ginger, garlic, peanut butter, coconut amino acids, vinegar, agave nectar and oil to the tall cup. Twist the extractor blade onto the cup to seal. Blend for 30 seconds or until smooth.

2. Use as a marinade immediately or store in an airtight container in the refrigerator for up to 1 week.

TIPS

To use as a marinade, add 1 lb (500 g) chicken or pork, cut into 1-inch (2.5 cm) cubes, to a large sealable plastic bag and pour ¼ cup (60 mL) marinade over top. Seal bag and refrigerate for 2 hours or up to 4 hours. Drain and discard marinade.

We suggest dulse or kelp flakes in this recipe because of the saltiness they add to the marinade. You can use any other type of seaweed that you prefer, provided it has a similar flavor profile.

Cranberry, Pineapple and Almond Relish

If you have ever just looked at that glob of relish during the holidays and wondered why there couldn't be something better, well, wonder no longer. This version of relish is packed with anti-inflammatory polyphenols, as well as vitamin C and potassium, which support healthy blood pressure.

MAKES 2 CUPS (500 ML)

- **Tall cup**

3	4- by ½-inch (10 by 1 cm) strips of orange zest	3
3 cups	fresh or canned pineapple chunks, with juice	750 mL
2 cups	fresh or thawed frozen cranberries	500 mL
1½ tsp	pomegranate powder	7 mL
3 tbsp	liquid honey	45 mL
1 tbsp	natural almond butter	15 mL
	Toasted slivered almonds (optional)	

1. Add orange peel, pineapple, cranberries, pomegranate powder, honey and almond butter to the tall cup. Twist the extractor blade onto the cup to seal. Blend for 10 seconds or until blended and chunky.

2. Transfer relish to a medium saucepan. Bring to a boil over medium-high heat, stirring occasionally. Reduce heat and simmer, stirring frequently, for 15 minutes or until thickened. (Sauce will also thicken as it cools.) Let cool to room temperature.

3. Transfer to an airtight container and refrigerate for at least 1 hour, until chilled, for up to 1 week. If desired, garnish with almonds just before serving.

TIPS

This is a great make-ahead condiment for any holiday gathering.

Choose cranberries that are firm, plump and deep red. They should not be shriveled, soft or discolored. Fresh cranberries can be refrigerated up to 3 to 4 weeks or frozen for up to 1 year.

To toast almonds, heat a small dry skillet over medium-high heat, add blanched almonds and cook, stirring constantly, for 2 to 3 minutes or until fragrant and lightly browned. Immediately transfer to a bowl and let cool before adding as garnish.

Avocado and Pineapple Salsa

For a new take on salsa, you must try this chunky, fruit-filled version paired with the creaminess of avocado. It's rich in nutrients that support fetal development and a healthy pregnancy. Serve with tortilla chips for dipping.

MAKES 1½ CUPS (375 ML)

- **Tall cup**

1	lime	1
4	strawberries	4
1½	avocados (see tips, page 140)	1½
1	kiwifruit, peeled and halved	1
1	slice red onion, rings separated	1
¼ cup	fresh or canned pineapple chunks, with juice	60 mL
½ tsp	kosher salt	2 mL
	Sriracha	
	Mint leaves (optional)	

Optional Nutrition Boost

Add 1½ tsp (7 mL) açaí powder after the pineapple.

1. Using a sharp paring knife, peel four 3- by ½-inch (7.5 by 1 cm) strips of lime zest. Squeeze juice from lime.

2. Add strips of lime zest, lime juice, strawberries, avocados, kiwi, onion, pineapple and salt to the tall cup. Twist the extractor blade onto the cup to seal. Blend for 10 seconds or until combined and chunky.

3. Transfer to a serving bowl and season to taste with Sriracha. If desired, garnish with mint just before serving.

TIPS

To keep your salsa chunky but combined, blend for 5 seconds, remove the cup from the base, shake ingredients gently and then continue blending until your desired consistency is reached.

The salsa can be stored in an airtight container in the refrigerator for up to 3 days. Wait to garnish with mint until just before serving.

Sweet Chile Dipping Sauce

This zesty little dipping sauce is delicious served with chicken satay, crab cakes or shrimp. It adds just enough spice and sweetness to complement these dishes. This is a tasty way to get your daily dose of iodine, which supports a healthy thyroid gland and therefore energy metabolism and production, and it supports a healthy mood.

MAKES ¾ CUP (175 ML)

- **Tall cup**

2	tomatoes (such as beefsteak), cored and halved	2
2 tbsp	seaweed flakes (such as dulse or kelp)	30 mL
1 tbsp	lime juice	15 mL
2	red chile peppers (such as Fresno or Chimayo), halved and seeded	2
2	cloves garlic	2
⅓ cup	unseasoned rice vinegar	75 mL
2 to 4 tbsp	coconut water	30 to 60 mL
1 tbsp	liquid honey	15 mL

1. Add tomatoes, seaweed flakes, lime juice, chile peppers, garlic, vinegar, 1 tbsp (15 mL) coconut water and honey to the tall cup. Twist the extractor blade onto the cup to seal. Blend for 30 seconds or until smooth.

2. If the dipping sauce is too thick, blend in additional coconut water, 1 tbsp (15 mL) at a time, until you achieve the desired consistency.

3. Transfer to a serving bowl and serve immediately or store in an airtight container in the refrigerator for up to 3 days.

TIPS

The red chile peppers used in this recipe have a medium spice level, although even among individual peppers, the Scoville heat units can vary widely. You can choose other red peppers to adjust spiciness.

Use kitchen gloves when handling chile peppers and avoid touching your eyes and skin.

Romesco Dipping Sauce with Tomatoes and Almonds

This rich and creamy sauce from northern Spain is often used as a dipping sauce for fish. We also really like this as a spread for toasted crusty bread, which makes it perfect for snacking on throughout the day.

MAKES 2 CUPS (500 ML)

- **Preheat oven to 375°F (190°C)**
- **Baking sheet, lined with heavy-duty foil**
- **Tall cup**

1	thick slice crusty white bread, crust removed and cut into 1-inch (2.5 cm) cubes	1
3	cloves garlic (unpeeled)	3
2	red bell peppers	2
1	large red tomato	1
½ cup	raw almonds	125 mL
1	ancho chile pepper, seeded and soaked (see tips)	1
	Kosher salt	
	Hot pepper flakes	
¼ cup	almond or extra virgin olive oil	60 mL
2 tbsp	red wine vinegar	30 mL

1. Arrange bread cubes, garlic, red peppers, tomato and almonds on prepared baking sheet, keeping each ingredient separate on the sheet. Bake in preheated oven until bread cubes are crusty and almonds are fragrant, about 10 minutes. Transfer bread cubes and almonds to a cutting board and let cool. Return garlic, red peppers and tomato to the oven and bake until garlic is soft and tomato is tender, about 20 minutes. Transfer garlic and tomato to the cutting board and let cool. Return red peppers to the oven and bake until red peppers are collapsed and toasted, about 15 minutes. Transfer red peppers to a bowl and cover loosely with plastic wrap or a paper bag. Let cool.

2. Remove skin and core from tomato, remove skin from garlic cloves and remove skin, stem, core and seeds from red peppers.

3. Add bread cubes, garlic, red peppers, tomato, ancho chile pepper, almonds, 1 tsp (5 mL) salt, ⅛ tsp (0.5 mL) hot pepper flakes, oil and vinegar to the tall cup. Twist the extractor blade onto the cup to seal. Blend for 30 seconds or until smooth.

4. Transfer to an airtight container and season to taste with salt and hot pepper flakes, if desired. Refrigerate for at least 2 hours, until chilled, or for up to 5 days.

TIPS

Seed the ancho chile, setting some aside if you want your sauce spicier. Discard the remaining seeds. Soak the chile in hot water for 30 minutes; drain and discard water.

Use kitchen gloves when handling chile peppers, and avoid touching your skin or eyes.

You can purchase almonds in the shell or shelled with or without the skin. When you shake almonds in the shell, there should be no rattling sound, which indicates aging. Cut shelled almonds in half and check for white solid meat. Do not use if the center is yellowish or has a honeycomb texture. Store fresh almonds in an airtight container in the refrigerator up to 6 months or freeze for up to 2 years.

Creamy Tomato Coconut Soup (page 154)

Tuscan White Bean Soup (page 159)

Strawberry, Pear and
Lime Ice Pops (page 183)

Gooey Almond Oat Balls (page 186) and
Chocolate-Covered Coconut Avocado Balls (page 185)

Happy Birthday Smoothie (page 190)

Virgin Piña Colada (page 194)

Blueberry Chia Parfait (page 203)

Nutty Choco-Caramel Tarts (page 206)

Creamy Beet, Ginger and Almond Dip

Try this gorgeous red beet dip with roasted vegetables and you will have found a new way to enjoy a triple dose of vegetables and superfoods without even skipping a beat — no pun intended.

MAKES 2 CUPS (500 ML)

- **Preheat oven to 425°F (220°C)**
- **Heavy-duty foil**
- **Tall cup**

1½ lbs	beets (about 5 medium), stems cut to a maximum of 2 inches (5 cm)	750 g
1 tbsp	fresh cilantro leaves	15 mL
1	1- by 1-inch (2.5 by 2.5 cm) piece of gingerroot	1
1 tsp	mint leaves	5 mL
2 tbsp	natural almond butter	30 mL
1 tbsp	flaxseed oil	15 mL
	Kosher salt and freshly ground black pepper	

1. Wrap beets individually in sheets of foil and place on a baking sheet, spacing apart. Roast in preheated oven for 1½ hours or until beets pierce easily with a fork. Unwrap beets and let cool. Cut ends and discard. Peel beets and cut into quarters.

2. Add beets, cilantro, ginger, mint, almond butter and oil to the tall cup. Twist the extractor blade onto the cup to seal. Blend for 30 seconds or until smooth.

3. Transfer to a serving bowl and season to taste with salt and pepper.

TIPS

Select beets that are firm and heavy for their size and have no nicks or soft spots. Their greens should be green, fresh-looking and not wilted. The greens are also edible; store them in the refrigerator, gently wrapped in paper towels.

Wear kitchen gloves when handling beets to prevent staining your hands.

A 1- by 1-inch (2.5 by 2.5 cm) piece of gingerroot yields about 1 tbsp (15 mL) grated gingerroot. You can find grated gingerroot in jars in well-stocked grocery stores and can use it in place of the fresh. Refrigerate after opening.

The dip can be stored in an airtight container in the refrigerator for up to 5 days.

Spicy Moroccan-Inspired Tomato Dip

This spicy, chunky tomato dip is wonderful served with pita wedges. Similar to the traditional dip, called matbucha, this one may become your new favorite alternative to salsa. This dip supports your brain and your cardiovascular system with its carotenoids and potassium.

MAKES 2 CUPS (500 ML)

- **Tall cup**

1	green bell pepper, roasted (see tip)	1
4	large tomatoes (such as beefsteak), cored and quartered	4
1	small jalapeño pepper, seeded	1
1	clove garlic, quartered	1
1	pitted date, quartered	1
½ tsp	hot pepper flakes	2 mL
½ tsp	kosher salt	2 mL
3 tbsp	sunflower oil or virgin olive oil	45 mL
2 tsp	paprika	10 mL
	Granulated sugar (optional)	
	Cilantro leaves (optional)	

1. Add green pepper, tomatoes, jalapeño, garlic and date to the tall cup. Twist the extractor blade onto the cup to seal. Pulse 4 to 5 times or until coarsely chopped.

2. Transfer mixture to a medium saucepan and add hot pepper flakes and salt. Cook over medium heat, stirring occasionally, for 10 minutes or until liquids are mostly evaporated. Add oil and paprika and cook, stirring, for 10 to 15 minutes or until mixture is thickened. If desired, add sugar to taste, stirring well. Remove from heat and let cool to room temperature.

3. Transfer to a serving bowl and, if desired, garnish with cilantro just before serving.

TIPS

To roast green pepper, arrange on a baking sheet lined with foil and bake for 30 to 40 minutes in a preheated 400°F (200°C) oven, turning once, or until collapsed and charred. Transfer to a bowl and cover with plastic wrap. Let cool and remove skin, core and seeds.

Substitute 1 tsp (5 mL) dulse flakes for the kosher salt.

The dip can be stored in an airtight container in the refrigerator for up to 5 days. Wait to garnish with cilantro until just before serving.

Creamy Kale and Feta Dip

Loaded with greens and proteins, this brightly seasoned dip is perfect for serving with vegetables or spreading on sliced French bread, crackers or pita wedges. The phytonutrients, vitamins and minerals in the kale support liver and mental health and reduce inflammation and the risk for cancer.

MAKES 2 CUPS (500 ML)

- **Tall cup**

1 cup	lightly packed baby kale leaves	250 mL
8 oz	crumbled feta cheese	250 g
1 tsp	ground turmeric	5 mL
½ tsp	dried oregano	2 mL
1	clove garlic	1
¼ cup	plain Greek yogurt	60 mL
¼ cup	flaxseed or extra virgin olive oil	60 mL
1½ tbsp	lemon juice	22 mL

Optional Nutrition Boost
Add 2 tbsp (30 mL) whey protein powder after the feta.

1. Add kale, feta, turmeric, oregano, garlic, yogurt, oil and lemon juice to the tall cup. Twist the extractor blade onto the cup to seal. Blend for 30 seconds or until smooth.

2. Transfer dip to a serving bowl and serve immediately, or transfer to an airtight container and store in the refrigerator for up to 3 days.

TIPS

Choose kale with smaller leaves that are moist, crisp and free of tiny holes. The leaves should be a rich green color with no yellow or brown spots.

To store kale, wrap unwashed leaves in damp paper towels and refrigerate for up to 3 days. Your kale may stay fresh longer, but it will develop a stronger taste the longer it is stored.

You may want to add 2 tsp (10 mL) liquid honey, stevia or agave nectar for sweetness if your kale has a stronger taste.

Mint Cashew Cream Dip

You will be delighted with this creamy, fresh-flavored dip that is also vegetarian and vegan. Packed with minerals, this dip feeds the brain, supports healthy moods and plays a role in healthy blood pressure. Grab some crunchy vegetables and fruit and start dipping your way to feeling great.

MAKES 1½ CUPS (375 ML)

- **Tall cup**

1 cup	raw cashews, soaked (see tip)	250 mL
2 tbsp	loosely packed fresh mint leaves	30 mL
2 tsp	fresh dill (optional)	10 mL
½ tsp	kosher salt	2 mL
⅓ cup	water (approx.)	75 mL
2 tbsp	lemon juice	30 mL
1 tbsp	flaxseed or hempseed oil	15 mL

1. Add soaked cashews, mint, dill (if using), salt, ⅓ cup (75 mL) water, lemon juice and flaxseed oil to the tall cup. Twist the extractor blade onto the cup to seal. Blend for 30 seconds or until smooth. If the dip is too thick, add more water, a little bit at a time, and blend until desired consistency is reached.

2. Transfer dip into a serving bowl and serve immediately, or transfer to an airtight container and store in the refrigerator for up to 1 week.

TIPS

To soak cashews, add cashews and 2 cups (500 mL) water to a medium bowl and let stand for 30 minutes or up to 2 hours. Drain and discard water. Rinse cashews and drain again.

A half lemon will yield about 2 tbsp (30 mL) lemon juice.

If using fresh fruit for dipping, sprinkle the fruit with a little cinnamon for a new twist.

African-Inspired Lentil Dip

This darling of a dip takes a little longer to make, yet it is so worth the wait for a healthy dip that is bursting with lemon and exotic flavors. This dip helps to maintain muscle mass with its protein content while providing a healthy dose of vitamins and minerals. Serve with lightly toasted pita wedges or your favorite crackers.

MAKES 5 CUPS (1.25 L)

- **Extra-tall cup**

2 cups	dried brown or red lentils, rinsed	500 mL
1	carrot, cut into 1-inch (2.5 cm) pieces	1
1	onion, coarsely chopped	1
4 cups	water	1 L
3 tbsp	natural cashew butter	45 mL
1	clove garlic, minced	1
2 tsp	grated gingerroot	10 mL
1 tsp	curry powder	5 mL
1 tbsp	lemon juice	15 mL
	Ground or freshly grated nutmeg	
2 tbsp	chopped fresh cilantro	30 mL

1. In a large saucepan over medium-high heat, bring lentils, carrot, onion and water to a boil. Reduce heat to medium-low and simmer, stirring occasionally, for 40 minutes or until lentils are tender and liquid is mostly evaporated. Let cool.

2. Transfer lentil mixture to extra-tall cup. Twist the extractor blade onto the cup to seal. Blend for 40 seconds or until smooth. Set aside.

3. In the same saucepan (no need to wash it), melt cashew butter over medium-low heat. Add garlic, ginger and curry powder and cook, stirring, for 3 minutes or until fragrant. Add lentil mixture and cook, stirring, for 5 minutes or until heated through. Remove from heat and stir in lemon juice.

4. Transfer to a serving bowl and garnish with nutmeg and cilantro. Serve warm or at room temperature.

TIPS

Choose lentils that are firm, uniform in color and not shriveled. Lentils come in a variety of colors and with slightly different flavors. Lentils should be stored in an airtight container in a cool, dry place and will keep for up to 1 year.

You can cook the dried lentils ahead of time and store them in an airtight container in the refrigerator for up to 1 week or in the freezer for up to 6 months. Let thaw in the refrigerator before using. Add cooked lentils to the saucepan 5 minutes before the end of cooking time in step 1.

The dip can be stored in an airtight container in the refrigerator for up to 5 days. Let come to room temperature before serving or, to serve warm, heat through over medium-low heat.

Time-Out Black Bean Dip

Everyone loves a good dip for game day and this one adds a tasty and healthy mix to the party. This dip wears many hats: it promotes regularity, benefits those with diabetes and helps to maintain healthy cholesterol and blood sugar levels.

MAKES 6 CUPS (1.5 L)		

• **Extra-tall cup**

2	cans (each 14 to 15 oz/398 to 425 mL) black beans, drained and rinsed	2
1	red onion, peeled and quartered	1
¼ cup	fresh cilantro leaves	60 mL
1	clove garlic	1
2 tbsp	balsamic vinegar	30 mL
1 tbsp	lime juice	15 mL
1 tbsp	sunflower oil or extra virgin olive oil	15 mL
	Kosher salt and freshly ground black pepper	

1. Add black beans, onion, cilantro (reserving a few leaves for garnish), garlic, vinegar, lime juice and oil to the extra-tall cup. Twist the extractor blade onto the cup to seal. Blend for 30 seconds or until smooth.

2. Transfer to a serving bowl and season to taste with salt and pepper. Garnish with reserved cilantro just before serving.

TIPS

If you want to use dried black beans in place of canned, you will need to soak and cook the dried beans. Add 2½ cups (625 mL) beans to a large bowl and cover with 9 cups (2.25 L) water. Let stand at room temperature for 12 hours or overnight. Drain and rinse beans. Add beans to a large stockpot, cover with water and boil for 1 to 1½ hours or until beans are softened. Drain and rinse beans under cold water, drain again and let cool. Continue with step 1.

If you can only find larger cans of black beans, use two 19-oz (540 mL) cans and measure 3 cups (750 mL) drained rinsed beans for this recipe; reserve extra for another use.

The dip can be stored in an airtight container in the refrigerator for up to 3 days. Let come to room temperature before serving. Wait to garnish with cilantro until just before serving.

Spicy White Bean Dip

This spirited dip starts with white kidney beans and gets a kick from jalapeño peppers, garlic and cayenne. It works as a midday snack or a great party presentation complementing black bean dips and salsa.

MAKES 3 CUPS (750 ML)

- **Tall cup**

2	jalapeño peppers, seeded	2
1	can (14 to 15 oz/398 to 425 mL) cannellini (white kidney) beans, drained and rinsed	1
2 tsp	dulse flakes	10 mL
1/8 tsp	cayenne pepper	0.5 mL
2	cloves garlic	2
1/4 cup	brewed white tea, cooled	60 mL
2 tbsp	balsamic vinegar	30 mL
1 tbsp	plain Greek yogurt	15 mL
	Hot pepper flakes	

1. Add jalapeños, cannellini beans, dulse flakes, cayenne pepper, garlic, tea, vinegar and yogurt to the tall cup. Twist the extractor blade onto the cup to seal. Blend for 30 seconds or until smooth.

2. Transfer to a serving bowl and garnish with hot pepper flakes.

TIPS

Wear kitchen gloves when handling jalapeño peppers and avoid touching your eyes and skin.

Jalapeños are considered a medium-spice pepper but can range from mild to very spicy. The older the pepper, the hotter it is. Younger peppers are bright, shiny and green. As the pepper ages, it changes to bright red. Growing conditions, such as sun, water and cross-pollination, can affect the spiciness of your peppers. You can add more spiciness by adding the seeds to your dip, to taste.

If you can only find larger cans of beans, use a 19-oz (540 mL) can and measure 1 1/2 cups (375 mL) drained rinsed beans for this recipe; reserve extra for another use.

The dip can be stored in an airtight container in the refrigerator for up to 3 days.

Chickpea and Yogurt Dip

Mix up this lighter variation of hummus and serve with pita wedges or fresh vegetables for dipping. With protein, fat, carbohydrate and B vitamins, this dip helps to fuel your body while providing the building blocks for growth and repair.

MAKES 2½ CUPS (625 ML)

- **Tall cup**

1	can (14 to 15 oz/398 to 425 mL) chickpeas, drained and rinsed	1
½ tsp	ground coriander	2 mL
Pinch	ground ginger	Pinch
¼ cup	plain Greek yogurt	60 mL
3 tbsp	sunflower oil	45 mL
1 tsp	red wine vinegar	5 mL
	Kosher salt and freshly ground black pepper	
	Coarsely chopped mint leaves	

Optional Nutrition Boost

Add 2 tbsp (30 mL) whey protein powder after the chickpeas.

1. Add chickpeas, coriander, ginger, yogurt, oil and vinegar to the tall cup. Season with salt and pepper. Twist the extractor blade onto the cup to seal. Blend for 20 seconds or until smooth.

2. Transfer dip to a serving bowl and garnish with mint just before serving.

TIPS

Coriander seeds are the seeds of the cilantro plant.

Flaxseed or hempseed oil are good substitutions for the sunflower oil.

If you can only find larger cans of chickpeas, use a 19-oz (540 mL) can and measure 1½ cups (375 mL) drained and rinsed chickpeas for this recipe; reserve extra for another use.

The dip can be stored in an airtight container in the refrigerator for up to 1 week. Wait to garnish with mint until just before serving.

Traditional Creamy Hummus

Why buy hummus when you can make this traditional super-powered hummus at home? Chickpeas are so nutrient-packed they're like a multivitamin with minerals, protein, carbohydrate and fiber to boot.

....

MAKES 2 CUPS (500 ML)		

- **Tall cup**

1	can (14 to 15 oz/398 to 425 mL) chickpeas, drained and rinsed	1
½ tsp	kosher salt	2 mL
2	cloves garlic	2
	Juice of 1 lime	
¼ cup	tahini	60 mL
2 tbsp	plain Greek yogurt	30 mL
	Extra virgin olive oil	
	Paprika	

1. Add chickpeas, salt, garlic, lime juice, tahini and yogurt to the tall cup. Twist the extractor blade onto the cup to seal. Blend for 20 seconds, or until combined.

2. Transfer hummus to a serving bowl. Using the back of a spoon, add a swirl to the top of the hummus. Drizzle olive oil into the swirl and garnish with paprika.

TIPS

Hummus can be stored in an airtight container in the refrigerator for up to 3 days. For better results, pour a thin layer of olive oil on top of the hummus.

If you can only find larger cans of chickpeas, use a 19-oz (540 mL) can and measure 1½ cups (375 mL) drained and rinsed chickpeas for this recipe; reserve extra for another use.

Pesto Almond Hummus

There are so many healthy reasons to eat hummus, and the almond butter and healthy oil take this one up a notch. Rich in magnesium, potassium and calcium, chickpeas may help to lower blood pressure and the fiber helps to balance cholesterol.

MAKES 2½ (625 ML)

- **Tall cup**

1	can (14 to 15 oz/398 to 425 mL) chickpeas, drained and rinsed	1
½ tsp	kosher salt	2 mL
¼ tsp	freshly ground black pepper	1 mL
1	clove garlic	1
2 tbsp	cold water	30 mL
1 tbsp	natural almond butter	15 mL
1 tbsp	cold-pressed sweet almond oil or sunflower oil	15 mL
1 cup	lightly packed fresh basil leaves	250 mL
	Grated Parmesan cheese or nutritional yeast (optional)	

Optional Nutrition Boost
Add 1 tsp (5 mL) wheatgrass powder or another green powder (see box, page 18) after the chickpeas.

1. Add chickpeas, salt, pepper, garlic, cold water, almond butter and oil to the tall cup. Twist the extractor blade onto the cup to seal. Blend for 20 seconds or until combined.

2. Add basil, reseal the extractor blade and blend for 5 seconds or until combined but flecks of basil remain.

3. Transfer hummus to a serving bowl and, if desired, garnish with Parmesan just before serving.

TIPS

If you want to use dried chickpeas in place of canned, you will need to soak and cook the dried chickpeas. Choose chickpeas that are whole, free of dark spots and are not split or cracked. Add ¾ cup (175 mL) chickpeas to a large bowl and cover with 2½ cups (625 mL) water. Let stand at room temperature overnight. Drain and rinse chickpeas. Add chickpeas to a medium stockpot, cover with water and boil for 1 to 1½ hours or until chickpeas are softened. Drain and rinse chickpeas under cold water and let cool. Continue with step 1.

If you can only find larger cans of chickpeas, use a 19-oz (540 mL) can and measure 1½ cups (375 mL) drained and rinsed chickpeas for this recipe; reserve extra for another use.

Hummus can be stored in an airtight container in the refrigerator for up to 3 days. For better results, pour a thin layer of olive oil on top of the hummus. Wait to garnish with Parmesan until just before serving.

Spinach, Hot Pepper and Yogurt Hummus

Hummus is a delightful-tasting and body-friendly dip for any time of the day and this variation adds spinach and hot pepper flakes for a more inviting taste. Fiber-rich, this hummus can help fill you up, which promotes satiety. Fiber is also our best ally to promote regularity. This version of hummus has lots of eye-loving carotenoids, like lutein.

MAKES 3 CUPS (750 ML)

- **Extra-tall cup**

1 cup	packed trimmed spinach	250 mL
1	can (14 to 15 oz/398 to 425 mL) chickpeas, drained and rinsed	1
½	red bell pepper	½
2 tsp	ground ginger	10 mL
¼ tsp	kosher salt	1 mL
¼ tsp	hot pepper flakes	1 mL
3 tbsp	raw cashews	45 mL
1	clove garlic	1
⅓ cup	plain yogurt	75 mL
3 tbsp	lemon juice	45 mL
2 tbsp	sunflower oil	30 mL
	Freshly ground black pepper	

1. Add spinach, chickpeas, red pepper, ginger, salt, hot pepper flakes, cashews, garlic, yogurt, lemon juice and oil to the extra-tall cup. Twist the extractor blade onto the cup to seal. Blend for 40 seconds or until smooth.

2. Transfer to a serving bowl and season to taste with pepper.

VARIATION

Roasted Red Pepper Hummus:
Replace the spinach and fresh red bell pepper with 2 roasted red bell peppers. To roast red peppers, arrange on a baking sheet lined with foil and bake in a 400°F (200°C) oven for 30 to 40 minutes, turning once, or until collapsed and charred. Transfer to a bowl, cover with plastic wrap and let cool. Remove and discard skin, core and seeds. Add red peppers to cup after the chickpeas.

TIPS

If you can only find larger cans of chickpeas, use a 19-oz (540 mL) can and measure 1½ cups (375 mL) drained and rinsed chickpeas for this recipe; reserve extra for another use.

Hummus can be stored in an airtight container in the refrigerator for up to 3 days. For better results, pour a thin layer of olive oil on top of the hummus.

Mango Guacamole

This tropical twist on guacamole gets a sweet and refreshing punch from bright, fresh mango. It is perfect for a midday snack. Your skin will love the fats, vitamin C and carotenoids (like lutein and beta-carotene) — just what it needs to look its healthiest.

MAKES 2 CUPS (500 ML)		

- **Tall cup**

2	avocados	2
½ cup	cubed mango	125 mL
3 tbsp	fresh cilantro leaves	45 mL
¼ tsp	kosher salt	1 mL
1 tbsp	lime juice	15 mL

1. Add avocados, mango, cilantro, salt and lime juice to the tall cup. Twist the extractor blade onto the cup to seal. Blend for 10 seconds or until coarsely blended.

2. Transfer to a serving bowl and serve immediately, or transfer to an airtight container and store in the refrigerator for up to 3 days.

TIPS

This recipe can easily be doubled. Use the extra-tall cup if doubling.

To choose a ripe avocado, place it in the palm of your hand and squeeze gently. It should be firm but give slightly. Color does not indicate ripeness, as some varieties turn dark green or black and others have a lighter green skin. Avoid avocados with dark blemishes.

To use avocados over several days, choose them at varying degrees of ripeness. You can accelerate ripening by placing them in a sealed brown paper bag at room temperature. They will ripen over 2 to 5 days. To ripen them even faster, add an apple or kiwi to the bag. Ripe avocados should be refrigerated and will last up to 3 days.

Guacamole with Tomatoes and Cilantro

Sassy, versatile, loved by many and good for you — how is that for a wonderful and easy dip? This guacamole delivers more than great taste, it supports eye health and helps to lower inflammation and blood pressure and reduce the risk for stroke.

MAKES 2 CUPS (500 ML)

- **Tall cup**

2	avocados (see tips, page 140)	2
1	plum (Roma) tomato, cored and quartered	1
1	poblano or chilaca pepper, seeded and quartered	1
½	red onion, rings separated	½
½ cup	fresh cilantro leaves	125 mL
½ tsp	kosher salt	2 mL
2 tbsp	lemon juice	30 mL
	Freshly ground black pepper	
	Paprika (preferably Hungarian)	

1. Add avocados, tomato, poblano pepper, onion, cilantro, salt and lemon juice to the tall cup. Twist the extractor blade onto the cup to seal. Pulse 5 to 7 times or until combined and chunky.

2. Transfer to a serving bowl and season to taste with pepper. Garnish with paprika just before serving.

TIPS

You can substitute 1 jalapeño pepper for the poblano pepper if you prefer a spicier guacamole.

Wear kitchen gloves when handling hot peppers and avoid touching your skin and eyes.

Any variety of firm, meaty tomato will work in this recipe.

The guacamole can be stored in an airtight container in the refrigerator for up to 3 days. Wait to garnish with paprika until just before serving.

Pineapple, Cashew and Chile Pepper Spread

This zesty cheese-like spread is sweet, crunchy and sports a bit of spiciness for an interesting appetizer offering. This spread provides bone-loving calcium, phosphorus, magnesium and protein. Spread it over your favorite crackers or serve with sliced vegetables for dipping.

MAKES 2 CUPS (500 ML)

- Small cup
- Tall cup

¼ cup	raw cashews	60 mL
1 tbsp	lime juice	15 mL
3	green onions, cut into 2-inch (5 cm) pieces	3
½	green bell pepper, halved	½
3 tbsp	chia seeds	45 mL
Pinch	cayenne pepper	Pinch
1¼ cups	plain Greek yogurt	300 mL
½ cup	fresh or drained canned pineapple chunks	125 mL
	Hot pepper flakes (optional)	

1. Add cashews and lime juice to the small cup. Twist the extractor blade onto the cup to seal. Pulse 3 to 4 times or until finely chopped. Set aside.

2. Add green onions, green pepper, chia seeds, cayenne pepper and yogurt to the tall cup. Twist the extractor blade onto the cup to seal. Blend for 20 seconds or until smooth.

3. Add pineapple to the tall cup and pulse 3 to 4 times or until coarsely combined.

4. Transfer to an airtight container and stir in cashew mixture. Refrigerate for at least 8 hours or up to 1 week. Transfer to a bowl and, if desired, garnish with hot pepper flakes before serving.

TIPS

For a decorative presentation, cut a whole fresh skin-on pineapple in half lengthwise and cut out the flesh from the shell. Use one half as your serving bowl, spritzing the inside of the shell with lemon juice to prevent it from darkening.

An average 5-lb (2.5 kg) pineapple will yield about 7 cups (1.75 L) of pineapple chunks. Store the unused pineapple in an airtight container in the refrigerator for up to 1 week. The remaining chunks can be eaten alone or used in other smoothies and dips.

Soups and Sauces

Chilled Avocado and Ginger
   Soup 144

Avocado Almost-Vichyssoise.........145

Chilled Peppery Avocado
   and Arugula Soup........................146

Cold Beet Soup...............................147

Carrot, Ginger and Pineapple
   Soup 148

Spicy Pumpkin Soup 149

Gazpacho...150

Cold Strawberry and Tomato
   Soup 151

Wild and Button Mushroom
   Soup 152

Roasted Pumpkin and Carrot
   Juice Soup.....................................153

Creamy Tomato Coconut Soup.....154

Pea Soup with Mushrooms,
   Watercress and Mint 155

Yellow Split Pea and Pumpkin
   Soup 156

Red Lentil, Chickpea and
   Tomato Soup 157

Zesty Chickpea, Tomato and
   Mushroom Soup 158

Tuscan White Bean Soup...............159

Garden-Fresh Tomato Sauce.........160

Roasted Vegetable Pasta Sauce
   with Tomatoes, Carrots and
   Mushrooms 161

Enchilada Sauce with Poblano
   Peppers and Black Beans 162

Creamy Mushroom Sauce 163

Arugula and Sweet Pea Pesto........163

Kale and Roasted Pepper Pesto.....164

Spicy Spinach Cilantro Sauce 165

Triple-Berry Sauce.........................166

Chilled Avocado and Ginger Soup

This creamy and delicate cold soup is perfect as a starter or served with a healthy green salad for lunch on a hot summer day. This soup is packed with blood pressure–lowering potassium, and the carotenoids can lower your risk for cancer, reduce inflammation and support healthy skin.

MAKES 4 SERVINGS

- **Extra-tall cup**

⅓ cup	loosely packed fresh cilantro leaves and tender stems	75 mL
1	avocado, halved	1
1	¾- by ¾-inch (2 by 2 cm) chunk of gingerroot	1
2½ cups	ready-to-use vegetable broth	625 mL
3 tbsp	plain yogurt, divided	45 mL
1 tbsp	lime juice	15 mL
½ tsp	Sriracha	2 mL
	Kosher salt	
1½ tbsp	finely chopped red onion, chilled	22 mL

> **Optional Nutrition Boost**
> Add 1 tsp (5 mL) seaweed flakes, such as dulse or kelp, after the ginger.

1. Add cilantro, avocado, ginger, broth, 2 tbsp (30 mL) yogurt, lime juice and Sriracha to the tall cup. Twist the extractor blade onto the cup to seal. Blend for 30 seconds or until smooth. Cover and refrigerate for 2 hours or until chilled.

2. Season to taste with salt. Spoon into bowls, top each with a dollop of the remaining yogurt and garnish with red onion.

TIPS

A ¾- by ¾-inch (2 by 2 cm) piece of gingerroot yields about 2 tsp (10 mL) grated gingerroot. You can find grated gingerroot in jars in well-stocked grocery stores and can use it in place of the fresh. Refrigerate after opening.

Use reduced-sodium broth, if you prefer.

When the soup has chilled, stir in additional Sriracha or lime juice to suit your taste.

Avocado Almost-Vichyssoise

Our new take on a classic potato soup gets a creamy boost from rich avocado and white beans with sautéed leeks for a delectable cold soup. This soup has lots of gut bacteria–loving fiber and prebiotics, which support a healthy gut, mood and immunity.

MAKES 3 TO 4 SERVINGS

- **Tall cup**

1 tbsp	coconut oil	15 mL
1	leek, white part only, cut into ½-inch (1 cm) slices, rings separated	1
1 cup	cannellini (white kidney) beans, drained and rinsed	250 mL
2 cups	ready-to-use vegetable broth	500 mL
1	avocado, halved	1
¼ cup	plain Greek yogurt	60 mL
1 tbsp	chopped fresh mint	15 mL

Optional Nutrition Boost
Add 1 tsp (5 mL) dulse granules after the beans.

1. In a large skillet, heat oil over medium heat until shimmering. Add leeks and cook, stirring, for 4 minutes or until tender. Stir in beans and broth; bring to a boil. Boil, stirring occasionally, for 10 minutes or until liquid is reduced by half. Let cool.

2. Add bean mixture and avocado to the tall cup. Twist the extractor blade onto the cup to seal. Blend for 30 seconds or until smooth. Cover and refrigerate for 2 hours or until chilled.

3. Spoon into bowls, top each with a dollop of yogurt and garnish with mint.

TIPS

To choose a ripe avocado, place it in the palm of your hand and squeeze gently. It should be firm but give slightly. Color does not indicate ripeness, as some varieties turn dark green or black and others have a lighter green skin. Avoid avocados with dark blemishes.

To use avocados over several days, choose them at varying degrees of ripeness. You can accelerate ripening by placing them in a sealed brown paper bag at room temperature. They will ripen over 2 to 5 days. To ripen them even faster, add an apple or kiwi to the bag. Ripe avocados should be refrigerated and will last up to 3 days.

Chilled Peppery Avocado and Arugula Soup

This crisp and creamy avocado soup gets a lift from arugula, celery and jalapeño pepper for a delectably spicy cold soup. This soup does double duty by reducing the risk for cataracts and macular degeneration while promoting healthy blood pressure and overall cardiovascular health.

MAKES 2 SERVINGS

- **Extra-tall cup**

1	lime	1
1 cup	packed arugula	250 mL
1	avocado, halved (see tips, page 140)	1
1	stalk celery, quartered	1
1	jalapeño pepper, seeded	1
1 tsp	grated gingerroot	5 mL
1 cup	coconut water	250 mL
	Dulse flakes	
	Cilantro leaves	

1. Cut the lime in half. Cut one half into slices; peel the remaining half and discard the peel.

2. Add arugula, avocado, celery, jalapeño, lime slices, lime half, ginger and coconut water to the extra-tall cup. Twist the extractor blade onto the cup to seal. Blend for 40 seconds or until smooth. Cover and refrigerate for 2 hours or until chilled.

3. Spoon into bowls, season to taste with dulse flakes and garnish with cilantro.

TIP

Choose gingerroot that is hard and snaps easily when bent. The root should feel heavy for its size. Store unpeeled gingerroot in a paper towel, changing when damp, in the refrigerator crisper for up to 3 weeks. Gingerroot should be peeled before using.

Cold Beet Soup

This Lithuanian-inspired beet soup is similar to the bright color and full flavors of the more common hot borscht. It is rich in liver-supporting nutrients and is wonderful during a hot day. This soup is stellar when it comes to supporting the health of your gut and gut bacteria.

MAKES 6 SERVINGS

- **Extra-tall cup**

4	medium beets (about 1 lb/ 500 g total), peeled	4
1	small onion, diced	1
1	medium carrot, shredded	1
1	clove garlic, minced	1
1 tsp	ground chicory	5 mL
2 cups	reduced-sodium ready-to-use vegetable broth	500 mL
2 cups	plain kefir	500 mL
2 tsp	liquid honey	10 mL
	Kosher salt and freshly ground black pepper	
	Plain Greek yogurt	
2 tbsp	chopped fresh chives	30 mL

Optional Nutrition Boost
Season with dulse powder instead of kosher salt.

1. In a medium saucepan, combine beets, onion, carrot, garlic, chicory, broth and kefir. Bring to a boil over medium-high heat. Reduce heat to medium-low and cook, covered, for about 30 minutes or until beets are fork-tender. Let cool.

2. Working in batches, add beet mixture to the extra-tall cup. Twist the extractor blade onto the cup to seal. Blend for 40 seconds or until smooth, then transfer to a bowl.

3. Once all of the beet mixture is puréed, stir in honey and season to taste with salt and pepper. Cover and refrigerate for 4 hours or until chilled.

4. Spoon into bowls, top each with a dollop of yogurt and garnish with chives.

TIPS

Wear kitchen gloves when peeling beets to avoid staining your hands.

Look for yogurt that contains live active yogurt cultures, as this type contains the most desirable health properties.

Soup can be stored in an airtight container in the refrigerator for up to 2 days.

Carrot, Ginger and Pineapple Soup

Bright, refreshing and crisp are just a few of the hallmarks of this body-loving soup. It's loaded with nutrients that support gut, bone and skin health and help reduce the risk for cancer and high blood pressure.

MAKES 2 SERVINGS

- **Tall cup**

1 tbsp	sunflower oil	15 mL
4	medium carrots, cut into ½-inch (1 cm) slices	4
1	1- by 1-inch (2.5 by 2.5 cm) piece gingerroot, thinly sliced	1
2 tsp	natural almond butter	10 mL
½ tsp	dulse powder	2 mL
¼ tsp	ground turmeric	1 mL
1 cup	unsweetened almond milk	250 mL
1 cup	unsweetened pineapple juice	250 mL
1 tbsp	chopped fresh cilantro	15 mL

1. In a large skillet, heat sunflower oil over medium heat until bubbling. Add carrots and ginger; cook, stirring occasionally, for 7 to 10 minutes or until crisp-tender. Let cool.

2. Add carrot mixture, almond butter, dulse, turmeric, almond milk and pineapple juice to the tall cup. Twist the extractor blade onto the cup to seal. Blend for 30 seconds or until smooth. Cover and refrigerate for 2 hours or until chilled.

3. Spoon into bowls and garnish with cilantro.

TIPS

This soup can also be served warm. In step 3, instead of chilling soup, return it to the skillet and warm over medium heat, stirring occasionally, for 5 minutes or until heated through.

Choose unpeeled carrots with fresh green stems attached. Carrots come in a variety of colors; choose ones with intense, deep color. The carrot should be thin with just slightly flared tops at the stems. They should not have splits, cracks, hairy roots or wilted leaves.

Spicy Pumpkin Soup

Blend up some pumpkin, ginger, garlic, and coconut and you have a creamy, mouthwatering soup that is good for you, too. This soup will help to give you glowing skin and reduce your risk for dementia and several cancers while supporting gut health.

MAKES 4 SERVINGS

- **Extra-tall cup**

1	can (14 oz/400 mL) full-fat coconut milk, chilled (see tips)	1
1	small onion, quartered	1
1	1- by 1-inch (2.5 by 2.5 cm) piece gingerroot	1
1 tsp	ground turmeric	5 mL
Pinch	cayenne pepper	Pinch
1	clove garlic	1
1½ cups	coconut water	375 mL
1¼ cups	puréed pumpkin (see tip, page 153) or canned pumpkin purée (not pie filling)	300 mL
1 tbsp	pumpkin seed oil or extra virgin olive oil	15 mL
2 tsp	lemon juice	10 mL
2 tsp	tomato paste	10 mL
	Kosher salt and freshly ground black pepper	
1 tbsp	plain yogurt	15 mL
2 tbsp	chopped peanuts	30 mL

1. Using a spoon, carefully remove the thick layer of coagulated cream from the top of the can of coconut milk and transfer to a bowl. Measure ⅓ cup (75 mL) of the remaining coconut milk and add to the cream; reserve extra coconut milk for another use.

2. Add onion, ginger, turmeric, cayenne pepper, garlic, coconut water, puréed pumpkin, coconut cream, coconut milk, pumpkin oil, lemon juice and tomato paste to the extra-tall cup. Twist the extractor blade onto the cup to seal. Blend for 40 seconds or until smooth. Cover and refrigerate for 2 hours or until chilled.

3. Season to taste with salt and pepper. Spoon into bowls, top each with a dollop of yogurt and garnish with peanuts.

TIPS

Chill the can of coconut milk thoroughly and avoid shaking before opening to avoid mixing the cream with the milk.

Any remaining coconut milk can be stored in an airtight container in the refrigerator for up to 5 days or frozen for up to 6 months for use in other recipes.

Gazpacho

This classic cold soup from the Andalusian region of Spain is abounding with tomatoes, cucumber, bell pepper and onion, a traditional combination that makes this soup perfect just about any time. This summertime favorite can help to reduce the risk for stroke, supports prostate health, helps to lower blood pressure and supports a healthy mood.

MAKES 4 SERVINGS

- **Extra-tall cup**

4	plum (Roma) tomatoes, cored and halved	4
2	garlic cloves, quartered	2
1	cucumber, cut into chunks	1
1	small red onion, quartered	1
1	green or red bell pepper, quartered	1
3 cups	tomato juice	750 mL
¼ cup	red wine vinegar	60 mL
2 tbsp	sunflower oil	30 mL
	Kosher salt and freshly ground black pepper	

1. Divide ingredients evenly in half and, in two batches, add tomatoes, garlic, cucumber, onion, bell pepper, tomato juice, vinegar and oil to the extra-tall cup. Twist the extractor blade onto the cup to seal. Blend for 40 seconds or until smooth. Cover and refrigerate for 2 hours or until chilled.

2. Season to taste with salt and pepper. Spoon into bowls.

TIPS

Gazpacho is an ideal make-ahead dish because it gets better with age. It can be stored in an airtight container in the refrigerator for up to 2 days.

You can seed the tomatoes and cucumbers, if you prefer.

Garnish with mint leaves for a sophisticated presentation.

Cold Strawberry and Tomato Soup

A refreshing and light first course that is sure to please the most distinguishing palates. It is a riff on a traditional strawberry gazpacho that is ideal at summertime parties. This soup supports energy production and metabolism while helping to lower the risk for high blood pressure and stroke.

	MAKES 6 SERVINGS	

- **Tall cup**
- **Fine-mesh sieve**

12	fresh basil leaves, divided	12
2	large heirloom tomatoes (about 2 lbs/1 kg total), peeled and quartered, divided	2
1	English cucumber, peeled and quartered, divided	1
1 lb	strawberries, divided	500 g
½ tsp	kelp powder (optional)	2 mL
1⅓ cups	water	325 mL
2 tbsp	sunflower oil	30 mL
1 tbsp	balsamic vinegar	15 mL
2 to 3 tbsp	granulated sugar	30 to 45 mL
	Freshly ground black pepper	

1. Add 6 basil leaves, half the tomatoes with juices, half the cucumber, half the strawberries, kelp (if using), water, oil and vinegar to the tall cup. Season to taste with sugar and pepper. Twist the extractor blade onto the cup to seal. Blend for 40 seconds or until smooth.

2. Strain mixture through the sieve into a bowl. Cover and refrigerate for 2 hours or until chilled.

3. Meanwhile, coarsely chop the remaining tomatoes and cucumber and thinly slice the remaining strawberries.

4. Spoon chilled soup into bowls and garnish with tomatoes, cucumber, strawberries and a basil leaf.

TIPS

To easily peel tomatoes, cut a small "x" in the bottom of each tomato. Drop them into a pot of boiling water for 10 seconds or until skin begins to wrinkle, then plunge them into a large bowl filled with ice water. Let tomatoes cool and cut out core, then peel off skin and discard.

When quartering tomatoes, use a sharp chef's knife to avoid squashing them.

Wild and Button Mushroom Soup

Impress your family and guests with this outstanding mushroom soup. You won't even have to tell them that it's good for them.

MAKES 4 SERVINGS

- **Extra-tall cup**

2 tbsp	sunflower oil	30 mL
1	small sweet onion (such as Vidalia), thinly sliced	1
8 oz	button mushrooms	250 g
1 oz	dried shiitake mushrooms, soaked and drained (see tip)	30 g
4 cups	ready-to-use vegetable broth	1 L
1	sprig flat-leaf (Italian) parsley	1
1 tsp	granulated sugar	5 mL
3 tbsp	natural almond butter	45 mL
2 tsp	balsamic vinegar	10 mL
	Freshly ground black pepper	
	Plain yogurt (optional)	

1. In a medium saucepan, heat oil over medium heat. Add onion and cook, stirring for 5 to 7 minutes or until translucent. Add button and shiitake mushrooms; cook, stirring occasionally, for 7 to 10 minutes or until only a little moisture from the mushrooms remains. (If onions begin to brown, add a small amount of the broth to saucepan.)

2. Stir in broth and parsley; bring to a boil over medium-high heat. Reduce heat and simmer for 1 hour. Discard parsley. Transfer to a large bowl and let cool.

3. Working in batches, add mixture to the extra-tall cup. Twist the extractor blade onto the cup to seal. Blend for 30 seconds or until smooth.

4. Return soup to the pan and stir in sugar, almond butter and vinegar. Bring to a simmer over medium heat, stirring occasionally. Season to taste with pepper.

5. Spoon into bowls and top each with a small dollop of yogurt, if desired, using the tip of a knife to slice through the yogurt to make a pretty pattern. Serve immediately.

TIPS

Soak the dried shiitake mushrooms in hot water for 15 minutes or until softened. You can discard the liquid or substitute an equal amount of mushroom liquid for the vegetable broth. After removing the mushrooms from the soaking liquid, strain the liquid through a coffee filter or cheesecloth to remove any grit before using.

Substitute a reduced-sodium vegetable broth for the regular broth and season to taste with kosher salt before serving.

Roasted Pumpkin and Carrot Juice Soup

Perfect for a chilly fall day, this colorful, richly flavored soup is delectable and good for you from the inside out. This soup helps to maintain healthy blood pressure, supports bone health and has B vitamins to support energy production.

MAKES 4 SERVINGS

* **Extra-tall cup**

3 tbsp	pumpkin seed oil, divided	45 mL
½	onion, sliced	½
1	clove garlic, sliced	1
1	sprig fresh thyme	1
1	bay leaf	1
3 cups	carrot juice	750 mL
1¾ cups	puréed pumpkin (see tip) or canned pumpkin purée (not pie filling)	425 mL
	Water (optional)	
	Kosher salt and freshly ground black pepper	
2 tbsp	raw green pumpkin seeds (pepitas), toasted (see tip)	30 mL
2 tbsp	chopped fresh cilantro	30 mL

1. In a large saucepan, heat 1 tbsp (15 mL) oil over medium-high heat until shimmering. Add onion and cook, stirring often, for 7 minutes or until lightly browned. Add garlic and cook, stirring, for 1 minute or until garlic is fragrant.

2. Stir in thyme sprig, bay leaf, carrot juice and pumpkin. If necessary, add water to cover ingredients completely. Bring to a boil, stirring occasionally. Transfer to a large bowl and let cool. Discard thyme sprig and bay leaf.

3. Add 1 tbsp (15 mL) oil to the extra-tall cup. Working in batches if necessary, add pumpkin mixture. Twist the extractor blade onto the cup to seal. Blend for 40 seconds or until smooth.

4. Return soup to the pan and bring to a simmer over medium heat, stirring occasionally. Simmer for 5 minutes or until heated through. Season to taste with salt and pepper.

5. Spoon into bowls and drizzle with remaining oil. Garnish with pumpkin seeds and cilantro.

TIPS

A 2½-lb (1.25 kg) pie pumpkin will yield enough pumpkin for this recipe.

Puréed pumpkin: Preheat oven to 350°F (180°C). Cut 1 pie pumpkin in half and remove seeds. Arrange, cut side down, on baking sheet lined with foil. Bake for 45 minutes to 1 hour or until pumpkin is soft when pressed and juices are beginning to caramelize. Let cool. Scoop out pumpkin flesh and drain in a fine-mesh sieve. Add to the "Max Line" of the extra-tall cup. Blend for 30 seconds or until smooth. Repeat with remaining pumpkin. Measure pumpkin into desired quantities and store in individual airtight containers in the refrigerator for up to 1 week or in the freezer for up to 3 months.

To toast pumpkin seeds, place them in a small skillet and cook over medium-high heat, stirring, for 2 to 3 minutes or until fragrant and lightly browned.

Creamy Tomato Coconut Soup

This homemade creamy tomato soup is better than anything you can find in a can, and it's packed with nutritious ingredients. Key nutrients in this soup help to maintain healthy blood pressure, lower inflammation, and support healthy mood, collagen production and skin health.

MAKES 4 SERVINGS

- **Extra-tall cup**

2 tbsp	coconut oil	30 mL
¼	onion, sliced	¼
1	clove garlic, minced	1
2 tbsp	tomato paste	30 mL
3 tbsp	fresh basil chiffonade, divided (see tip)	45 mL
Pinch	hot pepper flakes	Pinch
1	can (28 oz/796 mL) diced tomatoes, with juice	1
2 cups	ready-to-use vegetable broth	500 mL
1 cup	full-fat coconut milk	250 mL
	Kosher salt and freshly ground black pepper	

1. In a large saucepan, heat coconut oil over medium heat until bubbly. Add onion and cook, stirring, for 3 to 5 minutes or until translucent. Add garlic and cook, stirring, for 1 minute or until fragrant. Add tomato paste and cook, stirring, for 2 to 3 minutes or until paste is slightly caramelized.

2. Stir in 2 tbsp (30 mL) basil, hot pepper flakes, tomatoes and broth; bring to a boil over medium-high heat. Reduce heat and simmer for 30 to 40 minutes or until liquid is reduced by a quarter. Transfer to a large bowl and let cool.

3. Working in batches if necessary, add tomato mixture to the extra-tall cup. Twist the extractor blade onto the cup to seal. Blend for 20 seconds or until smooth.

4. Return soup to the pan and stir in coconut milk. Cook over medium-low heat, stirring occasionally, for 5 minutes or until heated through. Season to taste with salt and pepper.

5. Spoon into bowls and garnish with remaining basil.

TIP

To chiffonade basil, remove the stems and stack 10 or more leaves. Roll the stack lengthwise into a fairly tight cigar shape, then cut crosswise into thin strips. Fluff the strips.

Pea Soup with Mushrooms, Watercress and Mint

It's not your grandmother's pea soup, but this one will be on your "most memorable" list. Sweet green peas get treated with mushrooms, watercress, mint and coconut for a boost of umami. This soup delivers a good dose of blood pressure–supportive potassium, as well as phytonutrients that support liver health and reduce the risk for cancer.

MAKES 4 SERVINGS

• **Extra-tall cup**

1 tbsp	sunflower oil	15 mL
½	sweet onion (such as Vidalia), sliced	½
1 cup	sliced morel or trimmed shiitake mushrooms	250 mL
1 cup	chopped fresh mint leaves	250 mL
2½ cups	thawed frozen peas	625 mL
1¾ cups	chopped trimmed watercress	425 mL
	Kosher salt	
2¼ cups	coconut water	550 mL
	Water (optional)	
	Freshly ground black pepper	
2 tbsp	plain Greek yogurt	30 mL

Optional Nutrition Boost

Add ½ to 1 tsp (2 to 5 mL) green powder (see box, page 18) with the pea mixture in step 2.

1. In a large saucepan, heat oil over medium heat until shimmering. Add onion and mushrooms; cook, stirring occasionally, for 5 minutes or until onion is softened and mushrooms have started to release their moisture. Add mint and cook, stirring, for 1 minute. Add peas and watercress and season with salt. Stir in coconut water and cook, stirring occasionally, for 5 minutes or until peas are softened. Transfer to a large bowl and let cool.

2. Working in batches, add pea mixture to the extra-tall cup. Twist the extractor blade onto the cup to seal. Blend for 30 seconds or until smooth, then return to the pan.

3. Cook over medium-low heat, stirring occasionally, for 5 minutes or until heated through. Add water, 1 tbsp (15 mL) at a time, if needed, to reach your desired consistency. Season to taste with salt and pepper.

4. Spoon into bowls and top each with a dollop of Greek yogurt.

TIP

Choose watercress that has crisp and bright green leaves with no yellowing. Watercress is delicate and, as such, is best eaten within 1 day of purchase. Both the leaves and stems are edible, but the stems tend to get tougher later in the season.

Yellow Split Pea and Pumpkin Soup

This creamy, rich soup, packed with healthy, hearty ingredients, is perfect for a fireside dinner on a cool fall day.

- **Tall cup**

2 tbsp	sunflower oil	30 mL
1	large onion, chopped	1
1 tbsp	grated gingerroot	15 mL
2 cups	dried yellow split peas, rinsed and picked through	500 mL
6 cups	no-salt-added ready-to-use chicken or vegetable broth	1.5 L
1¼ cups	puréed pumpkin (see tip, page 153) or canned pumpkin purée (not pie filling)	300 mL
	Kosher salt and freshly ground black pepper	
½ cup	raw green pumpkin seeds (pepitas), toasted (see tip)	125 mL

1. In a large pot, heat oil over medium-high heat. Add onion and cook, stirring, for 5 to 7 minutes or until translucent. Add ginger and cook, stirring, for 1 minute or until fragrant.

2. Stir in split peas and broth; bring to a boil. Reduce heat to medium-low, cover and simmer, stirring occasionally, for 1 hour. Transfer to a large bowl and let cool.

3. Working in batches, add split pea mixture to the tall cup. Twist the extractor blade onto the cup to seal. Blend for 30 seconds or until smooth.

4. Return soup to pot and stir in puréed pumpkin. Bring to a simmer over medium heat. Simmer, stirring, for 15 minutes to blend the flavors. Season to taste with salt and pepper.

5. Spoon into bowls and garnish with pumpkin seeds.

VARIATION

Substitute 2 medium sweet potatoes, peeled and cubed, for the pumpkin purée. Add potatoes to the broth in step 1 before simmering.

TIP

To toast pumpkin seeds, heat a small dry skillet over medium-high heat, add raw pumpkin seeds and cook, stirring constantly, for 2 to 3 minutes or until fragrant and lightly browned. Immediately transfer to a bowl and let cool before use.

Red Lentil, Chickpea and Tomato Soup

When you are in the mood for a warm, comforting soup, this full-flavored vegetarian soup should be on your list. This soup supports healthy metabolism, promotes a healthy gut and can help to reduce the risk for osteoporosis.

MAKES 4 SERVINGS

- **Extra-tall cup**

2 tsp	cumin seeds	10 mL
2 tsp	hot pepper flakes	10 mL
1 tbsp	flaxseed oil	15 mL
1	red onion, sliced and rings separated	1
¾ cup	dried red lentils, rinsed	175 mL
1	can (14 oz/398 g) whole tomatoes, with juice	1
3 cups	water	750 mL
½	can (14 to 15 oz/398 to 425 mL) chickpeas, drained and rinsed	½
1½ tsp	dulse granules	7 mL
¼ cup	chopped fresh cilantro, divided	60 mL
¼ cup	plain Greek yogurt	60 mL

1. In a large saucepan, heat cumin seeds and hot pepper flakes over medium-high heat for 1 minute or until seeds are just starting to pop. Add oil and heat until shimmering. Add onion and cook, stirring, for 5 minutes or until translucent.

2. Stir in lentils, tomatoes and water; bring to a boil, stirring often. Reduce heat and simmer for 7 to 10 minutes or until lentils are just tender. Transfer to a large bowl and let cool.

3. Working in batches if necessary, add lentil mixture to the extra-tall cup. Twist the extractor blade onto the cup to seal. Blend for 20 seconds or until smooth.

4. Return soup to the pan and stir in chickpeas and dulse. Cook over medium-low heat, stirring occasionally, for 5 minutes or until heated through. Stir in 3 tbsp (45 mL) cilantro.

5. Spoon into bowls, top each with a dollop of yogurt and garnish with remaining cilantro.

TIP

Leftover chickpeas can be stored in an airtight container in the refrigerator for up to 1 week and in the freezer for up to 6 months.

Zesty Chickpea, Tomato and Mushroom Soup

This mouthwatering, heartwarming soup doesn't take hours of simmering, but it's just as satisfying and good for you as a good old-fashioned home-cooked soup. By supporting gut health and gut bacteria, this soup helps to promote regularity and a healthy immune system and moods.

MAKES 2 SERVINGS

- **Extra-tall cup**

1	can (14 to 15 oz/398 to 425 mL) chickpeas, drained and rinsed	1
1	tomato, cored and quartered	1
1	clove garlic	1
½	small onion, quartered	½
1 cup	maitake (hen-of-the-woods) mushrooms, shiitake mushroom caps or oyster mushrooms	250 mL
¼ cup	lightly packed fresh cilantro	60 mL
1 tsp	ground turmeric	5 mL
½ tsp	ground ginger	2 mL
1½ cups	full-fat coconut milk	375 mL
1 cup	coconut water	250 mL

1. Add chickpeas, tomato, garlic, onion, mushrooms, cilantro, turmeric, ginger, coconut milk and coconut water to the extra-tall cup. Twist the extractor blade onto the cup to seal. Blend for 40 seconds or until smooth.

2. Pour soup into a medium saucepan. Bring to a simmer over medium heat, stirring occasionally, and cook for 5 minutes or until heated through.

TIP

Choose maitake mushrooms that are young, pliable and damp. The mushroom can be very large, but the fingers can be removed from their tough stem and broken into smaller pieces.

Tuscan White Bean Soup

The aroma of simmering garlic will draw you to this sublime creamy soup. It's rich in nutrients that support bone and tooth health, healthy mood and energy production while reducing the risk for metabolic syndrome and diabetes.

MAKES 4 SERVINGS

- **Extra-tall cup**

2 tbsp	butter or coconut oil	30 mL
1 tbsp	sunflower oil	15 mL
2	shallots, chopped	2
2	cans (each 14 to 15 oz/398 to 425 mL) cannellini (white kidney) beans, drained and rinsed	2
2	sprigs fresh thyme	2
4 cups	reduced-sodium ready-to-use chicken or vegetable broth	1 L
4	cloves garlic, halved	4
½ cup	full-fat coconut milk	125 mL
	Dulse powder or kosher salt	
	Freshly ground black pepper	

1. In a large saucepan, heat butter and sunflower oil over medium heat until shimmering. Add shallots and cook, stirring, for 3 minutes or until softened.

2. Stir in beans, thyme and broth; bring to a simmer, stirring often. Add garlic and simmer, stirring occasionally, for 10 minutes or until garlic is softened. Discard thyme sprigs. Transfer to a large bowl and let cool.

3. Working in batches, add bean mixture to the extra-tall cup. Twist the extractor blade onto the cup to seal. Blend for 30 seconds or until smooth.

4. Return soup to the pan and stir in coconut milk. Season to taste with dulse and pepper. Cook over medium-low heat, stirring occasionally, for 5 minutes or until heated through.

TIPS

Serve with a bright green salad and toasted French bread slices.

If you can only find 19-oz (540 mL) cans of cannellini beans, you will need 3 cups (750 mL) rinsed drained beans for this recipe. Store the remaining beans in an airtight container in the refrigerator for up to 1 week or in the freezer for up to 6 months.

Garden-Fresh Tomato Sauce

This fresh and inviting tomato sauce is the perfect accompaniment to your favorite pasta dish. Rich in lycopene, this sauce supports prostate and skin health.

MAKES ABOUT 3 CUPS (750 ML)

- **Extra-tall cup**

2 tbsp	sunflower oil	30 mL
½	onion, sliced and rings separated	½
2	cloves garlic, thinly sliced	2
6	plum (Roma) tomatoes, cored and quartered	6
1	chipotle chile pepper in adobo sauce (optional)	1
½	carrot, cut into chunks	½
2 tsp	granulated sugar	10 mL
¼ cup	lightly packed fresh basil leaves	60 mL
½ tsp	dried oregano	2 mL
½ tsp	lemon juice	2 mL
	Kosher salt and freshly ground black pepper	

1. In a large saucepan, heat oil over medium-high heat until shimmering. Add onion and cook, stirring, for 6 minutes or until translucent. Add garlic and cook, stirring, for 1 minute or until fragrant. Add tomatoes, ancho chile pepper with sauce (if using) and carrot; cook, breaking up the tomatoes and stirring occasionally, for 7 to 9 minutes or until tomatoes are softened. Transfer to a large bowl and let cool.

2. Working in batches if necessary, add sugar, basil, oregano, lemon juice and cooled tomato mixture to the extra-tall cup. Twist the extractor blade onto the cup to seal. Blend for 30 seconds or until smooth.

3. Return soup to the pan and cook over medium-low heat, stirring occasionally, for 5 minutes or until heated through. Season to taste with salt and pepper.

TIPS

If you prefer a chunkier sauce, in step 2, instead of blending until smooth, pulse the ingredients 3 times or until your desired consistency is reached.

Serve over traditional wheat pasta or try serving with spiralized zucchini noodles for a lighter meal.

Roasted Vegetable Pasta Sauce with Tomatoes, Carrots and Mushrooms

This robust blend of tomatoes, carrots and mushrooms seasoned with aromatic basil and oregano will make your taste buds swoon. This sauce may help reduce the risk for hormone-dependent cancers while supporting adrenal health and reducing the risk for both kidney stones and high blood pressure. Serve warm over pasta.

MAKES 4 SERVINGS

- **Preheat oven to 450°F (230°C)**
- **Baking sheet, lined with heavy-duty foil**
- **Extra-tall cup**

5	plum (Roma) tomatoes, cored and halved	5
2	small carrots, quartered	2
1 cup	baby bella or cremini mushrooms	250 mL
2	cloves garlic (unpeeled)	2
2 tbsp	rice bran oil or peanut oil	30 mL
1 tsp	kosher salt	5 mL
1/4 tsp	freshly ground black pepper	1 mL
1/4 cup	firmly packed fresh basil leaves	60 mL
2 tbsp	firmly packed fresh oregano leaves	30 mL
6 tbsp	tomato paste	90 mL
	Water (optional)	

1. Arrange tomatoes and carrots on one side of the prepared baking sheet and mushrooms and garlic on the other side. Drizzle with oil, turning to coat vegetables. Season with salt and pepper. Roast for 15 to 20 minutes, stirring mushrooms and garlic halfway through, until tomatoes are tender. Let cool. Remove skin from garlic.

2. Working in batches if necessary, add roasted vegetables, basil, oregano and tomato paste to the extra-tall cup. Twist the extractor blade onto the cup to seal. Blend for 30 seconds or until smooth.

3. Pour sauce into a medium saucepan. Bring to a simmer over medium heat, stirring occasionally. Simmer for 5 minutes or until heated through. If desired, add water, a little bit at a time, until you reach your preferred consistency.

TIPS

Choose mushrooms that are not bruised, shriveled or slimy. The stems should be firm and uniform in color. The gills should be dry and almost fanlike. Store mushrooms in a paper bag in the refrigerator.

Wash mushrooms gently under running water just before using them. Do not let mushrooms sit in water.

Enchilada Sauce with Poblano Peppers and Black Beans

This hearty sauce makes the perfect filling for enchiladas. The ingredients famously meld together and this combination is much better for you than a processed, store-bought canned sauce.

MAKES ABOUT 4 CUPS (1 L)

- **Preheat broiler, with rack set 6 inches (15 cm) from heat source**
- **Baking sheet, lined with heavy-duty foil**
- **Tall cup**

2	poblano chile peppers	2
2	cloves garlic (unpeeled)	2
1	yellow bell pepper	1
2	plum (Roma) tomatoes, cored and quartered, divided	2
1	can (14 to 19 oz/398 to 540 mL) black beans, with liquid, divided	1
1 cup	ready-to-use vegetable broth, divided	250 mL
1 tsp	ground cumin	5 mL
½ tsp	seaweed powder, such as dulse or kelp	2 mL

1. Arrange poblano peppers, garlic and yellow pepper on prepared baking sheet. Broil, turning once, for 7 to 9 minutes or until the skins of the peppers are charred and the peppers are collapsing. Transfer peppers and garlic to a heatproof bowl and cover with plastic wrap. Let cool.

2. Peel outer skin from peppers, cut off tops and remove seeds and ribs; discard. Peel skin from garlic and discard.

3. Add half of each of the roasted vegetables to the tall cup. Add half each of the tomatoes, beans and broth. Twist the extractor blade onto the cup to seal. Blend for 40 seconds or until smooth. Pour into a large saucepan. Repeat with remaining roasted vegetables, tomato, beans and broth.

4. Add cumin and seaweed powder to saucepan. Bring to a simmer over medium heat. Simmer, stirring often, for 8 to 10 minutes or until liquids are reduced by half.

VARIATION

Add ¾ cup (175 mL) cooked chicken cubes to the enchilada sauce.

TIPS

For a spicier sauce, use 3 to 4 poblano peppers and eliminate the bell pepper. For a milder version, use 2 yellow bell peppers and eliminate the poblano peppers.

This sauce can be stored in an airtight container in the refrigerator for up to 5 days.

Creamy Mushroom Sauce

This simple recipe is rich, creamy and flavored with just the right balance of leek, garlic and parsley for a versatile sauce that goes well with dumplings or pasta.

MAKES 4 SERVINGS

- **Tall cup**

12 oz	button mushrooms	375 g
1	leek, white parts only, sliced into 2-inch (5 cm) sections	1
1	clove garlic	1
2 tbsp	peanut oil	30 mL
⅔ cup	ready-to-use vegetable broth	150 mL
¾ cup	heavy or whipping (35%) cream	175 mL
	Kosher salt and freshly ground black pepper	
	Chopped fresh parsley	
	Freshly grated Parmesan cheese	

1. Add mushrooms, leek and garlic to the tall cup. Twist the extractor blade onto the cup to seal. Blend for 20 seconds or until coarsely chopped.

2. In a large saucepan, heat oil over medium-high heat. Add mushroom mixture and cook, stirring, for 5 to 7 minutes or until softened. Stir in broth and bring to a boil, stirring. Add cream, reduce heat and simmer, stirring, until thickened to your desired consistency. Season to taste with salt and pepper.

3. Spoon into bowls and garnish with parsley and Parmesan. Serve immediately.

TIP

You can substitute 2 large shallots, roughly chopped, for the leeks.

Arugula and Sweet Pea Pesto

Sweet peas complement the peppery flavor of arugula to make a pesto that makes your palate tingle. This pesto has liver-supporting and anticancer nutrients, as well as nutrients that support healthy blood pressure and bone and eye health.

MAKES ABOUT 2 CUPS (500 ML)

- **Tall cup**

1 cup	firmly packed arugula	250 mL
1 cup	thawed frozen sweet peas	250 mL
2	cloves garlic	2
⅓ cup	extra virgin olive oil	75 mL
2 tbsp	natural almond butter	30 mL
2 tbsp	lemon juice	30 mL
½ cup	grated Parmesan cheese	125 mL
	Kosher salt and freshly ground black pepper	

1. Add arugula, peas, garlic, oil, almond butter and lemon juice to the tall cup. Twist the extractor blade onto the cup to seal. Blend for 30 seconds or until smooth.

2. Add Parmesan cheese, seal cup and pulse 5 to 7 times or until combined. Season to taste with salt and pepper.

TIPS

Choose arugula that is bright green and has no yellow or bruised spots. Younger arugula is milder and has a less peppery taste. Store arugula in a produce bag or lightly wrapped in paper towels in the refrigerator for up to 1 week.

Spread pesto on toasted French bread slices and add halved cherry tomatoes for a nutritional boost and an inviting presentation.

Kale and Roasted Pepper Pesto

A traditional basil pesto is wonderful, but add in baby kale, roasted pepper and almond butter and you have gone to new heights. This pesto contains several different cancer-fighting phytonutrients, which also support the liver in its natural detoxification role.

MAKES ABOUT 2½ CUPS (625 ML)

- **Extra-tall cup**

1	small roasted red bell pepper, drained	1
2 cups	lightly packed baby kale leaves	500 mL
1 cup	packed fresh basil leaves	250 mL
1 tsp	kosher salt	5 mL
3	cloves garlic	3
⅓ cup	extra virgin olive oil	75 mL
2 tbsp	lemon juice	30 mL
2 tbsp	natural almond butter	30 mL
½ cup	grated Parmesan cheese	125 mL

Optional Nutrition Boost
Add 1 tsp (5 mL) chlorella after the salt.

1. Add roasted pepper, kale, basil, salt, garlic, oil, lemon juice and almond butter to the extra-tall cup. Twist the extractor blade onto the cup to seal. Blend for 40 seconds or until smooth.

2. Add Parmesan, seal cup and pulse 5 to 7 times or until combined.

TIPS

Serve over wheat pasta or zucchini noodles. Garnish with roasted pine nuts and shaved Parmesan.

Spread on sandwiches or pizza dough for a fun and healthy twist.

Spicy Spinach Cilantro Sauce

Green, spicy and delectable are just a few of the trademarks of this gloriously flavored sauce that is the perfect accompaniment to grilled or roasted fish. Packed with anti-inflammatory carotenoids, this sauce helps any health condition where there is inflammation, such as diabetes, heart disease, dementia, cataracts and depression.

MAKES ABOUT 1 CUP (250 ML)

- **Tall cup**

1	lime, peeled and halved	1
3 cups	firmly packed fresh cilantro leaves and tender stems	750 mL
2 cups	firmly packed trimmed spinach	500 mL
½ cup	firmly packed fresh parsley leaves and tender stems	125 mL
2 tsp	seaweed flakes, such as dulse or kelp	10 mL
1 tsp	grated turmeric	5 mL
⅛ tsp	cayenne pepper	0.5 mL
2	cloves garlic	2
¼ cup	water	60 mL
½ cup	flaxseed or sunflower oil	125 mL
2 tbsp	balsamic vinegar	30 mL
2 tbsp	liquid honey	30 mL
	Kosher salt and freshly grated black pepper	

1. Add lime, cilantro, spinach, parsley, seaweed flakes, turmeric, cayenne pepper, garlic, water, oil, vinegar and honey to the tall cup. Twist the extractor blade onto the cup to seal. Blend for 30 seconds or until smooth. Season to taste with salt and pepper. Serve immediately.

TIPS

Choose spinach with thin, flexible leaves, indicating a younger and more tender plant. Leaves should be bright green with no dark spots or yellowing.

Flaxseed oil often gets a bad rap. But a good flaxseed oil should taste clean, crisp and slightly nutty. If the oil tastes or smells bitter or is overpowering, the oil is rancid and should not be used.

Sauce can be stored in an airtight container in the refrigerator for up to 3 days.

Triple-Berry Sauce

All of you berry lovers will want to add this simple yet delightful sauce to everything. Try it on Greek yogurt, chia pudding, pancakes or waffles — for starters. This well-rounded sauce supports gut health while promoting regularity and reducing the risk for high blood pressure, stroke and cancer.

MAKES ABOUT 2½ CUPS (625 ML)

- **Tall cup**

1 cup	strawberries	250 mL
1 cup	raspberries	250 mL
¾ cup	blueberries	175 mL
1 tbsp	chia seeds	15 mL
1 cup	coconut water	250 mL
1 tbsp	lemon juice	15 mL

Optional Nutrition Boost
Add 1 tsp (5 mL) pomegranate powder after the chia seeds.

1. Add strawberries, raspberries, blueberries, chia seeds, coconut water and lemon juice to the tall cup. Twist the extractor blade onto the cup to seal. Blend for 40 seconds or until smooth. Sauce can be served at room temperature or warmed.

TIP

Choose raspberries that are deeply colored and remove any stems. Berries with mold should be discarded. Raspberries are best enjoyed when just picked. Store unwashed raspberries in a single layer, lightly covered with paper towels, in the refrigerator for up to 3 days.

Kid-Friendly Recipes

Great Start Breakfast Smoothie....168

Strawberry Malt Smoothie 168

Triple-Threat Protein and
Berry Smoothie 169

Grape Kiwi Kid-Power Smoothie...170

Peachy Grape and Blueberry
Smoothie 171

Orange Cream Smoothie 171

Fruit Combo Smoothie...................172

Cardinal Red Fruit and
Vegetable Burst 172

Pineapple, Citrus and Carrot
Smoothie 173

Fruity Carrot Smoothie..................173

Garden Basket Veggie and
Fruit Smoothie 174

Zingy Green and Fruity
Energy Boost.................................174

Fruity Get-Your-Greens
Smoothie 175

Green Chocolate Milk 176

Guilt-Free Chocolate Delight 176

Sporty Peanut Butter Banana
Smoothie 177

Cranberry Pear Splash 177

Bountiful Berry, Spinach and
Cashew Smoothie Bowl...............178

Zesty Edamame Dip.......................179

BLT Bean Spread............................180

Spaghetti Beanballs 181

Peach, Blueberry and
Chia Parfait...................................182

Papaya Kiwi Frozen Yogurt............183

Strawberry, Pear and Lime
Ice Pops...183

Raspberry, Peach and Grape
Ice Pops...184

Chocolate-Covered Coconut
Avocado Balls 185

Gooey Almond Oat Balls...............186

Banana Coconut Lentil Balls.........187

Spiced Pineapple and Maca
Energy Balls..................................188

Great Start Breakfast Smoothie

This smoothie will help you get fruit, vegetables, protein and fiber into your family's diet before they even get out the door. And if you're running late, just pack it to go. Getting your daily dose of fiber isn't just about bran cereal!

	MAKES 1 TO 3 SERVINGS	
• Tall cup		
2	kiwifruits, peeled and halved	2
1	banana, halved	1
1	carrot, cut into thirds	1
¾ cup	raspberries	175 mL
¼ cup	large-flake (old-fashioned) rolled oats	60 mL
½ cup	plain yogurt	125 mL
1 tbsp	lemon juice	15 mL
	Coconut water	

1. Add kiwis, banana, carrot, raspberries, rolled oats, yogurt and lemon juice to the tall cup. Add coconut water to the "Max Line." Twist the extractor blade onto the cup to seal. Blend for 30 seconds or until smooth.

TIPS

Choose kiwis that are firm and unblemished. The kiwis should give to slight pressure when pressed with your thumb.

Choose rolled oats that are organic to avoid unwanted chemicals in your diet. Selecting a trusted brand will help you get rolled oats that have the best flavor and have not been overprocessed or dried out.

Strawberry Malt Smoothie

Infused with strawberry goodness, this creamy smoothie tastes like an old-fashioned malt but is new-age good for you.

	MAKES 1 TO 3 SERVINGS	
• Tall cup		
6	frozen strawberries	6
½	frozen banana	½
1	small pear, halved	1
¼ cup	plain Greek yogurt	60 mL
1 tbsp	malted milk powder (without added sweeteners)	15 mL
2	ice cubes (optional)	2
2 tsp	liquid honey	10 mL
	Unsweetened almond milk	

> **Optional Nutrition Boost**
> Add 2 tbsp (30 mL) whey protein powder after the yogurt.

1. Add strawberries, banana, pear, yogurt, milk powder, ice cubes (if using) and honey to the tall cup. Add almond milk to the "Max Line." Twist the extractor blade onto the cup to seal. Blend for 30 seconds or until smooth.

TIP

Strawberries don't ripen further after they're picked. Choose berries that are bright red and have a natural sheen and fresh green leaves and stems. Store strawberries in the refrigerator. Just before serving, rinse berries in cold water, with stems intact, and blot dry with paper towel. Remove hulls just before using. Strawberries taste best at room temperature.

Triple-Threat Protein and Berry Smoothie

When it's time to load your bases, this smoothie with a healthy blend of blueberries, blackberries and flax seeds is a grand slam, with protein for building and maintaining muscles and bones.

MAKES 1 TO 3 SERVINGS

- **Tall cup**

½ cup	frozen blueberries	125 mL
½ cup	frozen blackberries	125 mL
½ cup	plain or vanilla-flavored yogurt	125 mL
3 tbsp	vanilla or plain whey protein powder	45 mL
1 tbsp	ground flax seeds (flaxseed meal)	15 mL
2 tsp	liquid honey	10 mL
	Milk or plain kefir	

Optional Nutrition Boost
Add 1 tbsp (15 mL) wheat germ after the flax seeds.

1. Add blueberries, blackberries, yogurt, protein powder, flax seeds and honey to the tall cup. Add milk to the "Max Line." Twist the extractor blade onto the cup to seal. Blend for 40 seconds or until smooth.

TIPS

If using fresh berries, you may want to add 3 to 4 ice cubes to make the smoothie thicker.

Look for yogurt that contains live active yogurt cultures, as this type contains the most desirable health properties.

Whey protein powder can be found online and in specialty health-food stores.

Grape Kiwi Kid-Power Smoothie

A little bit of sweet and a little bit of tart makes for a kid-friendly smoothie that is cleansing and refreshing. This smoothie supports growing bones and promotes a healthy gut.

MAKES 1 TO 3 SERVINGS

- **Tall cup**

3	kiwifruits, peeled and halved	3
1	orange, peeled and seeded	1
1	pear (such as green d'Anjou or Bartlett), halved	1
2 cups	seedless red grapes	250 mL
2 to 3	ice cubes	2 to 3
½ cup	coconut water	125 mL

Optional Nutrition Boost
Add 1 tsp (5 mL) camu camu powder after the grapes.

1. Add kiwis, orange, pear, grapes, ice cubes and coconut water to the tall cup. Twist the extractor blade onto the cup to seal. Blend for 30 seconds or until smooth.

TIP

Choose kiwis that are firm and have unblemished skin. The size of the kiwi does not indicate ripeness or flavor, so choose any size that looks best to you. The kiwis should give slightly when pressed with your thumb.

Peachy Grape and Blueberry Smoothie

At the heart of this smoothie are sweet and succulent peaches complemented by the bright, slightly tart flavors of red grapes and blueberries. Don't tell your kids this smoothie helps to fight infections and heal cuts and bruises or that it supports their eyes and minds. You're the only one who needs to know.

MAKES 1 TO 3 SERVINGS

- **Tall cup**

2	small peaches, halved and pitted	2
1 cup	blueberries	250 mL
½ cup	seedless red grapes	125 mL
1 tsp	camu camu powder	5 mL
4 to 5	ice cubes	4 to 5
	Coconut water	

Optional Nutrition Boost
Add 2 tbsp (30 mL) whey protein powder after the grapes.

1. Add peaches, blueberries, grapes, camu camu powder and ice cubes to the tall cup. Add coconut water to the "Max Line." Twist the extractor blade onto the cup to seal. Blend for 40 seconds or until smooth.

TIPS

You can substitute frozen grapes, blueberries and 1½ cups (375 mL) peach slices for the fresh. Eliminate or reduce the number of ice cubes.

Yellow peaches have a yellow peel with a red blush. If you plan to use them the same day, choose peaches that are soft when lightly pressed with your finger. If the flesh is still firm, let the peaches stand 2 days at room temperature. Select peaches of varying ripeness to use over a few days.

Orange Cream Smoothie

What adult doesn't remember those heavenly cream-filled Popsicles? Share this smoothie recipe with your kids and enjoy it all over again. Unlike the frozen dessert, this smoothie nourishes muscles and bones.

MAKES 1 TO 3 SERVINGS

- **Tall cup**

½ cup	frozen mango chunks	125 mL
½ cup	frozen halved seedless red grapes	125 mL
1 cup	plain Greek yogurt	250 mL
½ cup	orange juice	125 mL
1 tsp	pure vanilla extract	5 mL
4	ice cubes	4
	Water	

Optional Nutrition Boost
Add 1 tbsp (15 mL) goji berries after the yogurt.

1. Add mango, grapes, yogurt, orange juice, vanilla and ice cubes to the tall cup. Add water to the "Max Line." Twist the extractor blade onto the cup to seal. Blend for 40 seconds or until smooth.

TIP

To easily halve grapes before freezing, arrange between two flat plates or container lids. Using a sharp knife, cut horizontally between the plates, cutting through the grapes.

Fruit Combo Smoothie

This symphony of sweet peaches and berries, tropical fruits and tangy cranberry juice makes this smoothie sing with flavor and vitamin C, potassium and skin-loving carotenoids.

MAKES 1 TO 3 SERVINGS

- **Tall cup**

2	peaches, halved and pitted	2
1	banana, halved	1
1 cup	quartered strawberries	250 mL
⅔ cup	pineapple chunks	150 mL
1 tsp	camu camu powder	5 mL
3 to 4	ice cubes	3 to 4
	Unsweetened cranberry juice (not a blend)	

Optional Nutrition Boost
Add 1 tbsp (15 mL) goji berries after the pineapple.

1. Add peaches, banana, strawberries, pineapple, camu camu powder and ice cubes to the tall cup. Add cranberry juice to the "Max Line." Twist the extractor blade onto the cup to seal. Blend for 30 seconds or until smooth.

TIPS

If your kids prefer peeled peaches, drop them into a pot of boiling water for 10 seconds, then immediately plunge into a bowl of ice water and let cool slightly. Use your fingers to peel off the skin.

You can substitute mango or papaya chunks for the pineapple.

Adjust the number of ice cubes depending on your desired thickness.

Cardinal Red Fruit and Vegetable Burst

Spinach, citrus and fresh berries meld for a refreshing and colorful smoothie. This is a tasty and easy way to get kids to eat their vegetables.

MAKES 1 TO 3 SERVINGS

- **Tall cup**

1½ cups	firmly packed trimmed spinach	375 mL
1	orange, peeled and seeded	1
¼	grapefruit, peeled and seeded	¼
¼ cup	sliced strawberries	60 mL
¼ cup	raspberries	60 mL
2 tbsp	goji berries	30 mL
1 tbsp	chia seeds	15 mL
	Coconut water	

1. Add spinach, orange, grapefruit, strawberries, raspberries, goji berries and chia seeds to the tall cup. Add coconut water to the "Max Line." Twist the extractor blade onto the cup to seal. Blend for 30 seconds or until smooth.

TIP

You can substitute frozen strawberries and/ or frozen raspberries for the fresh. Doing so will make your smoothie thicker and colder. Make sure no sugars have been added.

Pineapple, Citrus and Carrot Smoothie

School starts or the weather takes a nasty turn and suddenly we just aren't feeling as great. It's time to make this jam-packed superfood smoothie to give your system a boost. Bioflavonoids and vitamin C help to keep the immune system strong.

MAKES 1 TO 3 SERVINGS

- **Tall cup**

1	carrot, cut into thirds	1
1	clementine, peeled and seeded	1
½ cup	frozen mango chunks	125 mL
½ cup	frozen pineapple chunks	125 mL
1	½- by ½-inch (1 by 1 cm) piece gingerroot, peeled	1
1	¼- by ¼-inch (0.5 by 0.5 cm) piece fresh turmeric, peeled	1
1 tbsp	hemp seeds	15 mL
1½ tsp	camu camu powder	7 mL
2 tbsp	lemon juice	30 mL
	Coconut water	

1. Add carrot, clementine, mango, pineapple, ginger, turmeric, hemp seeds, camu camu powder and lemon juice to the tall cup. Add coconut water to the "Max Line." Twist the extractor blade onto the cup to seal. Blend for 40 seconds or until smooth.

TIP

Choose hemp seeds that are certified organic and non-GMO for the best quality and taste. Hemp seeds have a pleasing and slightly nutty taste, but unfortunately you're not always able to taste them before purchasing. Canadian growers produce some of the highest-quality hemp seeds.

Fruity Carrot Smoothie

Turn to this recipe when active kids need an energizing boost along with extra nutrients. Everyone can benefit from the carotenoids, vitamin C, fiber and potassium.

MAKES 1 TO 3 SERVINGS

- **Tall cup**

1	carrot, cut into thirds	1
1	pear, halved	1
¼ cup	frozen mango chunks	60 mL
¼ cup	frozen strawberries	60 mL
½ cup	plain Greek yogurt	125 mL
	Coconut water	

Optional Nutrition Boost

Add 1 tsp (5 mL) camu camu powder after the yogurt.

1. Add carrot, pear, mango, strawberries and yogurt to the tall cup. Add coconut water to the "Max Line." Twist the extractor blade onto the cup to seal. Blend for 40 seconds or until smooth.

TIP

A fully ripened pear will be slightly soft when you press a finger near the stem. It should not have any soft spots or blemishes. An unripe pear will ripen at room temperature within a few days. To speed up the process, place in a paper bag and store at room temperature. Once ripe, store in the refrigerator for up to 3 days.

Garden Basket Veggie and Fruit Smoothie

Your kids will enjoy this mini cornucopia of fruit and vegetables all blended up in a make-and-take beverage. This smoothie promotes regularity and a healthy gut and helps to keep eyes strong.

MAKES 1 TO 3 SERVINGS

- **Tall cup**

1 cup	packed trimmed kale leaves	250 mL
1 cup	packed baby spinach	250 mL
2	pitted prunes	2
1	banana, halved	1
1	pitted soft date, preferably Medjool	1
½ cup	frozen blueberries	125 mL
½ cup	frozen blackberries	125 mL
	Unsweetened rice milk	

Optional Nutrition Boost
Add 1 tsp (5 mL) maca powder after the blackberries.

1. Add kale, spinach, prunes, banana, date, blueberries and blackberries to the tall cup. Add rice milk to the "Max Line." Twist the extractor blade onto the cup to seal. Blend for 40 seconds or until smooth.

TIP

You can substitute hemp milk or almond milk for the rice milk.

Zingy Green and Fruity Energy Boost

Go ahead, we double dare you to sneak some power-packed vegetables into a refreshing, sweet smoothie. While the kids might not appreciate it now, they'll benefit from this smoothie's nutrients, which help to keep eyes healthy and support hearts at rest and play.

MAKES 1 TO 3 SERVINGS

- **Tall cup**

1 cup	lightly packed trimmed watercress	250 mL
1	pear, halved	1
1 cup	frozen sweet peas	250 mL
1 cup	seedless red grapes	250 mL
1	1- by 1-inch (2.5 by 2.5 cm) piece gingerroot, peeled	1
2 tbsp	lemon juice	30 mL
	Coconut water	

1. Add watercress, pear, peas, grapes, ginger and lemon juice to the tall cup. Add coconut water to the "Max Line." Twist the extractor blade onto the cup to seal. Blend for 30 seconds or until smooth.

TIP

Choose red grapes that are predominantly red, without any green or yellow patches. The grapes should be firm, plump and firmly attached to the stem. The stems should be green and flexible and not dried out. Don't worry if the grapes have a powder-white coating: it means they are moist and fresh.

Fruity Get-Your-Greens Smoothie

Help your family's bodies stay healthy and boost everyone's immune systems with this tasty smoothie.

- **Tall cup**

1 cup	lightly packed baby kale	250 mL
½ cup	frozen strawberries	125 mL
½ cup	frozen raspberries	125 mL
½ cup	frozen blueberries	125 mL
½ tsp	ground cinnamon	2 mL
1 tbsp	natural almond butter	15 mL
	Coconut water	

Optional Nutrition Boost

Add 1 tsp (5 mL) green powder (see box, page 18) after the blueberries.

1. Add kale, strawberries, raspberries, blueberries, cinnamon and almond butter to the tall cup. Add coconut water to the "Max Line." Twist the extractor blade onto the cup to seal. Blend for 40 seconds or until smooth.

TIP

You can substitute trimmed spinach, watercress or Swiss chard for the baby kale.

Green Chocolate Milk

For all of the chocolate-milk lovers out there, this is a wonderful way to introduce your kids —
and yourself — to green smoothies. They'll never know they're drinking their vegetables.

MAKES 1 TO 3 SERVINGS

- **Tall cup**

1 cup	firmly packed trimmed spinach	250 mL
2	pitted soft dates, preferably Medjool	2
½	banana	½
1 tbsp	cacao powder	15 mL
1 tsp	maca powder	10 mL
2 tbsp	natural cashew butter	30 mL
2	ice cubes	2
	Unsweetened almond milk	

1. Add spinach, dates, banana, cacao powder, maca powder, cashew butter and ice cubes to the tall cup. Add almond milk to the "Max Line." Twist the extractor blade onto the cup to seal. Blend for 30 seconds or until smooth.

TIPS

While a variety of fresh dates will work in this recipe, Medjool dates are softer and sweeter than many other varieties.

Choose dates that are plump, soft and have shiny skin. They should not have any evidence of crystalizing sugar on their skin.

Guilt-Free Chocolate Delight

You can let your kids have a chocolate treat without giving up on everything healthy. This blend of banana, chocolate and almonds will appeal to kids of all ages.

MAKES 1 TO 3 SERVINGS

- **Tall cup**

1	frozen banana, halved	1
¾ cup	plain yogurt	175 mL
1 tbsp	cacao powder	15 mL
1 tbsp	chocolate or vanilla whey protein powder	15 mL
2 tbsp	natural almond butter	30 mL
	Unsweetened almond milk	
	Slivered almonds	
	Cacao nibs (optional)	

1. Add banana, yogurt, cacao powder, whey protein powder and almond butter to the tall cup. Add almond milk to the "Max Line." Twist the extractor blade onto the cup to seal. Blend for 30 seconds or until smooth. Garnish with slivered almonds and cacao nibs (if using).

TIPS

Whey protein is commonly available in three varieties: whey protein concentrate, which contains 70% to 90% protein; whey protein isolate, which contains at least 90% protein; and whey protein hydrolysate, which is the purest form. As the percent of protein increases, so does the digestibility and expense. Whey isolate and whey hydrolysate are both lower in lactose and can often be tolerated by those with lactose intolerance. Try different varieties and choose the one that works best for you.

Pea, hemp, rice, soy or egg-white protein can be substituted for the whey protein.

Sporty Peanut Butter Banana Smoothie

Help kids' bodies power ahead during — and recover quicker after — sports activities with this blend of bananas, peanut butter and protein powder. It has the protein they need to maintain muscle and the carbohydrate they require for energy.

MAKES 1 TO 3 SERVINGS

- Tall cup

⅔ cup	lightly packed trimmed spinach	150 mL
1	frozen banana, halved	1
½ cup	plain or vanilla yogurt	125 mL
1 tsp	whey or hemp protein powder	5 mL
2 tbsp	natural peanut butter	30 mL
	Unsweetened almond milk	

1. Add spinach, banana, yogurt, protein powder and peanut butter to the tall cup. Add almond milk to the "Max Line." Twist the extractor blade onto the cup to seal. Blend for 30 seconds or until smooth.

TIP

Choose peanut butter with no added oils or sugars. If there is a thin layer of oil on top of the butter, stir before using. Select full-fat peanut butter, as fillers such as sugar and starches replace the healthy fats found naturally in peanuts in light and low-fat products. Check the ingredient list carefully and purchase one that contains only peanuts: although the jar may say "all natural," it may contain undesirable natural additives.

Cranberry Pear Splash

A fun and festive slushy drink that is an inviting nonalcoholic beverage but looks like a grown-up cocktail.

MAKES 6 SERVINGS

- Tall cup

¼ cup	fresh cranberries	60 mL
2 tbsp	granulated sugar	30 mL
4 to 5	ice cubes	4 to 5
¾ cup	unsweetened pear juice	175 mL
½ cup	unsweetened cranberry juice (not a blend)	125 mL
1 tbsp	orange juice	15 mL

> **Optional Nutrition Boost**
> Add 1 tsp (5 mL) pomegranate powder after the sugar.

1. Add cranberries, sugar, ice cubes, pear juice, cranberry juice and orange juice to the tall cup. Twist the extractor blade onto the cup to seal. Blend for 20 seconds or until combined and slushy.

TIPS

Frozen cranberries can be used in place of fresh. Reduce the ice cubes to 2 to 3 cubes.

Serve in stemware for a festive look.

Bountiful Berry, Spinach and Cashew Smoothie Bowl

If you're looking for a way to get your kids to dive into a healthy breakfast instead of running out the door, just set this bowl in front of them and watch them dig in. They won't know they're getting the nutrients they need for healthy eyes or a healthy gut — or the nutrients they need for energy — but that's okay.

MAKES 1 TO 2 SERVINGS

- **Tall cup**

Smoothie

1 cup	firmly packed trimmed spinach	250 mL
1	frozen banana, halved, divided	1
1 cup	mixed frozen berries	250 mL
1 tbsp	pea, hemp or whey protein powder	15 mL
1 tsp	ground chicory root	5 mL
1 tsp	coconut oil	5 mL
⅔ cup	unsweetened almond milk, divided	150 mL

Topping

1 tbsp	cashews	15 mL
1 tbsp	goji berries	15 mL
1 tbsp	unsweetened shredded coconut	15 mL
¼ cup	blueberries	60 mL
	Assorted fresh raspberries, blackberries or sliced strawberries (optional)	

1. *Smoothie:* Add spinach, half the banana, berries, protein powder, chicory root, coconut oil and ⅓ cup (75 mL) almond milk to the tall cup. Twist the extractor blade onto the cup to seal. Blend for 30 seconds or until thick and smooth. If smoothie is too thick, add additional almond milk, 1 tbsp (15 mL) at a time, and blend until the desired consistency is reached.

2. *Topping:* Using a silicone spatula, transfer smoothie to a bowl or bowls. Slice remaining banana half. Arrange banana, cashews, goji berries, coconut and blueberries on top of smoothie. If desired, arrange additional fresh berries on top.

TIPS

Smoothie bowls are much thicker than traditional smoothies.

Ask your kids to arrange the topping ingredients in step 2 into any fun shape or pattern they choose. Caution: allow enough time in the morning to let your kids "play with their food."

Zesty Edamame Dip

This fiery edamame dip gets its zing from wasabi paste and a combination of garlic, cilantro and chili sauce for an interesting twist on a blended bean dip.

MAKES ABOUT 1 CUP (250 ML)

- **Tall cup**

1 cup	frozen shelled edamame, thawed	250 mL
¼ cup	lightly packed cilantro leaves	60 mL
2	green onions (green and white parts), cut into 3-inch (7.5 cm) sections	2
1	clove garlic	1
2 tbsp	lime juice	30 mL
2 tsp	unseasoned rice vinegar	10 mL
1 tsp	chili sauce	5 mL
¼ tsp	wasabi paste (see tip)	1 mL
	Coconut water	
	Kosher salt and freshly ground black pepper	
	Additional cilantro leaves (optional)	

Optional Nutrition Boost
Add 1 tbsp (15 mL) matcha powder after the garlic.

1. Add edamame, cilantro, green onions, garlic, lime juice, vinegar, chili sauce and wasabi to the tall cup. Twist the extractor blade onto the cup to seal. Blend for 30 seconds or until smooth. Add coconut water, 1 tbsp (15 mL) at a time, and blend until your desired consistency is reached. Cover and refrigerate for 2 hours or until chilled.

2. Season to taste with salt and pepper and stir. Transfer to a serving bowl. If desired, garnish with additional cilantro.

VARIATION

Add 1 halved avocado after the edamame in step 1 for an additional boost of flavor and nutrients.

TIP

This dip is quite spicy, but it is a good way to introduce spicy foods to your kids. The first time you make it, start with just a pinch of wasabi paste and taste-test it before adding more. Gradually increase the amount of wasabi in subsequent batches.

BLT Bean Spread

This take on a classic BLT sandwich is an inviting spread for an after-school or midday snack. In addition to the savory taste, it is gluten-free and bursting with nutrients. Serve with crackers or sliced French bread.

MAKES ABOUT 2 CUPS (500 ML)

- **Extra-tall cup**

1 cup	lightly packed baby spinach	250 mL
1¾ cups	rinsed drained cannellini (white kidney) beans	425 mL
½ tsp	kosher salt	2 mL
½ tsp	freshly ground black pepper	2 mL
2 tbsp	tahini	30 mL
2 tbsp	lemon juice	30 mL
2 tsp	extra virgin olive oil	10 mL
2	cloves garlic	2
¼ cup	unsweetened brewed green tea, cooled	60 mL
3	slices bacon, cooked and crumbled	3
1	plum (Roma) tomato, peeled and diced	1

1. Add spinach, cannellini beans, salt, pepper, tahini, lemon juice, oil, garlic and green tea to the extra-tall cup. Twist the extractor blade onto the cup to seal. Blend for 30 seconds or until smooth. Cover and refrigerate for 2 hours or until chilled.

2. Transfer mixture to a serving bowl and sprinkle with bacon and tomatoes.

TIP

You can substitute chickpeas for the cannellini beans in this recipe. Or, for an earthier flavor, use an equal amount of black beans.

Spaghetti Beanballs

These vegetarian beanballs are a great alternative to traditional meatballs. Served with tomato sauce, they make a hearty addition to a bowl of spaghetti or hoagie roll.

MAKES 6 SERVINGS

- **Preheat oven to 400°F (200°C)**
- **Tall cup**
- **Baking sheet, lined with foil and sprayed with nonstick cooking spray**

1¾ cups	canned soybeans, drained and rinsed	425 mL
½ cup	wheat germ, divided	125 mL
2 tbsp	grated Parmesan cheese	30 mL
1½ tbsp	lightly packed basil leaves	22 mL
1 tsp	onion powder	5 mL
1	clove garlic	1
¼ cup	unsweetened soy milk	60 mL

1. Add soybeans, ⅓ cup (75 mL) wheat germ, Parmesan, basil, onion powder, garlic and soy milk to the tall cup. Twist the extractor blade onto the cup to seal. Blend for 30 seconds or until coarsely combined.

2. Using your hands, roll mixture into 1½ inch (4 cm) balls. Roll balls in remaining wheat germ. Arrange balls, 1 inch (2.5 cm) apart, on prepared baking sheet.

3. Bake in preheated oven for 12 to 15 minutes or until firm and hot in the center and wheat germ is lightly browned.

TIPS

For a gluten-free version, use gluten-free panko (Japanese bread crumbs) or other gluten-free cracker crumbs in place of the wheat germ.

Serve with Garden-Fresh Tomato Sauce (page 160), over noodles or in a hoagie roll.

Store beanballs in an airtight container in the refrigerator for up to 3 days or in the freezer for up to 3 months. Let thaw overnight in the refrigerator. Reheat by simmering in tomato sauce for 10 minutes.

Peach, Blueberry and Chia Parfait

Layer upon layer of lusciousness that is also superfood-powered goodness for kids' bodies — how exciting is that? What doesn't this parfait have? It's like a multivitamin with minerals in a glass! Just make sure to plan ahead, because you need to soak the chia seeds ahead of time.

- Small cup
- 2 tall cups
- 2 parfait glasses (about 10 oz/300 mL each)

Chia Pudding

3 tbsp	chia seeds	45 mL
¼ tsp	ground cinnamon	1 mL
⅔ cup	unsweetened almond milk	150 mL
1 tbsp	pure maple syrup	15 mL
⅛ tsp	pure vanilla extract	0.5 mL

Peach Purée

1	frozen banana, halved	1
1 cup	frozen peach slices	250 mL
1 tsp	grated gingerroot	5 mL
½ cup	unsweetened almond milk	125 mL

Blueberry Purée

1	frozen banana, halved	1
1	pitted soft date	1
¾ cup	frozen blueberries	175 mL
½ cup	unsweetened almond milk	125 mL

> **Optional Nutrition Boost**
> Top the parfaits with 2 tsp (10 mL) cacao nibs.

1. *Chia Pudding:* Add chia seeds, cinnamon, almond milk, maple syrup and vanilla to the small cup. Twist the extractor blade onto the cup to seal. Blend for 20 seconds or until smooth. Cover and refrigerate for 8 to 10 hours or until mixture becomes a pudding consistency.

2. *Peach Purée:* Add banana, peaches, ginger and almond milk to a tall cup. Twist the extractor blade onto the cup to seal. Blend for 20 seconds or until smooth. Set aside.

3. *Blueberry Purée:* Add banana, date, blueberries and almond milk to the other tall cup. Twist the extractor blade onto the cup to seal. Blend for 20 seconds or until smooth.

4. Spoon about 1 inch (2.5 cm) of chia pudding into each parfait glass. Add a 1- to 2-inch (2.5 to 5 cm) layer of peach purée, another layer of chia pudding, and a 1- to 2-inch (2.5 to 5 cm) layer of blueberry purée. Continue layering until glasses are full.

TIPS

If you don't have 2 tall cups, after step 2 transfer the peach purée to a small bowl and rinse out the tall cup before continuing with step 3.

Equal amounts of frozen raspberries or strawberries can be substituted for the blueberries in the blueberry purée.

You can use any size parfait glass, but you may have more or fewer servings depending on their size.

Reserve several blueberries for garnish, if desired.

Papaya Kiwi Frozen Yogurt

This fruity frozen yogurt is tasty as a snack or dessert and introduces less-common fruits to kids. It helps to build strong bones, teeth and muscles and supports healthy gums.

MAKES 6 SERVINGS

- **Extra-tall cup**

1 cup	frozen kiwifruit chunks	250 mL
1 cup	frozen papaya chunks	250 mL
1 cup	plain Greek yogurt	250 mL
2 tbsp	coconut sugar or granulated sugar	30 mL
½ cup	coconut milk	125 mL
¼ cup	cacao nibs (optional)	60 mL

Optional Nutrition Boost
Add 1 tsp (5 mL) maca powder after the coconut sugar.

1. Add kiwi, papaya, yogurt, coconut sugar and coconut milk to the extra-tall cup. Twist the extractor blade onto the cup to seal. Blend for 40 seconds or until smooth.

2. Spoon mixture into an airtight container and freeze for 30 minutes. Stir in cacao nibs, if using. Cover and freeze for 3 hours or until a soft ice cream consistency or for up 1 week.

Strawberry, Pear and Lime Ice Pops

These bright and inviting ice pops will grab any kid's attention. They're a cool and tasty way to get the goodness of vitamin C, potassium and fiber.

MAKES 12 ICE POPS

- **Tall cup**
- **Twelve ¼-cup (60 mL) ice pop molds and sticks**

2	pears (such as d'Anjou), halved	2
2¼ cups	frozen strawberries	550 mL
¼ cup	granulated sugar or coconut sugar	60 mL
¾ tsp	grated lime zest	3 mL
Pinch	kosher salt	Pinch
¼ cup	lime juice	60 mL

Optional Nutrition Boost
Add 1½ tsp (7 mL) pomegranate powder after the lime zest.

1. Add pears, strawberries, sugar, lime zest, salt and lime juice to the tall cup. Twist the extractor blade onto the cup to seal. Blend for 40 seconds or until smooth.

2. Pour mixture into ice pop molds, cover and insert sticks. Freeze for 4 hours or until solid. Quickly dip molds into hot water to release pops.

TIPS

One lime will yield enough juice and zest for this recipe.

Small (about ¼-cup/60 mL) paper or plastic cups and wooden sticks can be used in place of the molds.

Leftover ice pops can be frozen for up to 1 week.

Raspberry, Peach and Grape Ice Pops

Layers of sweet raspberry and peach give these pops a tempting presentation. Kids need more than calcium for healthy teeth and bones; magnesium and vitamin C are important too. And these ice pops deliver both.

MAKES 8 ICE POPS

- Small cup
- Tall cup
- Eight ½-cup (125 mL) ice pop molds and sticks

1 cup	frozen raspberries	250 mL
6 tbsp	granulated sugar, divided	90 mL
1¼ cups	unsweetened red grape juice, divided	300 mL
2 cups	frozen peach chunks	500 mL
Pinch	kosher salt	Pinch

Optional Nutrition Boost
Add 1 tsp (5 mL) açaí powder after the sugar in step 1.

1. Add raspberries, 2 tbsp (30 mL) sugar and 6 tbsp (90 mL) red grape juice to the small cup. Twist the extractor blade onto the cup to seal. Blend for 20 seconds or until smooth.

2. Spoon 1 tbsp (15 mL) mixture into each ice pop mold. Freeze for 1 hour or until solid.

3. Add peaches, remaining sugar, remaining grape juice and salt to the tall cup. Twist the extractor blade onto the cup to seal. Blend for 30 seconds or until smooth.

4. Pour peach mixture over frozen raspberries in ice pop molds, dividing evenly. Cover and insert sticks. Freeze for 4 hours or until solid. Quickly dip molds into hot water to release pops.

TIPS

If you don't want to layer the raspberry and peach purées, blend all ingredients together in the extra-tall cup or divide into two different sets of ice pops. Pour into molds, cover, insert sticks and freeze for 4 hours.

Small (about ½ cup/125 mL) paper or plastic cups and wooden sticks can be used in place of the molds.

Leftover ice pops can be frozen for up to 1 week.

Chocolate-Covered Coconut Avocado Balls

These delectable, creamy snack balls are wonderful as a midday pick-me-up or when your family is craving a little treat. Getting your potassium isn't just about bananas; avocados also have lots and they support a healthy heart and eyesight on top of that.

MAKES 12 BALLS

- Tall cup
- 8-inch (20 cm) square plastic container or glass baking dish
- Small ice cream scoop or melon baller
- Baking sheet, lined with parchment paper and topped with a wire rack

2	avocados, halved	2
¼ cup	unsweetened flaked coconut	60 mL
½ cup	coconut butter, melted	125 mL
3 tbsp	pure maple syrup	45 mL
½ tsp	vanilla bean paste or pure vanilla extract	2 mL
4 oz	bittersweet (dark) chocolate, chopped	125 g

Optional Nutrition Boost

Add 1 tsp (5 mL) maca powder after the coconut.

1. Add avocados, coconut, coconut butter, maple syrup and vanilla bean paste to the tall cup. Twist the extractor blade onto the cup to seal. Blend for 30 seconds or until smooth.

2. Spread mixture into the square plastic container. Freeze for 3 hours or until firm.

3. Add chocolate chunks to a wide, shallow microwave-safe dish and heat on Medium (50%) power for 1 minute. Remove from microwave and stir. Continue heating in 30-second intervals, stirring after each, until melted.

4. Using small ice cream scoop, scoop avocado mixture into 1½-inch (4 cm) balls. Using a fork, dip balls in melted chocolate and arrange on rack over prepared baking sheet. Place baking sheet in freezer for 1 hour or until chocolate sets. Store balls in an airtight container in the refrigerator for up to 5 days (a white sheen, or bloom, may develop on the chocolate, which is okay).

TIPS

Coconut butter is made from the flesh of the coconut and is a different product than coconut oil.

Vanilla bean paste has a more concentrated flavor than pure vanilla extract and has small flecks of vanilla. Use pure vanilla extract if you prefer a less strong flavor.

To melt chocolate on the stove, place it in the top of a double boiler or a heatproof bowl over simmering water. Heat, stirring, for 3 to 5 minutes or until melted.

After dipping in chocolate, let the balls stand until chocolate is slightly set and roll balls in unsweetened shredded coconut before freezing.

Gooey Almond Oat Balls

These little gems are perfect to pack in lunch boxes or anytime kids need a quick and healthy snack. It's a tasty way for them to get the fiber and nutrients they need for growing, active bodies.

MAKES 15 BALLS

- **Extra-tall cup**
- **Baking sheet, lined with parchment paper**

1 cup	large-flake (old-fashioned) rolled oats	250 mL
¼ cup	dried cranberries	60 mL
¼ cup	sunflower seeds	60 mL
2 tbsp	unsalted peanuts	30 mL
2 tbsp	cacao nibs	30 mL
½ cup	creamy natural peanut butter	125 mL
¼ cup	liquid honey	60 mL
	Cacao powder (optional)	

Optional Nutrition Boost

Add 1 tsp (5 mL) maca powder after the cacao nibs.

1. Add rolled oats, cranberries, sunflower seeds, peanuts, cacao nibs, peanut butter and honey to the extra-tall cup. Twist the extractor blade onto the cup to seal. Pulse 8 to 10 times or until combined.

2. Twist off the extractor blade. Cover cup and refrigerate for 30 minutes.

3. Scoop out rounded spoonfuls of the mixture and use your hands to form 1½-inch (4 cm) balls. Arrange on prepared baking sheet. Refrigerate for 30 minutes or until firm. If desired, roll balls in cacao powder. Store balls in an airtight container in the refrigerator for up to 2 weeks.

TIP

When forming the balls with your hands, work quickly to avoid softening the mixture too much.

Banana Coconut Lentil Balls

These flavorful balls not only make a nutritious little snack, but they are vegan and gluten-free.

- **Extra-tall cup**
- **Baking sheet, lined with parchment paper**

1	banana, halved	1
1 cup	unsweetened flaked coconut	250 mL
½ cup	cooked green (Puy) lentils	125 mL
¼ cup	raw sunflower seeds, divided	60 mL
½ tsp	ground cinnamon	2 mL
3 tbsp	liquid honey	45 mL
½ cup	almond flour (almond meal)	125 mL
3 tbsp	cacao nibs	45 mL
1 tbsp	coconut oil, melted and cooled slightly	15 mL

Optional Nutrition Boost

Add 1 tsp (5 mL) maca powder after the cinnamon.

1. Add banana, flaked coconut, lentils, 3 tbsp (45 mL) sunflower seeds, cinnamon and honey to the extra-tall cup. Twist the extractor blade onto the cup to seal. Blend for 40 seconds or until smooth. Transfer mixture to a medium bowl. Add remaining sunflower seeds, flour, cacao nibs and coconut oil, stirring to combine.

2. Scoop out rounded spoonfuls of the mixture and use your hands to form 1½-inch (4 cm) balls. Arrange balls on prepared baking sheet. Refrigerate for 30 minutes or until firm. Store balls in an airtight container in the refrigerator for up to 2 weeks or in the freezer for up to 3 months.

TIP

When forming the balls with your hands, work quickly to avoid softening the mixture too much.

Spiced Pineapple and Maca Energy Balls

These zesty and enjoyable energy balls are a wonderful pick-me-up or after-school snack. They provide the fiber and nutrients kids need for growing, immunity and red blood cell production.

MAKES 16 BALLS

- **Extra-tall cup**
- **Baking sheet, lined with parchment paper**

1 cup	pitted soft dates, preferably Medjool	250 mL
1 cup	raw cashews	250 mL
½ cup	dried pineapple	125 mL
2 tbsp	maca powder	30 mL
1 tbsp	grated orange zest	15 mL
½ tsp	ground cinnamon	2 mL
½ tsp	ground ginger	2 mL
½ tsp	ground chicory root	2 mL
Pinch	ground nutmeg	Pinch
Pinch	kosher salt	Pinch
¼ cup	orange juice (approx.)	60 mL
	Unsweetened desiccated coconut (optional)	
	Cacao powder (optional)	

1. Add dates, cashews, pineapple, maca powder, orange zest, cinnamon, ginger, chicory root, nutmeg, salt and orange juice to the tall cup. Twist the extractor blade onto the cup to seal. Pulse 7 to 9 times or until combined and sticky. Add more orange juice if the mixture is too crumbly and will not clump together.

2. Scoop out rounded spoonfuls of the mixture and use your hands to form 1½-inch (4 cm) balls. Arrange on prepared baking sheet. Refrigerate for 30 minutes or until firm. Roll balls in desiccated coconut or cacao powder, if desired. Store balls in an airtight container in the refrigerator for up to 2 weeks.

TIP

Desiccated coconut is coconut that has been flaked or shredded and then dried to remove most of the moisture. You can use unsweetened flaked or shredded coconut in its place.

Desserts

Happy Birthday Smoothie 190

Peppermint Patty Shake 190

Banana Cream Yogurt Shake 191

Raspberry Chocolate Milkshake ...191

Chocolate Banana Butterscotch
    Milkshake 192

Cacao Maple Oatmeal Malt..........192

Chocolate Peanut Butter
    Yogurt Delight.............................193

Peachy Spiced Chocolate Treat 193

Virgin Piña Colada.........................194

Mango Almond Lassi.....................194

Strawberry Pineapple Sorbet.........195

Just Peachy Blueberry and
    Almond Sorbet............................196

Bountiful Berry Sorbet with
    Ginger and Mint..........................197

Fall Cranberry Pear Sorbet 198

Mayan Chocolate Mango
    Maca Dessert...............................199

Exotic Mango, Banana and
    Avocado Pudding 199

Chocolate Pudding with
    Goji Berries 200

Avocado Lentil Chocolate
    Pudding...201

Red Velvet Parfait 201

Mango, Pineapple, Coconut and
    Cashew Cream Parfait................202

Blueberry Chia Parfait 203

Sliced Peaches with Blueberry
    Cashew Cream 204

Coconut Pineapple Cream Pie.......205

Nutty Choco-Caramel Tarts 206

Funky Chunky Monkey Bars 207

Sweet and Nutty Superfood
    Balls...208

Nutty Date Truffles 209

Happy Birthday Smoothie

Why not celebrate your birthday and many more to come with this birthday cake–inspired smoothie?

MAKES 1 SERVING

- **Tall cup**

1	frozen banana, halved	1
3 tbsp	vanilla whey protein powder	45 mL
½ cup	unsweetened vanilla almond milk	125 mL
2 tsp	natural almond butter	10 mL
1 tsp	pure vanilla extract	5 mL
1 tsp	pure maple syrup	5 mL
	Shredded coconut (see tip) or cacao nibs (optional)	

1. Add banana, protein powder, almond milk, almond butter, vanilla and maple syrup to the tall cup. Twist the extractor blade onto the cup to seal. Blend for 20 seconds or until smooth.

2. Spoon into a serving glass and sprinkle with shredded coconut or cacao nibs, if desired.

TIP

Adding natural color to shredded coconut makes a festive topping for this smoothie. To naturally dye shredded coconut, combine 1 tbsp (15 mL) coconut with: 1 tsp (5 mL) beet juice for red; ⅛ tsp (0.5 mL) ground turmeric and 1 tsp (5 mL) water for vibrant yellow; 1 tsp (5 mL) carrot juice for orange; or ⅛ tsp (0.5 mL) spirulina and 1 tsp (5 mL) water for green. Stir well to color coconut. Arrange coconut on a baking sheet and let stand for 2 hours or until dry.

Peppermint Patty Shake

Make your taste buds swoon with the abundance of chocolate flavor graced with a hint of peppermint. This is a tasty way to love your heart and brain while supporting gut health.

MAKES 1 SERVING

- **Tall cup**

1	frozen banana, halved	1
2 tbsp	chocolate whey protein powder	30 mL
2 tbsp	cacao powder	30 mL
Pinch	kosher salt	Pinch
1 cup	plain kefir	250 mL
¼ tsp	peppermint extract	1 mL

Optional Nutrition Boost
Add 1 tsp (5 mL) maca powder after the cacao powder.

1. Add banana, protein powder, cacao powder, salt, kefir and peppermint extract to the tall cup. Twist the extractor blade onto the cup to seal. Blend for 20 seconds or until smooth.

TIP

You can use almond, cashew or hazelnut milk in place of the kefir.

Banana Cream Yogurt Shake

Dive into this healthy riff on banana cream pie and you'll be pleasantly surprised at how wonderfully delicious it is. It's a tasty way to support your gut, gut bacteria and blood pressure.

- **Tall cup**

1	frozen banana, halved	1
½ cup	plain Greek yogurt	125 mL
2 tbsp	pasteurized egg white powder	30 mL
1 tsp	pure vanilla extract	5 mL
1 tsp	agave nectar	5 mL
	Unsweetened almond milk	
¼	fresh banana, sliced	¼
2 tsp	granola	10 mL

1. Add frozen banana, yogurt, egg white powder, vanilla and agave nectar to the tall cup. Add almond milk to the "Max Line." Twist the extractor blade onto the cup to seal. Blend for 20 seconds or until smooth. Garnish with sliced fresh banana and granola.

TIPS

Egg white powder can be purchased online or in specialty food markets.

Substitute 1 crushed graham cracker for the granola.

Raspberry Chocolate Milkshake

When you marry raspberries and chocolate in a creamy milkshake, get ready for sheer bliss. This shake has the clout it needs to build strong bones and muscles with anti-inflammatory polyphenols. Fiber and protein can help to keep hunger in check, too.

- **Tall cup**

1½ cups	frozen raspberries	375 mL
1 cup	plain Greek yogurt	250 mL
¼ cup	cacao powder	60 mL
3	ice cubes	3
2 tsp	pure maple syrup	10 mL
	Unsweetened vanilla almond milk	

1. Add raspberries, yogurt, cacao powder, ice cubes and maple syrup to the tall cup. Add almond milk to the "Max Line." Twist the extractor blade onto the cup to seal. Blend for 20 seconds or until smooth.

TIPS

You can use fresh raspberries in place of frozen, but the milkshake will be less thick.

For a thicker milkshake, add more ice cubes.

Chocolate Banana Butterscotch Milkshake

Transport yourself to an old-fashioned ice cream parlor with this dreamy combination of chocolate and banana, with maca powder providing a butterscotch flavor.

MAKES 1 SERVING

- **Tall cup**

1	frozen banana, halved	1
1 tbsp	cacao powder	15 mL
1 tbsp	chia seeds	15 mL
1 tsp	maca powder	5 mL
4	ice cubes	4
1 cup	unsweetened almond milk	250 mL
2 tsp	natural almond butter	10 mL
2 tsp	pure maple syrup	10 mL
½ tsp	pure vanilla extract	2 mL
	Cacao nibs	
	Frozen sweet cherry (optional)	

1. Add banana, cacao powder, chia seeds, maca powder, ice cubes, almond milk, almond butter, maple syrup and vanilla to the tall cup. Twist the extractor blade onto the cup to seal. Blend for 30 seconds or until smooth. Garnish with cacao nibs and cherry (if using).

TIP

Egg white powder can be purchased online or in specialty food markets.

> **Optional Nutrition Boost**
> Add 1 tbsp (15 mL) pasteurized egg white powder after the chia seeds.

Cacao Maple Oatmeal Malt

Cacao powder, maple syrup and rolled oats join forces for a filling chocolate-flavored malt that is entirely satisfying. It also helps to balance cholesterol, supports healthy blood pressure and keeps you feeling full.

MAKES 1 SERVING

- **Tall cup**

1	frozen banana, halved	1
½ cup	large-flake (old-fashioned) rolled oats	125 mL
3 tbsp	chocolate whey protein powder	45 mL
1 tbsp	cacao powder	15 mL
½ cup	unsweetened almond milk	125 mL
1 tbsp	pure maple syrup	15 mL
	Cacao nibs (optional)	

> **Optional Nutrition Boost**
> Add 1 tsp (5 mL) maca powder after the cacao powder.

1. Add banana, oats, protein powder, cacao powder, almond milk and maple syrup to the tall cup. Twist the extractor blade onto the cup to seal. Blend for 30 seconds or until smooth. Garnish with cacao nibs, if desired. Serve with a spoon.

VARIATION

Peanut Butter Cacao Oatmeal Malt: Add 2 tbsp (30 mL) creamy natural peanut butter for a flavor twist.

TIPS

Cashew milk, hazelnut milk, soy milk or coconut milk can be used in place of the almond milk. If your malt is too thick, blend in additional almond milk, 1 tbsp (15 mL) at a time, until your desired consistency is reached.

Chocolate Peanut Butter Yogurt Delight

Delight in this classic pairing of chocolate and peanut butter in a sweet and creamy dessert. What a fantastic way to nourish your bones and muscles and support your gut and healthy blood pressure.

MAKES 2 SERVINGS

- **Tall cup**

1	frozen banana, halved	1
¾ cup	plain Greek yogurt	175 mL
3 tbsp	cacao powder	45 mL
¾ cup	unsweetened almond milk	175 mL
2 tbsp	natural peanut butter	30 mL
1 tbsp	pure maple syrup	15 mL

Optional Nutrition Boost
Add 2 tbsp (30 mL) chocolate or vanilla whey protein powder and/or 1 tsp (5 mL) maca powder after the cacao powder.

1. Add banana, yogurt, cacao powder, almond milk, peanut butter and maple syrup to the tall cup. Twist the extractor blade onto the cup to seal. Blend for 20 seconds or until smooth. Serve with a spoon.

TIP

You can use cashew or hazelnut milk in place of the almond milk.

Peachy Spiced Chocolate Treat

Transport yourself to Latin America and spice up dessert with this slushy blend of peaches, chocolate and chile pepper. It's a tasty way to support your bones and teeth while getting the nutrients you need for healthy eyes.

MAKES 2 SERVINGS

- **Tall cup**

2	peaches, peeled, halved and pitted	2
1 cup	plain or vanilla yogurt	250 mL
1 tbsp	cacao powder	15 mL
1 tsp	ancho chile powder (see tip)	5 mL
¼ tsp	ground cinnamon	1 mL
4	ice cubes	4
2	prunes	2
	Unsweetened almond milk	

Optional Nutrition Boost
Add 2 tsp (10 mL) maca powder after the cacao powder.

1. Add peaches, yogurt, cacao powder, ancho chile powder, cinnamon, ice cubes and prunes to the tall cup. Add almond milk to the "Max Line." Twist the extractor blade onto the cup to seal. Blend for 30 seconds or until smooth.

TIPS

You can adjust the amount of ancho chile powder to your desired spice level. If you're not sure how much chile you'll enjoy, start by adding ¼ tsp (1 mL), then gradually add more to taste, blending after each addition. If you can't find ancho chile powder, you can substitute regular chili powder.

Add pure maple syrup, to taste, if you would like a sweeter drink.

Virgin Piña Colada

Pineapple and coconut pair up in a frozen mocktail that will bring a smile to your face while supporting healthy bones, teeth and gums.

MAKES 1 SERVING

- **Tall cup**

1	can (14 oz/400 mL) full-fat coconut milk, chilled (see tips)	1
⅔ cup	frozen pineapple chunks	150 mL
1 tbsp	unsweetened shredded coconut	15 mL
6	ice cubes	6
1 tsp	rum extract or almond extract	5 mL

1. Using a spoon, carefully remove the thick layer of coagulated cream from the top of the can of coconut milk and transfer to a bowl. Measure out 2 tbsp (30 mL) cream and add to the tall cup. Measure ¼ cup (60 mL) of the remaining coconut milk and set aside. Reserve extra coconut cream and coconut milk for another use.

2. Add pineapple, coconut, ice cubes, reserved coconut milk and rum extract to the coconut cream in the tall cup. Twist the extractor blade onto the cup to seal. Blend for 30 seconds or until smooth.

TIPS

Chill the can of coconut milk thoroughly and avoid shaking before opening to avoid mixing the cream with the milk.

Any remaining coconut milk can be stored in an airtight container in the refrigerator for up to 5 days or frozen for up to 6 months for use in other recipes.

Add a colorful paper cocktail umbrella to each drink for a festive flair.

Mango Almond Lassi

The lassi, a traditional drink of India, is a sweet and savory combination of mango and yogurt and makes a satisfying after-dinner drink. This version promotes healthy skin and reduces the risk for cancer.

MAKES 2 SERVINGS

- **Tall cup**

1	mango, cut into chunks	1
½ cup	plain yogurt	125 mL
1½ tsp	ground cardamom	7 mL
Pinch	kosher salt (optional)	Pinch
4	ice cubes	4
2 tsp	liquid honey	10 mL
¼ cup	unsweetened almond milk	60 mL

1. Add mango, yogurt, cardamom, salt (if using), ice cubes, honey and almond milk to the tall cup. Twist the extractor blade onto the cup to seal. Blend for 20 seconds or until smooth.

TIP

Two cups (500 mL) of frozen mango chunks can be used in place of fresh. Reduce the ice cubes to 1 or 2, depending upon your desired thickness.

Strawberry Pineapple Sorbet

Refreshing and flavorful, this easy-to-make sorbet is the perfect hot-weather dessert and delivers anti-inflammatory and anti-cancer polyphenols.

MAKES 4 SERVINGS

• **Extra-tall cup**

2¼ cups	frozen strawberries	550 mL
¾ cup	frozen pineapple chunks	175 mL
2 tsp	granulated sugar	10 mL
¾ cup	orange juice	175 mL
1 tsp	pure vanilla or almond extract	5 mL

Optional Nutrition Boost
Add 1½ tsp (7 mL) pomegranate powder after the sugar.

1. Add strawberries, pineapple, sugar, orange juice and vanilla to the extra-tall cup. Twist the extractor blade onto the cup to seal. Pulse 7 to 9 times or until just combined.

2. Transfer mixture to an airtight container and freeze for 30 to 60 minutes or until firm but not solid. Scoop sorbet into bowls.

VARIATION

Strawberry Pineapple Ice Pops:
After pulsing in step 1, transfer mixture to ice pop molds, cover and insert sticks. Freeze for 4 hours or until solid. Store in the freezer for up to 2 weeks. Quickly dip molds into hot water to release pops. Small (about ¼ cup/60 mL) paper or plastic cups and wooden sticks can be used in place of the molds.

Just Peachy Blueberry and Almond Sorbet

Sorbet is one of those treats that are tasty as a snack, between courses, as a dessert and, well, just about anytime. The pairing of peaches and blueberries and the excellent superfood qualities make this one even better.

MAKES 4 SERVINGS

- **Extra-tall cup**

1½ cups	frozen sliced peaches	375 mL
1 cup	frozen blueberries	250 mL
1 cup	coconut water	250 mL
2 tbsp	liquid honey	30 mL
1 tbsp	natural almond butter	15 mL
1 tsp	almond extract or pure vanilla extract	5 mL

Optional Nutrition Boost
Add 4 tsp (20 mL) açaí powder after the blueberries.

1. Add peaches, blueberries, coconut water, honey, almond butter and almond extract to the extra-tall cup. Twist the extractor blade onto the cup to seal. Pulse 6 to 8 times or until just combined.

2. Transfer mixture to an airtight container and freeze for 30 minutes to 1 hour or until firm but not solid. Scoop sorbet into bowls.

VARIATION

Just Peachy Ice Pops: After pulsing in step 1, transfer mixture to ice pop molds, cover and insert sticks. Freeze for 4 hours or until solid. Quickly dip molds into hot water to release pops. Small (about ¼ cup/60 mL) paper or plastic cups and wooden sticks can be used in place of the molds.

Bountiful Berry Sorbet with Ginger and Mint

For the berry lover in all of us, this downright delicious and nutritious sorbet gets a pick-me-up from hints of ginger and mint. Many of the ingredients in this sorbet help to reduce the risk for cancer, support healthy moods and promote digestive health.

MAKES 4 SERVINGS

- **Extra-tall cup**

½ cup	frozen blackberries	125 mL
½ cup	frozen raspberries	125 mL
½ cup	frozen strawberries	125 mL
¼ cup	partially thawed frozen açaí purée	60 mL
¼ cup	lightly packed fresh mint leaves	60 mL
2 tbsp	granulated or coconut sugar	30 mL
1	¾- by ¾-inch (2 by 2 cm) piece gingerroot	1
½ cup	brewed green tea, chilled	125 mL

Optional Nutrition Boost
Add 4 tsp (20 mL) camu camu powder after the ginger.

1. Add blackberries, raspberries, strawberries, açaí purée, mint, sugar, ginger and tea to the extra-tall cup. Twist the extractor blade onto the cup to seal. Blend for 15 seconds or until just combined.

2. Transfer mixture to an airtight container and freeze for 30 minutes to 1 hour or until firm but not solid. Scoop sorbet into bowls.

VARIATION

Bountiful Berry Ice Pops: After pulsing in step 1, transfer mixture to ice pop molds, cover and insert sticks. Freeze for 4 hours or until solid. Quickly dip molds into hot water to release pops. Small (about ¼ cup/60 mL) paper or plastic cups and wooden sticks can be used in place of the molds.

Fall Cranberry Pear Sorbet

When cranberries are in season, this sorbet should be at the top of your list as a dessert or festive brunch addition. Who knew a mouthwatering dessert could also support digestive and gut health and mood while reducing the risk for cancer and cardiovascular disease?

MAKES 4 SERVINGS

- **Extra-tall cup**

1	pear (such as Bartlett or Taylor's gold), halved	1
1½ cups	fresh cranberries	375 mL
½ tsp	ground cinnamon	2 mL
½ tsp	ground star anise	2 mL
4	ice cubes	4
¾ cup	coconut water	175 mL
1 tbsp	pure maple syrup	15 mL

Optional Nutrition Boost
Add 1½ tsp (7 mL) pomegranate powder after the cranberries.

1. Add pear, cranberries, cinnamon, star anise, ice cubes, coconut water and maple syrup to the extra-tall cup. Twist the extractor blade onto the cup to seal. Blend for 20 seconds or until just combined.

2. Transfer mixture to an airtight container and freeze for 30 minutes to 1 hour or until firm but not solid. Scoop sorbet into bowls.

TIP

You can use frozen cranberries in place of the fresh and omit the ice cubes. If the sorbet is not thick enough before freezing, add 1 or 2 ice cubes and blend until your desired consistency.

Mayan Chocolate Mango Maca Dessert

This sumptuous dessert includes cacao and maca, revered for their health and medicinal values in ancient civilizations, as well as the tropical, refreshing taste of mango. Here is a delicious way to nourish your immune system and keep blood pressure in check while helping to reduce inflammation.

MAKES 2 SERVINGS

- **Tall cup**

1	frozen banana, halved	1
1 cup	frozen mango chunks	250 mL
2 tbsp	cacao powder	30 mL
2 tsp	maca powder	10 mL
1 tsp	ground cinnamon	5 mL
2	ice cubes	2
¾ cup	unsweetened almond milk	175 mL
2 tbsp	natural almond butter	30 mL
	Fresh mint leaves (optional)	

1. Add banana, mango, cacao powder, maca powder, cinnamon, ice cubes, almond milk and almond butter to the tall cup. Twist the extractor blade onto the cup to seal. Blend for 30 seconds or until creamy.

2. Spoon into serving dishes and garnish with mint leaves, if desired.

TIP

For a smoothie version of this dessert, omit the ice cubes and add additional almond milk, 1 tbsp (15 mL) at a time, until your desired consistency is reached.

Exotic Mango, Banana and Avocado Pudding

This delectable, exotic dessert abounds with tropical fruit flavors and turmeric, a spice that has been valued for its health properties for thousands of years. Packed with anti-inflammatory compounds, potassium and antioxidants, this pudding supports a healthy cardiovascular system.

MAKES 4 SERVINGS

- **Extra-tall cup**

2	frozen bananas, halved	2
2 cups	frozen mango chunks	500 mL
2	small avocados	2
1	pitted soft date, preferably Medjool	1
2 tsp	turmeric powder	10 mL
2 tbsp	coconut oil	30 mL
2 tbsp	lemon juice	30 mL
1 tsp	pure vanilla extract	5 mL
	Water	

1. Add bananas, mango, avocados, date, turmeric, coconut oil, lemon juice and vanilla extract to the extra-tall cup. Add water to the "Max Line." Twist the extractor blade onto the cup to seal. Blend for 20 seconds or until smooth. Serve immediately.

TIPS

While a variety of fresh dates will work in this recipe, Medjool dates are softer and sweeter than many other varieties.

Choose dates that are plump, soft and have shiny skin. They should not have any evidence of crystalizing sugar on their skin.

Half of a fresh lemon will yield about 2 tbsp (30 mL) lemon juice.

Chocolate Pudding with Goji Berries

After you try this easy and delectable superfood pudding, you will completely forget about all the processed products you once enjoyed. This dessert nourishes your skin and provides fiber to support digestive and gut health.

- **Extra-tall cup**

4	large pitted soft dates, preferably Medjool	4
½ cup	cacao powder	125 mL
⅓ cup	chia seeds	75 mL
¼ cup	goji berries, divided	60 mL
½ tsp	ground chicory root	2 mL
⅛ tsp	kosher salt	0.5 mL
1½ cups	unsweetened almond milk	375 mL
1 tsp	pure vanilla extract	5 mL
2 tbsp	cacao nibs	30 mL

1. Add dates, cacao powder, chia seeds, 2 tbsp (30 mL) goji berries, chicory root, salt, almond milk and vanilla to the extra-tall cup. Twist the extractor blade onto the cup to seal. Blend for 30 seconds or until smooth. Cover and refrigerate 12 hours or until mixture is thickened to your liking.

2. Spoon into bowls and garnish with cacao nibs and remaining goji berries.

TIPS

While a variety of fresh dates will work in this recipe, Medjool dates are softer and sweeter than many other varieties.

Choose dates that are plump, soft and have shiny skin. They should not have any evidence of crystalizing sugar on their skin.

Leftover pudding can be stored in the refrigerator for up to 3 days.

Avocado Lentil Chocolate Pudding

If you've never tried a pudding made with lentils, this one is the perfect way to start your adventure. The avocado enhances the creamy texture, while the coconut and cacao infuse it with flavor.

MAKES 4 SERVINGS

- **Tall cup**

¼ cup	dried red lentils, cooked (see tip) and cooled	60 mL
2	avocados, halved	2
½ cup	coconut sugar	125 mL
3 tbsp	cacao powder	45 mL
⅓ cup	coconut milk	75 mL
2 tsp	pure vanilla extract	10 mL
¼ cup	dried cranberries	60 mL

1. Add lentils, avocados, coconut sugar, cacao powder, coconut milk and vanilla to the tall cup. Twist the extractor blade onto the cup to seal. Blend for 30 seconds or until smooth. Cover and refrigerate for 2 to 3 hours or until well chilled.

2. Spoon into bowls and garnish with cranberries.

TIP

To cook ¼ cup (60 mL) dried red lentils, rinse them and add to a medium saucepan. Cover with ¾ cup (175 mL) water and bring to a boil over high heat. Reduce heat to medium-low, cover and simmer for 5 to 7 minutes or until tender but firm. Let cool to room temperature before adding to the extra-tall cup.

Red Velvet Parfait

A feast for the taste buds as well as the eyes, this winning combination of red and white parfait layers is both visually appealing and prepared with nutritious ingredients.

MAKES 2 SERVINGS

- **Tall cup**
- **2 parfait glasses (each about 10 oz/ 300 mL)**

1	frozen banana, halved	1
1	small red beet, peeled and halved	1
1 cup	plain Greek yogurt, divided	250 mL
2 tbsp	packed mint leaves	30 mL
½ cup	unsweetened almond milk	125 mL
2 tsp	liquid honey	10 mL

1. Add banana, beet, half the yogurt, mint leaves, almond milk and honey to the tall cup. Twist the extractor blade onto the cup to seal. Blend for 30 seconds or until smooth.

2. Dividing evenly between parfait glasses, layer beet mixture and remaining yogurt.

TIPS

Wear kitchen gloves when peeling and halving the beet to avoid staining your hands.

For a thicker, colder beet mixture, add 3 to 4 ice cubes to the tall cup before the almond milk.

You can substitute another type of milk, such as cashew, hazelnut, soy or dairy, for the almond milk.

Mango, Pineapple, Coconut and Cashew Cream Parfait

Enjoy the colorful, mouthwatering layers of this parfait for a festive dessert. This dessert helps to promote healthy skin and keep your eyesight sharp while providing heart-loving healthy fats and vitamin E.

MAKES 2 SERVINGS

- Tall cup
- Small cup
- 2 parfait glasses (each about 10 oz/ 300 mL)

⅔ cup	dried unsweetened mango chunks	150 mL
⅔ cup	raw cashews	150 mL
6 tbsp	coconut water	90 mL
1 tbsp	liquid honey	15 mL
2 tsp	orange juice	10 mL
Pinch	kosher salt	Pinch
½ cup	chopped fresh mango	125 mL
½ cup	chopped fresh or canned pineapple, with juice	125 mL
2 tbsp	unsweetened shredded coconut	30 mL
	Additional unsweetened shredded coconut	
	Fresh mint leaves	

Optional Nutrition Boost

Add 1½ tsp (7 mL) açaí powder with the dried mango in step 3.

1. In a small bowl, add dried mango and cover with warm water. Let stand 2 hours, until softened. In another small bowl, add cashews and cover with warm water. Let stand 2 hours, until softened.

2. Drain cashews, discarding water. Add cashews, coconut water, honey, orange juice and salt to the tall cup. Twist the extractor blade onto the cup to seal. Blend for 20 seconds or until smooth. Set cashew cream aside.

3. Drain dried mango, discarding water, and add to the small cup. Twist the extractor blade onto the cup to seal. Blend for 20 seconds or until smooth.

4. Dividing evenly between parfait glasses, layer fresh mango, cashew cream, pineapple, shredded coconut and puréed mango. Garnish with additional shredded coconut and mint leaves.

TIP

If desired, for a deeper flavor, toast the shredded coconut in a small skillet over medium heat, stirring, for 1 minute or until lightly browned.

Blueberry Chia Parfait

This layered chia parfait is so beautiful it is hard to believe it is also so good for you. Each layer offers a little bit of everything. The parfait supports your gut and mood and helps balance cholesterol, maintain blood pressure and reduce inflammation.

MAKES 4 SERVINGS

- Small cup
- Tall cup
- 4 parfait glasses (each about 10 oz/ 300 mL)

Chia Pudding

3 tbsp	chia seeds	45 mL
⅔ cup	unsweetened almond milk	150 mL
1½ tsp	pure maple syrup	7 mL
⅛ tsp	pure vanilla extract	0.5 mL

Green Smoothie Layer

2	frozen bananas, halved	2
½ cup	large-flake (old-fashioned) rolled oats	125 mL
1 tsp	spirulina powder	5 mL
¼ cup	unsweetened almond milk	60 mL

Blueberry Smoothie Layer

2	frozen bananas, halved	2
½ cup	frozen blueberries	125 mL
½ cup	large-flake (old-fashioned) rolled oats	125 mL
2 tbsp	pasteurized egg white powder	30 mL
¾ cup	unsweetened almond milk	175 mL
⅓ cup	granola	75 mL
3	prunes, chopped	3
4	strawberries, sliced	4
	Mint leaves (optional)	

1. *Chia Pudding:* Add chia seeds, almond milk, maple syrup and vanilla to the small cup. Twist the extractor blade onto the cup to seal. Blend for 20 seconds or until smooth. Cover and refrigerate for at least 1 hour or up to 24 hours for a thicker consistency.

2. *Green Smoothie Layer:* Add bananas, oats, spirulina powder and almond milk to the tall cup. Twist the extractor blade onto the cup to seal. Blend for 20 seconds or until smooth. Scrape into a measuring cup or bowl and set aside. Wash and dry the tall cup.

3. *Blueberry Smoothie Layer:* Add bananas, blueberries, rolled oats, egg white powder and almond milk to the tall cup. Twist the extractor blade onto the cup to seal. Blend for 20 seconds or until smooth.

4. Layer the ingredients in each parfait glass, following this order and dividing evenly: granola, chia pudding, prune, green smoothie, strawberries and blueberry smoothie. Garnish with mint leaves, if desired.

TIPS

Chia pudding can be refrigerated for up to 24 hours before using. The longer the chia mixture stands, the thicker the pudding becomes. If it becomes too thick, stir in additional unsweetened almond milk, 1 tbsp (15 mL) at a time, until desired consistency is reached.

If you have 2 tall cups, there's no need to transfer the green smoothie layer to a cup before making the blueberry layer; just use the second tall cup.

Egg white powder can be purchased online or in specialty food markets.

Sliced Peaches with Blueberry Cashew Cream

Chin-dripping peaches are the perfect foundation for this alluring topping of blueberry cashew cream. This dessert is full of cardiovascular-boosting nutrients that help to reduce the risk for dementia, stroke and heart disease.

MAKES 4 SERVINGS

- **Tall cup**

1 cup	blueberries	250 mL
½ cup	raw cashews, soaked (see tip)	125 mL
¼ cup	prunes, soaked	60 mL
¼ cup	coconut water	60 mL
2 tbsp	pure maple syrup	30 mL
1 tbsp	sunflower oil	15 mL
1 tsp	lemon juice	5 mL
4	peaches, peeled (see tip) and sliced	4

Optional Nutrition Boost
Garnish with 2 tsp (10 mL) hemp seeds.

1. Add blueberries, cashews, prunes, coconut water, maple syrup, sunflower oil and lemon juice to the tall cup. Twist the extractor blade onto the cup to seal. Blend for 40 seconds or until smooth and creamy.

2. Arrange peach slices in individual serving dishes and spoon blueberry cashew cream over top.

TIPS

To soak the cashews and prunes, place them in a large bowl with 4 cups (1 L) water and let stand, stirring once, for 30 minutes. Drain and rinse before adding to the tall cup.

To easily peel peaches, add to a pot of boiling water for 10 seconds and then immediately plunge into a bowl of ice water. The peel should come off easily using your fingers or by rubbing with the palm of your hand.

Coconut Pineapple Cream Pie

What could be better than a piña colada? A piña colada–inspired pie of course, and one that is good for you, too. But you may want to keep that our little secret!

	MAKES 12 SERVINGS	

- **Preheat oven to 350°F (180°C)**
- **Extra-tall cup**

1 cup	dried red lentils, cooked (see tip) and cooled	250 mL
8 oz	brick-style cream cheese, softened	250 g
1 tsp	cornstarch	5 mL
½ tsp	kosher salt	2 mL
⅓ cup	liquid honey	75 mL
1 tbsp	sunflower oil	15 mL
1 tsp	pure vanilla extract	5 mL
1	can (14 oz/398 mL) unsweetened crushed pineapple, drained	1
½ cup	unsweetened shredded coconut	125 mL
1	9-inch (23 cm) prepared graham cracker pie crust	1

1. Add lentils, cream cheese, cornstarch, salt, honey, oil and vanilla to the extra-tall cup. Twist the extractor blade onto the cup to seal. Blend for 40 seconds or until smooth. Pour mixture into a large bowl. Add pineapple and coconut, stirring until combined.

2. Pour mixture into prepared crust and smooth the top. Bake in preheated oven for 20 minutes or until a tester inserted in the center comes out clean. Let stand until cool. Refrigerate for at least 30 minutes, until chilled, or for up to 2 days. Cut into 12 wedges to serve.

VARIATION

Banana Coconut Cream Pie: Omit the pineapple and use 2 bananas. Cut the bananas in half. Cut one of the halves into ½-inch (1 cm) slices and arrange slices in a layer on the bottom of the graham cracker crust before adding the filling. Add the remaining bananas in step 1 before adding the lentils to the extra-tall cup.

TIP

To cook 1 cup (250 mL) dried red lentils, rinse them and add to a large saucepan. Cover with 3 cups (750 mL) water and bring to a boil over high heat. Reduce heat to medium-low, cover and simmer for 5 to 7 minutes or until tender but firm. Let cool to room temperature before adding to the extra-tall cup.

Nutty Choco-Caramel Tarts

While these mouthwatering chocolate tarts are a delightful dessert, they are also a great pick-me-up as a midday snack. And they provide nutrients to support your muscles, bone and skin.

- Tall cup
- 6-cup muffin pan, cups lined with plastic wrap

Crust

6	pitted soft dates, preferably Medjool (see tips, page 200)	6
2 cups	raw almonds	500 mL
Pinch	kosher salt	Pinch
1 tbsp	agave nectar	15 mL

Filling

1 cup	raw almonds	250 mL
1 cup	cacao powder	250 mL
1 cup	coconut cream (see tip)	250 mL
½ cup	coconut oil	125 mL
¼ cup	light (fancy) molasses	60 mL
	Hard or semihard salted caramel chocolate candies (such as Werther's Original), crushed	

Optional Nutrition Boost
Add 2 tbsp (30 mL) maca powder after the molasses.

1. *Crust:* Add dates, almonds, salt and agave nectar to the tall cup. Twist the extractor blade onto the cup to seal. Blend for 30 seconds or until crumbly and sticky. Divide dough into six equal pieces and press one piece into the bottom and halfway up the sides of each prepared muffin cup to form crusts. Refrigerate for 30 minutes. Wash and dry the tall cup.

2. *Filling:* Add almonds, cacao powder, coconut cream, coconut oil and molasses to the tall cup. Twist the extractor blade onto the cup to seal. Blend for 30 seconds or until smooth. Spoon mixture into crusts and, using the back of spoon, smooth tops. Garnish with crushed candies. Refrigerate for 2 hours or until firm.

TIPS

You can find canned coconut cream at many well-stocked grocery stores. To make your own, thoroughly chill 4 cans (each 14 oz/400 mL) full-fat coconut milk; avoid shaking cans before opening to avoid mixing the cream with the milk. Using a spoon, carefully remove the thick layer of coagulated cream from the top of 3 cans of coconut milk and transfer to a bowl. If needed, repeat with the fourth can to yield the 1 cup (250 mL) cream required for this recipe. Reserve extra coconut cream and coconut milk; store in an airtight container in the refrigerator for up to 5 days or in the freezer for up to 6 months for use in other recipes.

You can use cacao nibs in place of the hard candies.

The tarts can be stored in an airtight container in the refrigerator for up to 1 week or in the freezer for up to 1 month.

Funky Chunky Monkey Bars

When that sweet tooth is calling out to you, satisfy it guilt-free with these delectable bars. Full of nutrients, these bars offer a convenient way to get lots of vitamin E, potassium, B vitamins, fiber and polyphenols.

MAKES 8 BARS

- Tall cup
- 8-inch (20 cm) square metal baking pan, lined with parchment paper long enough to overhang the edges

Bottom Layer

2	frozen bananas, halved	2
2	pitted soft dates, preferably Medjool (see tips, page 200)	2
½ tsp	kosher salt	2 mL
1 cup	natural almond butter	250 mL
1 tsp	pure vanilla extract	5 mL
½ cup	slivered almonds	125 mL
¼ cup	cacao nibs	60 mL

Filling

1 cup	pitted soft dates, preferably Medjool	250 mL
½ cup	raw cashews, soaked (see tip)	125 mL
½ tsp	kosher salt	2 mL
⅔ cup	unsweetened almond milk	150 mL
½ cup	coconut cream (see tip)	125 mL
3 tbsp	natural peanut butter	45 mL
2 tsp	pure vanilla extract	10 mL

Topping

⅔ cup	natural peanut butter	150 mL
2 tbsp	pure maple syrup	30 mL
¾ cup	unsalted roasted cashews or peanuts, lightly crushed	175 mL

1. *Bottom layer:* Add bananas, dates, salt, almond butter and vanilla to the tall cup. Twist the extractor blade onto the cup to seal. Blend for 20 seconds or until smooth. Using a spatula, spread mixture evenly over the base of the prepared baking pan. Sprinkle with slivered almonds and cacao nibs. Wash and dry the tall cup.

2. *Filling:* Add dates, cashews, salt, almond milk, coconut cream, peanut butter and vanilla to the tall cup. Twist the extractor blade onto the cup to seal. Blend for 30 seconds or until smooth. Pour filling over the bottom layer. Freeze for 4 hours or until firm.

3. *Topping:* In a small bowl, combine peanut butter and maple syrup, stirring well. Spread mixture over top of filling. Sprinkle with cashews. Holding the edges of the parchment paper, lift bars out of the pan. Cut into bars before serving.

TIPS

To soak cashews, add cashews and 2 cups (500 mL) water to a medium bowl and let stand for 30 minutes. Drain and rinse cashews before adding to the tall cup.

You can find canned coconut cream at many well-stocked grocery stores. To make your own, thoroughly chill 2 cans (each 14 oz/400 mL) full-fat coconut milk; avoid shaking cans before opening to avoid mixing the cream with the milk. Using a spoon, carefully remove the thick layer of coagulated cream from the top of the cans of coconut milk and transfer to a bowl. Measure out ½ cup (125 mL) cream and reserve extra coconut cream and coconut milk; store in an airtight container in the refrigerator for up to 5 days or in the freezer for up to 6 months for use in other recipes.

The bars can be stored in an airtight container in the refrigerator for up to 3 days or in the freezer for up to 2 months.

Sweet and Nutty Superfood Balls

As the saying goes: good things come in small packages. And these delicious, super-powered balls are a delightful example. This dessert or snack — rich in magnesium, vitamin E and polyphenols — supports healthy blood pressure and overall cardiovascular health and immunity.

MAKES 20 BALLS

- **Extra-tall cup**
- **Baking sheet, lined with parchment paper**

3	pitted soft dates, preferably Medjool	3
1 cup	raw cashews or almonds	250 mL
½ cup	cacao powder	125 mL
¼ cup	large-flake (old-fashioned) rolled oats	60 mL
2 tsp	maca powder	10 mL
Pinch	kosher salt	Pinch
½ cup	natural almond butter	125 mL
¼ cup	unsweetened cashew milk	60 mL
2 tbsp	coconut oil	30 mL
1 tsp	pure vanilla extract	5 mL
	Desiccated coconut or cacao powder (optional)	

1. Add dates, cashews, cacao powder, rolled oats, maca powder, salt, almond butter, cashew milk, coconut oil and vanilla to the extra-tall cup. Twist the extractor blade onto the cup to seal. Blend for 20 seconds or until smooth.

2. Remove rounded spoonfuls of mixture and use your hands to form 1½-inch (4 cm) balls. Arrange on prepared baking sheet. Refrigerate for 30 minutes or until firm. If desired, roll balls in coconut or cacao powder.

TIPS

While a variety of fresh dates will work in this recipe, Medjool dates are softer and sweeter than many other varieties.

Choose dates that are plump, soft and have shiny skin. They should not have any evidence of crystalizing sugar on their skin.

The balls can be stored in an airtight container in the refrigerator for up to 2 weeks or in the freezer for up to 2 months.

Nutty Date Truffles

Truffles are one of the most intriguing little desserts, and they always seem to impress guests. You can even prep these and wrap them in little gift boxes for any occasion — each one is like an indulgent bite-size multivitamin.

- Extra-tall cup
- Baking sheet, lined with parchment paper

2 cups	large pitted soft dates, preferably Medjool	500 mL
1¼ cups	unsweetened shredded coconut, divided	300 mL
1 cup	blanched almonds	250 mL
½ cup	raw green pumpkin seeds (pepitas)	125 mL
½ cup	raw cashews	125 mL
1 tsp	kosher salt	5 mL
2 tbsp	coconut oil	30 mL
1 tsp	pure vanilla extract	5 mL
¼ cup	cacao powder	60 mL

Optional Nutrition Boost
Add 1 tbsp (15 mL) maca powder after the salt.

1. Add dates, 1 cup (250 mL) shredded coconut, almonds, pumpkin seeds, cashews, salt, coconut oil and vanilla to the extra-tall cup. Twist the extractor blade onto the cup to seal. Pulse 8 to 10 times or until combined but still coarse.

2. Remove rounded spoonfuls of mixture and use your hands to form into 1½-inch (4 cm) balls. Roll half the balls in cacao powder and half in remaining shredded coconut. Arrange truffles on prepared baking sheet. Freeze for 30 minutes or until firm. Let stand at room temperature for 10 minutes before serving.

TIPS

While a variety of fresh dates will work in this recipe, Medjool dates are softer and sweeter than many other varieties.

Choose dates that are plump, soft and have shiny skin. They should not have any evidence of crystalizing sugar on their skin.

The truffles can be stored in an airtight container in the refrigerator for up to 1 week or in the freezer for up to 3 months.

Appendix 1: General Health Benefits of Superfoods

	INCREASED ENERGY	IMMUNE SUPPORT	IMPROVED LONGEVITY	MOOD SUPPORT	RADIANT SKIN
FRUITS					
AVOCADOS	•	•	•	•	•
BANANAS	•		•		
BLACKBERRIES	•	•	•	•	•
BLUEBERRIES	•	•	•	•	
CRANBERRIES	•		•		
DATES	•			•	
GOJI BERRIES	•			•	•
GRAPES, RED	•		•		
KIWIFRUIT	•			•	
MANGOS	•	•			•
PEACHES	•				
PEARS	•		•		
PINEAPPLE	•	•			•
PRUNES	•	•		•	•
RASPBERRIES	•		•		
STRAWBERRIES	•			•	
VEGETABLES					
ARUGULA	•	•	•	•	•
BEETS	•	•	•	•	
BOK CHOY	•		•		•
CARROTS	•	•	•		•
KALE	•	•	•	•	•
MUSHROOMS	•	•	•	•	
PUMPKIN	•	•	•	•	•
SEAWEEDS	•	•			
SPINACH	•	•	•	•	•
TOMATOES	•	•	•	•	
WATERCRESS	•	•	•	•	•
LEGUMES					
BLACK BEANS	•	•	•	•	
CANNELLINI (WHITE KIDNEY) BEANS	•	•	•	•	
CHICKPEAS	•	•	•	•	
GREEN PEAS	•	•	•	•	
LENTILS	•	•	•	•	
SOYBEANS	•	•	•	•	
SPLIT PEAS	•	•	•	•	

	INCREASED ENERGY	IMMUNE SUPPORT	IMPROVED LONGEVITY	MOOD SUPPORT	RADIANT SKIN
GRAINS AND SEEDS					
ROLLED OATS	•		•	•	
CHIA SEEDS	•	•	•	•	
FLAX SEEDS	•	•	•	•	•
GREEN PUMPKIN SEEDS (PEPITAS)	•	•	•	•	•
HEMP SEEDS	•	•	•	•	•
SUNFLOWER SEEDS	•	•	•	•	
NUTS AND NUT BUTTERS					
ALMONDS AND ALMOND BUTTER	•	•	•	•	•
CASHEWS AND CASHEW BUTTER	•	•	•	•	•
PEANUT BUTTER	•	•	•	•	•
CACAO, SPICES AND HERBS					
CACAO POWDER AND NIBS		•	•	•	•
CHICORY ROOT				•	
CHILE PEPPERS		•	•		•
CILANTRO		•	•	•	•
CINNAMON					
GINGER				•	
MINT					
TURMERIC		•	•	•	
LIQUIDS					
COCONUT WATER	•				
KEFIR	•	•		•	
MILK	•				
TEA		•	•		
PROTEIN FOODS					
EGG WHITES	•	•	•	•	
VEGAN PROTEIN POWDER	•	•	•	•	
WHEY PROTEIN POWDER	•	•	•	•	
YOGURT	•	•	•	•	

	ADDICTION RECOVERY	ANEMIA	ASTHMA	BRAIN HEALTH	BLOOD PRESSURE	BONE HEALTH	CANCER RISK REDUCTION	CANCER TREATMENT SUPPORT	CARDIOVASCULAR HEALTH	CHOLESTEROL & TRIGLYCERIDES	CONSTIPATION & HEMORRHOIDS	DIABETES PREVENTION	
FRUITS													
AVOCADOS	•	•	•	•	•	•	•	•	•				
BANANAS	•				•	•	•		•	•			
BLACKBERRIES	•			•	•		•	•	•			•	
BLUEBERRIES			•	•	•	•	•	•	•			•	
CRANBERRIES			•	•			•		•			•	
DATES					•				•		•		
GOJI BERRIES				•	•	•	•		•	•	•		
GRAPES, RED												•	
KIWIFRUIT	•	•	•	•	•	•			•				
MANGOS			•		•		•	•	•		•		
PEACHES			•		•		•		•			•	
PEARS	•			•	•	•	•		•		•		
PINEAPPLES					•	•			•		•		
PRUNES	•			•	•	•	•	•	•	•	•		
RASPBERRIES	•			•	•	•	•		•		•		
STRAWBERRIES	•				•		•		•				
VEGETABLES													
ARUGULA	•	•	•	•	•		•	•	•			•	
BEETS			•	•	•	•	•	•	•		•		
BOK CHOY	•		•	•	•	•	•	•	•				
CARROTS			•	•	•		•	•	•	•	•	•	
KALE	•	•	•	•	•	•	•	•	•		•		
MUSHROOMS	•					•	•	•	•				
PUMPKIN	•	•	•	•	•	•	•	•	•		•		
SEAWEEDS							•		•				
SPINACH	•	•	•	•	•	•	•	•	•		•		
TOMATOES	•	•	•	•	•	•	•		•		•		
WATERCRESS		•	•	•	•		•		•	•			

	DIABETES MANAGEMENT	ECLAMPSIA & PRE-ECLAMPSIA	EYE HEALTH	FALL PREVENTION & RECOVERY	GASTROINTESTINAL & DIGESTIVE HEALTH	INFLAMMATION	JOINT HEALTH	KIDNEY STONES	LIVER HEALTH	MUSCLE HEALTH & SARCOPENIA	PREGNANCY	STRESS	WEIGHT MANAGEMENT	WOUND REPAIR
		•	•		•			•	•		•			
		•		•			•	•			•		•	
		•	•		•	•	•	•	•					
	•		•			•	•		•					
						•	•							
		•						•						
	•	•	•			•	•	•	•					
		•							•					
		•						•			•	•		•
	•	•			•	•	•	•	•		•	•		•
					•	•	•	•			•			
		•				•		•						•
	•	•			•	•	•	•			•			•
	•	•			•		•	•						•
		•							•					•
	•	•	•			•	•		•		•			
	•	•	•	•	•	•	•	•	•				•	
		•	•	•					•		•			•
	•	•	•		•	•	•				•		•	
	•	•	•	•		•			•		•			•
		•						•	•			•		
		•	•			•					•	•		
				•							•		•	
	•	•	•			•	•		•		•			
	•	•				•		•					•	•
		•	•			•			•		•			

	ADDICTION RECOVERY	ANEMIA	ASTHMA	BRAIN HEALTH	BLOOD PRESSURE	BONE HEALTH	CANCER RISK REDUCTION	CANCER TREATMENT SUPPORT	CARDIOVASCULAR HEALTH	CHOLESTEROL & TRIGLYCERIDES	CONSTIPATION & HEMORRHOIDS	DIABETES PREVENTION	
LEGUMES													
BLACK BEANS	•	•		•	•	•	•	•	•	•	•	•	
CANNELLINI (WHITE KIDNEY) BEANS	•	•		•	•	•	•	•	•	•	•	•	
CHICKPEAS	•	•		•		•	•	•	•	•		•	
GREEN PEAS	•	•		•	•	•	•	•	•	•	•	•	
LENTILS	•	•		•	•	•	•	•	•	•	•	•	
SOYBEANS	•	•		•	•	•	•	•	•	•	•	•	
SPLIT PEAS	•	•		•	•	•	•	•	•	•	•	•	
GRAINS AND SEEDS													
ROLLED OATS	•	•		•	•	•	•	•	•	•	•	•	
CHIA SEEDS	•			•	•	•	•	•	•	•	•	•	
FLAX SEEDS	•			•	•	•	•	•	•	•	•	•	
GREEN PUMPKIN SEEDS (PEPITAS)	•	•		•	•	•	•	•	•		•	•	
HEMP SEEDS	•	•		•	•	•	•	•	•		•		
SUNFLOWER SEEDS	•	•		•	•	•	•	•	•		•	•	
NUTS AND NUT BUTTERS													
ALMONDS AND ALMOND BUTTER	•			•	•	•	•	•	•	•		•	
CASHEWS AND CASHEW BUTTER	•			•	•	•	•	•	•	•	•	•	
PEANUT BUTTER	•			•	•	•	•	•	•	•		•	
CACAO, SPICES AND HERBS													
CACAO POWDER AND NIBS		•		•	•				•			•	
CHICORY ROOT	•					•			•				
CHILE PEPPERS				•	•		•		•				
CILANTRO			•	•			•		•				
CINNAMON				•	•							•	
GINGER				•	•		•	•	•			•	
MINT				•	•		•	•	•			•	
TURMERIC				•	•		•	•	•			•	

	DIABETES MANAGEMENT	ECLAMPSIA & PRE-ECLAMPSIA	EYE HEALTH	FALL PREVENTION & RECOVERY	GASTROINTESTINAL & DIGESTIVE HEALTH	INFLAMMATION	JOINT HEALTH	KIDNEY STONES	LIVER HEALTH	MUSCLE HEALTH & SARCOPENIA	PREGNANCY	STRESS	WEIGHT MANAGEMENT	WOUND REPAIR
	•	•		•	•	•	•	•		•	•	•	•	•
	•	•		•	•	•	•	•		•	•	•	•	•
	•	•		•	•	•	•			•	•	•	•	
	•	•		•	•	•	•			•	•	•	•	•
	•	•		•	•		•	•		•	•		•	
	•	•		•	•	•	•			•	•	•	•	•
	•	•		•	•	•	•	•		•	•	•		•
	•	•		•	•	•	•			•	•	•	•	
	•	•		•	•	•			•	•	•	•	•	•
	•	•			•		•	•		•	•		•	
	•		•	•		•	•		•	•	•	•	•	
	•		•	•		•	•		•	•	•	•	•	
	•		•	•		•	•		•	•	•	•	•	•
	•	•		•	•	•	•		•		•	•	•	•
	•	•					•		•	•	•	•	•	
	•		•	•		•	•		•		•		•	
	•	•		•		•					•			
			•		•	•	•		•					•
		•				•	•	•	•					•
	•					•	•							
	•					•			•					
	•					•	•		•					
						•	•		•					
	•					•	•		•					

	ADDICTION RECOVERY	ANEMIA	ASTHMA	BRAIN HEALTH	BLOOD PRESSURE	BONE HEALTH	CANCER RISK REDUCTION	CANCER TREATMENT SUPPORT	CARDIOVASCULAR HEALTH	CHOLESTEROL & TRIGLYCERIDES	CONSTIPATION & HEMORRHOIDS	DIABETES PREVENTION
LIQUIDS												
COCONUT WATER					•	•			•			
KEFIR					•	•		•	•		•	
MILK					•	•		•	•			
TEA				•	•				•			
PROTEIN FOODS												
EGG WHITES	•					•		•	•			•
VEGAN PROTEIN POWDER	•					•		•	•			•
WHEY PROTEIN POWDER	•				•	•		•	•			•
YOGURT	•				•	•		•	•			•

Resources

American Institute for Cancer Research
www.aicr.org

The American Journal of Clinical Nutrition
ajcn.nutrition.org

American Society for Nutrition
www.nutrition.org

Annual Review of Nutrition
www.annualreviews.org/journal/nutr

British Journal of Nutrition
www.cambridge.org/core/journals/british-journal-of-nutrition

GrassrootsHealth
www.grassrootshealth.net

Harvard T.H. Chan School of Public Health
www.hsph.harvard.edu/nutritionsource

Journal of the Academy of Nutrition and Dietetics
www.andjrnl.org

The Journal of Nutrition
jn.nutrition.org

Linus Pauling Institute
lpi.oregonstate.edu

National Institutes of Health, Office of Dietary Supplements
ods.od.nih.gov

Pulse Canada
www.pulsecanada.com

Vitamin D Council
www.vitamindcouncil.org

World Cancer Research Fund International
www.wcrf.org

	Diabetes Management	Eclampsia & Pre-Eclampsia	Eye Health	Fall Prevention & Recovery	Gastrointestinal & Digestive Health	Inflammation	Joint Health	Kidney Stones	Liver Health	Muscle Health & Sarcopenia	Pregnancy	Stress	Weight Management	Wound Repair
								•						
		•		•	•			•		•	•	•		•
		•		•				•		•	•	•		•
						•			•					
	•			•					•	•	•	•	•	•
		•		•						•	•		•	
		•		•				•	•	•	•	•	•	
		•		•				•		•	•	•	•	

Library and Archives Canada Cataloguing in Publication

Haugen, Marilyn, author
    175 best superfood blender recipes : using your NutriBullet / Marilyn Haugen & Doug Cook, RD, MHSc.

Includes index.
ISBN 978-0-7788-0559-5 (paperback)

    1. Blenders (Cooking). 2. Cooking (Natural foods).
3. Cookbooks. I. Cook, Doug, 1964-, author II. Title.
III. Title: One hundred seventy-five best superfood blender recipes. IV. Title: Using your NutriBullet.

TX840.B5.H38 2017   641.5'893   C2016-906336-4

Index

A

açaí, 36
Beet, Citrus and Açaí Berry Smoothie, 80
Bountiful Berry Sorbet with Ginger and Mint, 197
Hydrating Spinach, Berry and Orange Smoothie, 106
addictions, 41, 212, 214, 216
alfalfa grass, 18
almond butter, 29. *See also* nut butters
Arugula and Sweet Pea Pesto, 163
Berry and Almond Smoothie, 67
Berry-Berry-Berry Smoothie, 67
Carrot, Ginger and Pineapple Soup, 148
Chai-Spiced Almond Cacao Smoothie, 111
Chocolate Banana Butterscotch Milkshake, 192
Chocolate Delight, Guilt-Free, 176
Chocolaty Almond and Date Smoothie, 109
Cranberry, Pineapple and Almond Relish, 125
Creamy Almond Chocolate Smoothie, 109
Creamy Beet, Ginger and Almond Dip, 129
Happy Birthday Smoothie, 190
Just Peachy Blueberry and Almond Sorbet, 196
Kale and Roasted Pepper Pesto, 164
Mayan Chocolate Mango Maca Dessert, 199
Pesto Almond Hummus, 138
Strawberry Almond Dressing, 120
Wild and Button Mushroom Soup, 152
almond milk. *See also* smoothies
Berry, Spinach and Cashew Smoothie Bowl, Bountiful, 178
Blueberry Chia Parfait, 203
Carrot, Ginger and Pineapple Soup, 148
Funky Chunky Monkey Bars, 207
Peach, Blueberry and Chia Parfait, 182
almonds, 29. *See also* almond butter; almond milk; nuts
Banana Coconut Lentil Balls, 187
Chocolate and Almond Smoothie with Cacao Nibs, 110
Chocolate, Blackberry, Banana Superfood Smoothie Bowl, 113
Greek-Inspired Almond "Feta" Vinaigrette, 117
Romesco Dipping Sauce with Tomatoes and Almonds, 128
Strawberry Grape Smoothie, 66
anemia, 212, 214, 216
apples
Apple, Blueberry and Kale with Flax Seeds, 70
Fiber-Powered Kale, Apple and Ginger Smoothie, 84
Ginger, Lime and Arugula Pick-Me-Up, 82
Apricot Berry Green Smoothie, 73
arugula, 18, 210, 212–13
Arugula and Sweet Pea Pesto, 163
Chilled Peppery Avocado and Arugula Soup, 146
Ginger, Lime and Arugula Pick-Me-Up, 82
Pear, Camu Camu and Arugula Smoothie, 72
Spicy Tomato Avocado Smoothie, 105
asthma, 212, 214, 216
avocado, 11, 210, 212–13
Avocado Almost-Vichyssoise, 145
Avocado and Pineapple Salsa, 126
Avocado Lentil Chocolate Pudding, 201
Chilled Avocado and Ginger Soup, 144
Chilled Peppery Avocado and Arugula Soup, 146
Chocolate-Covered Coconut Avocado Balls, 185
Cooling Avocado, Cucumber and Grapefruit Smoothie, 102
Guacamole with Tomatoes and Cilantro, 141
Mango, Banana and Avocado Pudding, Exotic, 199
Mango Guacamole, 140
Pear, Camu Camu and Arugula Smoothie, 72
Pineapple, Avocado and Watercress Smoothie, 76
Pumpkin, Date and Flaxseed Smoothie, 104
Spicy Tomato Avocado Smoothie, 105
Spinach, Cucumber and Avocado Smoothie, Rejuvenating, 85
Zesty Edamame Dip (variation), 179

B

bananas, 12, 210, 212–13
Apricot Berry Green Smoothie, 73
Ayurveda-Inspired Chia Seed and Coconut Smoothie, 100
Banana, Blueberry and Orange Smoothie, 74
Banana, Peach, Citrus and Goji Berry Smoothie, 75
Banana and Mango Green Smoothie, 75
Banana Coconut Lentil Balls, 187
Banana Cream Yogurt Shake, 191
Beet, Banana and Oat Smoothie, 79
Berry, Spinach and Cashew Smoothie Bowl, Bountiful, 178
Berry Banana Smoothie Bowl, 112
Blackberry Pear Smoothie, 62
Blueberry, Pineapple and Spinach Boost, 65
Blueberry Chia Parfait, 203
Blueberry Muffin Smoothie, 62
Cacao Maple Oatmeal Malt, 192
Carrot, Raspberry and Oatmeal Breakfast, 80
Chocolate and Almond Smoothie with Cacao Nibs, 110
Chocolate, Blackberry, Banana Superfood Smoothie Bowl, 113
Chocolate Banana Butterscotch Milkshake, 192
Chocolate Peanut Butter Yogurt Delight, 193
Chocolaty Almond and Date Smoothie, 109
Coconut Pineapple Cream Pie (variation), 205
Cranberry, Blueberry and Kale Smoothie, 92
Creamy Almond Chocolate Smoothie, 109
Creamy Banana, Blueberry and Papaya Smoothie, 74
Fruit Combo Smoothie, 172
Funky Chunky Monkey Bars, 207
Garden Basket Veggie and Fruit Smoothie, 174
Grape, Carrot and Peach Smoothie, 69
Great Start Breakfast Smoothie, 168
Guilt-Free Chocolate Delight, 176
Happy Birthday Smoothie, 190
Kiwi, Goji Berry and Cacao Green Smoothie, 78
Mango, Banana and Avocado Pudding, Exotic, 199
Mayan Chocolate Mango Maca Dessert, 199
Oatmeal, Peach and Yogurt Smoothie, 72
Oats, Greens and Camu Camu Smoothie Bowl, 86
Oats, Greens and Matcha Smoothie Bowl, 87
Peach, Blueberry and Chia Parfait, 182
Peanut Butter Banana Smoothie, Sporty, 177
Peppermint Patty Shake, 190
Pineapple, Mango and Bok Choy Smoothie, 99
Protein-Powered Kale, Berry, Hemp and Yogurt Smoothie, 83
Pumped-Up Fall Harvest Pumpkin Breakfast Bowl, 88
Pumpkin, Oat and Pomegranate Smoothie Bowl, 114
Raspberry, Peach and Chia Seed Smoothie, 90

Red Velvet Parfait, 201
Spinach, Pineapple and
Mint Smoothie, 106
Strawberry, Camu Camu
and Oolong Smoothie, 93
Tropical Kiwi, Coconut
and Chia Seed Smoothie,
101
barley grass powder, 18
basil
Kale and Roasted Pepper
Pesto, 164
Pesto Almond Hummus,
138
Tomato Vinaigrette, 116
beans, 23–24, 25, 210,
214–15. See also
chickpeas
Avocado Almost-
Vichyssoise, 145
BLT Bean Spread, 180
Enchilada Sauce with
Poblano Peppers and
Black Beans, 162
Spaghetti Beanballs, 181
Spicy White Bean Dip,
135
Time-Out Black Bean Dip,
134
Tuscan White Bean Soup,
159
Zesty Edamame Dip, 179
beets, 18–19, 210, 212–13
Beet, Banana and Oat
Smoothie, 79
Beet, Citrus and Açaí
Berry Smoothie, 80
Blackberry, Beet and Chia
Seed Smoothie, 90
Cold Beet Soup, 147
Creamy Beet, Ginger and
Almond Dip, 129
Raspberry, Beet and Mint
Protein Smoothie, 65
Red Velvet Parfait, 201
berries (mixed). See also
specific types of berries
Apricot Berry Green
Smoothie, 73
Berry and Almond
Smoothie, 67
Berry and Protein-
Powered Greens, 94
Berry Banana Smoothie
Bowl, 112
Berry-Berry-Berry
Smoothie, 67
Berrylicious Swiss Chard
and Chia Smoothie, 68
Black Forest Berry Blast,
94
Bountiful Berry, Spinach
and Cashew Smoothie
Bowl, 178
Bountiful Berry Sorbet
with Ginger and Mint,
197

Cardinal Red Fruit and
Vegetable Burst, 172
Cranberry, Blueberry and
Kale Smoothie, 92
Dreamy Berry and Kale
Smoothie, 66
Fruity Get-Your-Greens
Smoothie, 175
Garden Basket Veggie and
Fruit Smoothie, 174
Oats, Greens and Matcha
Smoothie Bowl, 87
Protein-Powered Kale,
Berry, Hemp and Yogurt
Smoothie, 83
Triple-Berry Sauce, 166
Triple-Threat Protein and
Berry Smoothie, 169
blackberries, 12, 210,
212–13. See also berries
Blackberry, Beet and Chia
Seed Smoothie, 90
Blackberry Pear
Smoothie, 62
Chocolate, Blackberry,
Banana Superfood
Smoothie Bowl, 113
blended foods, 6–10. See
also smoothies
equipment needed, 58–59
health benefits, 37–53
pantry staples, 59
substitutions, 60
blood pressure, 45, 212,
214, 216
blood sugar, 46–47. See also
diabetes
blueberries, 12–13, 210,
212–13. See also berries
Apple, Blueberry and Kale
with Flax Seeds, 70
Banana, Blueberry and
Orange Smoothie, 74
Blueberry, Pineapple and
Spinach Boost, 65
Blueberry and Coconut
Protein Smoothie, 63
Blueberry Chia Parfait,
203
Blueberry Muffin
Smoothie, 62
Blueberry Sesame
Dressing, 118
Creamy Banana,
Blueberry and Papaya
Smoothie, 74
Just Peachy Blueberry and
Almond Sorbet, 196
Oats, Greens and Camu
Camu Smoothie Bowl, 86
Peach, Blueberry and Chia
Parfait, 182
Peachy Grape and
Blueberry Smoothie, 171
Protein Powerhouse with
Blueberries and Flax
Seeds, 64

Pumpkin, Oat and
Pomegranate Smoothie
Bowl, 114
Simply Satisfying
Blueberry Mango
Smoothie, 91
Sliced Peaches with
Blueberry Cashew
Cream, 204
bok choy, 19, 210, 212–13
Cucumber Pineapple
Green Smoothie, 82
Pear, Cranberry and Bok
Choy Smoothie, 95
Pineapple, Mango and
Bok Choy Smoothie, 99
bone and tooth health, 42,
212, 214, 216
brain health, 43, 212, 214,
216

C

cacao powder and nibs,
30–31, 211, 214–15
Avocado Lentil Chocolate
Pudding, 201
Banana Coconut Lentil
Balls, 187
Black Forest Berry Blast,
94
Blueberry Mango
Smoothie, Simply
Satisfying, 91
Cacao Maple Oatmeal
Malt, 192
Chai-Spiced Almond
Cacao Smoothie, 111
Chocolate and Almond
Smoothie with Cacao
Nibs, 110
Chocolate, Blackberry,
Banana Superfood
Smoothie Bowl, 113
Chocolate Banana
Butterscotch Milkshake,
192
Chocolate Peanut Butter
Yogurt Delight, 193
Chocolate Pudding with
Goji Berries, 200
Chocolaty Almond and
Date Smoothie, 109
Creamy Almond
Chocolate Smoothie, 109
Funky Chunky Monkey
Bars, 207
Gooey Almond Oat Balls,
186
Green Chocolate Milk,
176
Guilt-Free Chocolate
Delight, 176
Iced Mocha Smoothie,
85
Kiwi, Goji Berry and
Cacao Green Smoothie,
78

Land and Sea Green
Smoothie with Chocolate
and Berries, 107
Mayan Chocolate Mango
Maca Dessert, 199
Nutty Choco-Caramel
Tarts, 206
Nutty Date Truffles, 209
Peachy Spiced Chocolate
Treat, 193
Peanut Butter Chocolate
Smoothie, 108
Peppermint Patty Shake,
190
Raspberry Chocolate
Milkshake, 191
Sweet and Nutty
Superfood Balls, 208
camu camu powder, 36
Fruit Combo Smoothie,
172
Oats, Greens and Camu
Camu Smoothie Bowl, 86
Peachy Grape and
Blueberry Smoothie, 171
Pear, Camu Camu and
Arugula Smoothie, 72
Pineapple, Citrus and
Carrot Smoothie, 173
Strawberry, Camu Camu
and Oolong Smoothie, 93
cancer, 43–45, 212, 214,
216
cardiovascular health, 45,
212, 214, 216
carrots, 19, 210, 212–13
African-Inspired Lentil
Dip, 133
Carrot, Ginger and
Pineapple Soup, 148
Carrot, Mango, Citrus and
Ginger Smoothie with
Hemp Seeds, 81
Carrot, Raspberry and
Oatmeal Breakfast, 80
Carrot Ginger Dressing,
121
Fruity Carrot Smoothie,
173
Grape, Carrot and Peach
Smoothie, 69
Great Start Breakfast
Smoothie, 168
Land and Sea Green
Smoothie with Chocolate
and Berries, 107
Mango, Strawberry
and Carrot Smoothie,
Refreshing, 97
Pineapple, Citrus and
Carrot Smoothie, 173
Roasted Pumpkin and
Carrot Juice Soup, 153
Roasted Vegetable Pasta
Sauce with Tomatoes,
Carrots and Mushrooms,
161

cashews, 29–30. *See also*
nut butters; nuts
Ayurveda-Inspired Chia
Seed and Coconut
Smoothie, 100
Berry, Spinach and
Cashew Smoothie Bowl,
Bountiful, 178
Mango, Pineapple,
Coconut and Cashew
Cream Parfait, 202
Mint Cashew Cream Dip,
132
Oats, Greens and Camu
Camu Smoothie Bowl,
86
Pineapple, Cashew and
Chile Pepper Spread, 142
Sliced Peaches with
Blueberry Cashew
Cream, 204
Spiced Pineapple and
Maca Energy Balls, 188
Spinach, Hot Pepper and
Yogurt Hummus, 139
celery, 11
Chilled Peppery Avocado
and Arugula Soup, 146
cheese
Arugula and Sweet Pea
Pesto, 163
Coconut Pineapple Cream
Pie, 205
Creamy Kale and Feta
Dip, 131
Kale and Roasted Pepper
Pesto, 164
Spaghetti Beanballs, 181
chia seeds, 26–27. *See also*
seeds
Ayurveda-Inspired Chia
Seed and Coconut
Smoothie, 100
Beet, Banana and Oat
Smoothie, 79
Berry and Kale Smoothie,
Dreamy, 66
Berrylicious Swiss Chard
and Chia Smoothie, 68
Blackberry, Beet and Chia
Seed Smoothie, 90
Black Forest Berry Blast,
94
Blueberry Chia Parfait,
203
Cardinal Red Fruit and
Vegetable Burst, 172
Chocolate, Blackberry,
Banana Superfood
Smoothie Bowl, 113
Chocolate Banana
Butterscotch Milkshake,
192
Chocolate Pudding with
Goji Berries, 200
Grape, Carrot and Peach
Smoothie, 69

Peach, Blueberry and Chia
Parfait, 182
Pineapple, Cashew and
Chile Pepper Spread, 142
Pineapple, Mango and
Goji Berry Smoothie, 77
Raspberry, Peach and
Chia Seed Smoothie, 90
Triple-Berry Sauce, 166
Tropical Kiwi, Coconut
and Chia Seed Smoothie,
101
chickpeas, 24, 210, 214–15
Chickpea and Yogurt Dip,
136
Hummus, Traditional
Creamy, 137
Pesto Almond Hummus,
138
Red Lentil, Chickpea and
Tomato Soup, 157
Spinach, Hot Pepper and
Yogurt Hummus, 139
Zesty Chickpea, Tomato
and Mushroom Soup,
158
chicory root powder, 31,
211, 214–15
Bountiful Berry, Spinach
and Cashew Smoothie
Bowl, 178
Chocolate, Blackberry,
Banana Superfood
Smoothie Bowl, 113
Chocolate Pudding with
Goji Berries, 200
Hydrating Spinach, Berry
and Orange Smoothie,
106
children, 8, 167–88
chlorella powder, 18
chocolate. *See also* cacao
powder and nibs
Chocolate-Covered
Coconut Avocado Balls,
185
cholesterol, 45, 212, 214,
216
cilantro, 31–32, 211,
214–15
Black Bean Dip, Time-
Out, 134
Chilled Avocado and
Ginger Soup, 144
Cilantro Jalapeño Ranch
Dressing, 122
Guacamole with
Tomatoes and Cilantro,
141
Mango Guacamole, 140
Pineapple, Mango and
Bok Choy Smoothie, 99
Spicy Spinach Cilantro
Sauce, 165
Tex-Mex Salad Dressing,
123
Zesty Edamame Dip, 179

cinnamon, 32, 211, 214–15
Banana and Mango Green
Smoothie, 75
Berry Banana Smoothie
Bowl, 112
Blackberry Pear
Smoothie, 62
Mayan Chocolate Mango
Maca Dessert, 199
citrus, 59. *See also specific
citrus fruits*
coconut. *See also* coconut
milk and cream; coconut
water
Banana Coconut Lentil
Balls, 187
Berry, Spinach and
Cashew Smoothie Bowl,
Bountiful, 178
Berry Banana Smoothie
Bowl, 112
Chocolate, Blackberry,
Banana Superfood
Smoothie Bowl, 113
Chocolate-Covered
Coconut Avocado Balls,
185
Coconut Pineapple Cream
Pie, 205
Fiber-Powered Kale,
Apple and Ginger
Smoothie, 84
Mango, Pineapple,
Coconut and Cashew
Cream Parfait, 202
Nutty Date Truffles, 209
Pineapple, Mango and
Goji Berry Smoothie,
77
Pumped-Up Fall Harvest
Pumpkin Breakfast Bowl,
88
Tropical Kiwi, Coconut
and Chia Seed Smoothie,
101
coconut milk and cream
Avocado Lentil Chocolate
Pudding, 201
Berrylicious Swiss Chard
and Chia Smoothie, 68
Blueberry and Coconut
Protein Smoothie, 63
Creamy Tomato Coconut
Soup, 154
Funky Chunky Monkey
Bars, 207
Nutty Choco-Caramel
Tarts, 206
Papaya Kiwi Frozen
Yogurt, 183
Pear, Cranberry and Bok
Choy Smoothie, 95
Spicy Pumpkin Soup, 149
Virgin Piña Colada, 194
Zesty Chickpea, Tomato
and Mushroom Soup,
158

coconut water, 33,
211, 216–17. *See also*
smoothies
Chilled Peppery Avocado
and Arugula Soup, 146
Fall Cranberry Pear
Sorbet, 198
Just Peachy Blueberry
and Almond Sorbet,
196
Pea Soup with
Mushrooms, Watercress
and Mint, 155
Strawberry Almond
Dressing, 120
Sweet Chile Dipping
Sauce, 127
Triple-Berry Sauce, 166
constipation, 49, 212, 214,
216
cranberries, 13, 210,
212–13. *See also* berries
Avocado Lentil Chocolate
Pudding, 201
Cranberry, Pineapple and
Almond Relish, 125
Cranberry Pear Splash,
177
Fall Cranberry Pear
Sorbet, 198
Gooey Almond Oat Balls,
186
Pear, Cranberry and Bok
Choy Smoothie, 95
Pumped-Up Fall Harvest
Pumpkin Breakfast Bowl,
88
Pumpkin Cranberry
Protein Smoothie, 103
cucumber
Cold Strawberry and
Tomato Soup, 151
Cooling Avocado,
Cucumber and
Grapefruit Smoothie,
102
Cucumber Pineapple
Green Smoothie, 82
Gazpacho, 150
Rejuvenating Spinach,
Cucumber and Avocado
Smoothie, 85

D

dates, 13, 210, 212–13. *See
also* fruit, dried
Ayurveda-Inspired Chia
Seed and Coconut
Smoothie, 100
Berry Banana Smoothie
Bowl, 112
Chai-Spiced Almond
Cacao Smoothie, 111
Chocolate Pudding with
Goji Berries, 200
Chocolaty Almond and
Date Smoothie, 109

Cooling Avocado, Cucumber and Grapefruit Smoothie, 102
Funky Chunky Monkey Bars, 207
Green Chocolate Milk, 176
Iced Mocha Smoothie, 85
Land and Sea Green Smoothie with Chocolate and Berries, 107
Nutty Choco-Caramel Tarts, 206
Nutty Date Truffles, 209
Oats, Greens and Camu Camu Smoothie Bowl, 86
Oats, Greens and Matcha Smoothie Bowl, 87
Pumpkin, Date and Flaxseed Smoothie, 104
Spiced Pineapple and Maca Energy Balls, 188
Sweet and Nutty Superfood Balls, 208
diabetes, 46, 212–13, 214–15, 216–17
digestion, 50, 213, 214, 216
dips and spreads, 126–42, 179–80
dressings (salad), 116–23

E
egg whites, 34, 211, 216–17
energy balls and bars, 185–88, 207–8
eye health, 46–47, 213, 215, 217

F
falls, 47–48, 213, 215, 217
fertility, 51. See also pregnancy
fiber, 49, 54, 56
flax seeds, 27. See also seeds
Apple, Blueberry and Kale with Flax Seeds, 70
Blueberry Muffin Smoothie, 62
Creamy Almond Chocolate Smoothie, 109
Protein Powerhouse with Blueberries and Flax Seeds, 64
Pumpkin, Date and Flaxseed Smoothie, 104
Triple-Threat Protein and Berry Smoothie, 169
fruit, 11–17, 210, 212–13. See also berries; specific fruits
fruit, dried. See also dates; goji berries; prunes
Apricot Berry Green Smoothie, 73
Avocado Lentil Chocolate Pudding, 201

Garden Basket Veggie and Fruit Smoothie, 174
Gooey Almond Oat Balls, 186
Pumped-Up Fall Harvest Pumpkin Breakfast Bowl, 88
Spiced Pineapple and Maca Energy Balls, 188
fruit juices
Carrot, Ginger and Pineapple Soup, 148
Cranberry Pear Splash, 177
Fruit Combo Smoothie, 172
Ginger, Lime and Arugula Pick-Me-Up, 82
Orange Cream Smoothie, 171
Raspberry, Peach and Grape Ice Pops, 184
Sparkling Pineapple Mango Refresher, 98
Strawberry Pineapple Sorbet, 195
Zesty Edamame Dip, 179

G
garlic
Arugula and Sweet Pea Pesto, 163
BLT Bean Spread, 180
Greek-Inspired Almond "Feta" Vinaigrette, 117
Hummus, Traditional Creamy, 137
Kale and Roasted Pepper Pesto, 164
Romesco Dipping Sauce with Tomatoes and Almonds, 128
Spicy Spinach Cilantro Sauce, 165
Sweet Chile Dipping Sauce, 127
Tomato Vinaigrette, 116
Tuscan White Bean Soup, 159
Zesty Edamame Dip, 179
gastrointestinal system, 48–50, 213, 215, 217
gingerroot, 32, 211, 214–15
African-Inspired Lentil Dip, 133
Ayurveda-Inspired Chia Seed and Coconut Smoothie, 100
Berry Sorbet with Ginger and Mint, Bountiful, 197
Carrot, Ginger and Pineapple Soup, 148
Carrot, Mango, Citrus and Ginger Smoothie with Hemp Seeds, 81
Carrot Ginger Dressing, 121

Chilled Avocado and Ginger Soup, 144
Creamy Beet, Ginger and Almond Dip, 129
Fiber-Powered Kale, Apple and Ginger Smoothie, 84
Ginger, Lime and Arugula Pick-Me-Up, 82
Oats, Greens and Matcha Smoothie Bowl, 87
Pear, Cranberry and Bok Choy Smoothie, 95
Pineapple, Citrus and Carrot Smoothie, 173
Pineapple, Ginger and Peanut Butter Marinade, 124
Pumpkin Cranberry Protein Smoothie, 103
Spicy Pumpkin Soup, 149
Yellow Split Pea and Pumpkin Soup, 156
Zingy Green and Fruity Energy Boost, 174
goji berries, 14, 210, 212–13. See also berries
Banana, Peach, Citrus and Goji Berry Smoothie, 75
Chocolate Pudding with Goji Berries, 200
Cucumber Pineapple Green Smoothie, 82
Kiwi, Goji Berry and Cacao Green Smoothie, 78
Pineapple, Mango and Goji Berry Smoothie, 77
Raspberry, Beet and Mint Protein Smoothie, 65
grapefruit
Banana, Peach, Citrus and Goji Berry Smoothie, 75
Cardinal Red Fruit and Vegetable Burst, 172
Cooling Avocado, Cucumber and Grapefruit Smoothie, 102
grapes (red), 14, 210, 212–13
Berry-Berry-Berry Smoothie, 67
Grape, Carrot and Peach Smoothie, 69
Grape Kiwi Kid-Power Smoothie, 170
Hydrating Spinach, Berry and Orange Smoothie, 106
Orange Cream Smoothie, 171
Peachy Grape and Blueberry Smoothie, 171
Pear, Camu Camu and Arugula Smoothie, 72
Pineapple, Grape and Spinach Smoothie, 76

Red and Green Smoothie with Pepitas, 70
Red Grape, Peach and Raspberry Smoothie, 69
Strawberry Grape Smoothie, 66
Zingy Green and Fruity Energy Boost, 174
greens. See also specific greens
Apricot Berry Green Smoothie, 73
Berrylicious Swiss Chard and Chia Smoothie, 68
Garden Basket Veggie and Fruit Smoothie, 174
Red and Green Smoothie with Pepitas, 70

H
hemorrhoids, 212, 214, 216
hemp seeds, 28
Carrot, Mango, Citrus and Ginger Smoothie with Hemp Seeds, 81
Pineapple, Citrus and Carrot Smoothie, 173
Protein-Powered Kale, Berry, Hemp and Yogurt Smoothie, 83
Pumpkin Cranberry Protein Smoothie, 103
Spinach, Pineapple and Mint Smoothie, 106
herbs. See also specific herbs
Greek-Inspired Almond "Feta" Vinaigrette, 117
Roasted Vegetable Pasta Sauce with Tomatoes, Carrots and Mushrooms, 161

I
ice pops, 183–84, 195, 197
immune system, 38–39
inflammation, 50–51, 213, 215, 217
insulin resistance, 46

J
joint health, 213, 215, 217

K
kale, 20, 210, 212–13. See also greens
Apple, Blueberry and Kale with Flax Seeds, 70
Berry and Kale Smoothie, Dreamy, 66
Cranberry, Blueberry and Kale Smoothie, 92
Creamy Kale and Feta Dip, 131
Fiber-Powered Kale, Apple and Ginger Smoothie, 84
Fruity Get-Your-Greens Smoothie, 175

kale *(continued)*
  Kale and Roasted Pepper
    Pesto, 164
  Oats, Greens and Camu
    Camu Smoothie Bowl, 86
  Protein-Powered Kale,
    Berry, Hemp and Yogurt
    Smoothie, 83
  Tropical Kiwi, Coconut
    and Chia Seed Smoothie,
    101
kefir, 33, 211, 216–17
  Cold Beet Soup, 147
  Peppermint Patty Shake,
    190
  Red Grape, Peach and
    Raspberry Smoothie, 69
kidney stones, 213, 215, 217
kiwifruit, 14–15, 210,
    212–13
  Avocado and Pineapple
    Salsa, 126
  Breakfast Smoothie, Great
    Start, 168
  Grape Kiwi Kid-Power
    Smoothie, 170
  Kiwi, Goji Berry and
    Cacao Green Smoothie,
    78
  Mango Agua Fresca, 96
  Oats, Greens and Camu
    Camu Smoothie Bowl, 86
  Papaya Kiwi Frozen
    Yogurt, 183
  Pear, Kiwi and Key Lime
    Smoothie, 71
  Strawberry, Camu Camu
    and Oolong Smoothie, 93
  Tropical Kiwi, Coconut
    and Chia Seed Smoothie,
    101

L

legumes, 23–26, 210, 214–15.
  See also beans; lentils; peas
lemon
  Ayurveda-Inspired Chia
    Seed and Coconut
    Smoothie, 100
  Beet, Citrus and Açaí
    Berry Smoothie, 80
  Greek-Inspired Almond
    "Feta" Vinaigrette, 117
lentils, 24–25, 210, 214–15
  African-Inspired Lentil
    Dip, 133
  Avocado Lentil Chocolate
    Pudding, 201
  Banana Coconut Lentil
    Balls, 187
  Coconut Pineapple Cream
    Pie, 205
  Red Lentil, Chickpea and
    Tomato Soup, 157
lime
  Avocado and Pineapple
    Salsa, 126

Chilled Peppery Avocado
    and Arugula Soup, 146
  Ginger, Lime and Arugula
    Pick-Me-Up, 82
  Pear, Kiwi and Key Lime
    Smoothie, 71
  Sparkling Pineapple
    Mango Refresher, 98
  Spicy Spinach Cilantro
    Sauce, 165
  Strawberry, Pear and Lime
    Ice Pops, 183
  Tex-Mex Salad Dressing,
    123
  Zesty Edamame Dip, 179
liver health, 213, 215, 217

M

maca powder, 36
  Chocolate Banana
    Butterscotch Milkshake,
    192
  Green Chocolate Milk,
    176
  Mayan Chocolate Mango
    Maca Dessert, 199
  Spiced Pineapple and
    Maca Energy Balls, 188
  Sweet and Nutty
    Superfood Balls, 208
Magic Bullet blender, 58
mangos, 15, 210, 212–13
  Banana and Mango Green
    Smoothie, 75
  Blueberry Mango
    Smoothie, Simply
    Satisfying, 91
  Carrot, Mango, Citrus and
    Ginger Smoothie with
    Hemp Seeds, 81
  Exotic Mango, Banana and
    Avocado Pudding, 199
  Fruity Carrot Smoothie,
    173
  Mango, Pineapple,
    Coconut and Cashew
    Cream Parfait, 202
  Mango Agua Fresca, 96
  Mango Almond Lassi, 194
  Mango Guacamole, 140
  Mayan Chocolate Mango
    Maca Dessert, 199
  Orange Cream Smoothie,
    171
  Pear, Kiwi and Key Lime
    Smoothie, 71
  Pineapple, Citrus and
    Carrot Smoothie, 173
  Pineapple, Mango and
    Bok Choy Smoothie, 99
  Pineapple, Mango and
    Goji Berry Smoothie, 77
  Refreshing Mango,
    Strawberry and Carrot
    Smoothie, 97
  Sparkling Pineapple
    Mango Refresher, 98

matcha powder. *See* tea
milk (dairy and nondairy),
    33, 34, 211, 216–17. *See
    also* smoothies; *specific
    nondairy milks*
mint, 32, 211, 214–15
  Beet, Citrus and Açaí
    Berry Smoothie, 80
  Berry and Protein-
    Powered Greens, 94
  Berry Sorbet with Ginger
    and Mint, Bountiful, 197
  Blackberry, Beet and Chia
    Seed Smoothie, 90
  Kiwi, Goji Berry and
    Cacao Green Smoothie,
    78
  Mango, Strawberry
    and Carrot Smoothie,
    Refreshing, 97
  Mango Agua Fresca, 96
  Mint Cashew Cream Dip,
    132
  Pea Soup with
    Mushrooms, Watercress
    and Mint, 155
  Raspberry, Beet and Mint
    Protein Smoothie, 65
  Red Velvet Parfait, 201
  Spinach, Pineapple and
    Mint Smoothie, 106
Mocha Smoothie, Iced, 85
moringa leaf powder, 18
muscle health, 213, 215, 217
mushrooms, 20, 210,
    212–13
  Creamy Mushroom Sauce,
    163
  Pea Soup with
    Mushrooms, Watercress
    and Mint, 155
  Roasted Vegetable Pasta
    Sauce with Tomatoes,
    Carrots and Mushrooms,
    161
  Wild and Button
    Mushroom Soup, 152
  Zesty Chickpea, Tomato
    and Mushroom Soup,
    158

N

nut butters, 29–30, 211,
    214–15. *See also* almond
    butter; peanut butter
  African-Inspired Lentil
    Dip, 133
  Funky Chunky Monkey
    Bars, 207
  Green Chocolate Milk,
    176
NutriBullet blenders, 58–59
nuts, 29–30, 211, 214–15.
  See also almonds;
    cashews; nut butters
  Nutty Choco-Caramel
    Tarts, 206

Nutty Date Truffles, 209
  Pumped-Up Fall Harvest
    Pumpkin Breakfast Bowl,
    88
  Sweet and Nutty
    Superfood Balls, 208

O

oats, 26, 211, 214–15
  Beet, Banana and Oat
    Smoothie, 79
  Blueberry Chia Parfait,
    203
  Blueberry Muffin
    Smoothie, 62
  Breakfast Smoothie, Great
    Start, 168
  Cacao Maple Oatmeal
    Malt, 192
  Carrot, Raspberry and
    Oatmeal Breakfast, 80
  Gooey Almond Oat Balls,
    186
  Oatmeal, Peach and
    Yogurt Smoothie, 72
  Oats, Greens and Camu
    Camu Smoothie Bowl, 86
  Oats, Greens and Matcha
    Smoothie Bowl, 87
  Pumpkin, Oat and
    Pomegranate Smoothie
    Bowl, 114
  Sweet and Nutty
    Superfood Balls, 208
orange
  Banana, Blueberry and
    Orange Smoothie, 74
  Beet, Citrus and Açaí
    Berry Smoothie, 80
  Cardinal Red Fruit and
    Vegetable Burst, 172
  Carrot, Mango, Citrus and
    Ginger Smoothie with
    Hemp Seeds, 81
  Carrot, Raspberry and
    Oatmeal Breakfast, 80
  Cranberry, Pineapple and
    Almond Relish, 125
  Grape Kiwi Kid-Power
    Smoothie, 170
  Hydrating Spinach, Berry
    and Orange Smoothie,
    106
  Mango, Strawberry
    and Carrot Smoothie,
    Refreshing, 97
  Orange Cream Smoothie,
    171
  Pineapple, Citrus and
    Carrot Smoothie, 173
  Pineapple, Ginger and
    Peanut Butter Marinade,
    124
  Spiced Pineapple and
    Maca Energy Balls, 188
  Strawberry Pineapple
    Sorbet, 195

P

papayas
Creamy Banana,
Blueberry and Papaya
Smoothie, 74
Papaya Kiwi Frozen
Yogurt, 183
parfaits, 182, 201–3
peaches, 15, 210, 212–13
Banana, Peach, Citrus
and Goji Berry Smoothie,
75
Blueberry and Coconut
Protein Smoothie, 63
Fruit Combo Smoothie,
172
Grape, Carrot and Peach
Smoothie, 69
Just Peachy Blueberry and
Almond Sorbet, 196
Oatmeal, Peach and
Yogurt Smoothie, 72
Oats, Greens and Matcha
Smoothie Bowl, 87
Peach, Blueberry and Chia
Parfait, 182
Peachy Grape and
Blueberry Smoothie, 171
Peachy Spiced Chocolate
Treat, 193
Raspberry, Peach and
Grape Ice Pops, 184
Red Grape, Peach and
Raspberry Smoothie, 69
Sliced Peaches with
Blueberry Cashew
Cream, 204
Strawberry, Camu Camu
and Oolong Smoothie, 93
peanut butter, 30. See also
nut butters
Berry Banana Smoothie
Bowl, 112
Cacao Maple Oatmeal
Malt (variation), 192
Chocolate Peanut Butter
Yogurt Delight, 193
Gooey Almond Oat Balls,
186
Peanut Butter Chocolate
Smoothie, 108
Pineapple, Ginger and
Peanut Butter Marinade,
124
Sporty Peanut Butter
Banana Smoothie, 177
pears, 16, 210, 212–13
Blackberry Pear
Smoothie, 62
Fall Cranberry Pear
Sorbet, 198
Fruity Carrot Smoothie,
173
Grape Kiwi Kid-Power
Smoothie, 170
Pear, Camu Camu and
Arugula Smoothie, 72

Pear, Cranberry and Bok
Choy Smoothie, 95
Pear, Kiwi and Key Lime
Smoothie, 71
Raspberry, Peach and
Chia Seed Smoothie, 90
Strawberry, Pear and Lime
Ice Pops, 183
Strawberry Malt
Smoothie, 168
Tomato Vinaigrette, 116
Zingy Green and Fruity
Energy Boost, 174
peas, green, 24, 210, 214–15
Arugula and Sweet Pea
Pesto, 163
Pea Soup with
Mushrooms, Watercress
and Mint, 155
Zingy Green and Fruity
Energy Boost, 174
peas, split, 26, 210, 214–15
Yellow Split Pea and
Pumpkin Soup, 156
peppers, 31, 211, 214–15
Chilled Peppery Avocado
and Arugula Soup, 146
Cilantro Jalapeño Ranch
Dressing, 122
Enchilada Sauce with
Poblano Peppers and
Black Beans, 162
Gazpacho, 150
Guacamole with
Tomatoes and Cilantro,
141
Kale and Roasted Pepper
Pesto, 164
Pineapple, Cashew and
Chile Pepper Spread, 142
Romesco Dipping Sauce
with Tomatoes and
Almonds, 128
Spicy Moroccan-Inspired
Tomato Dip, 130
Spicy White Bean Dip,
135
Spinach, Hot Pepper and
Yogurt Hummus, 139
Sweet Chile Dipping
Sauce, 127
phytonutrients, 6, 18, 20, 40
pineapple, 16, 210, 212–13
Avocado and Pineapple
Salsa, 126
Blueberry, Pineapple and
Spinach Boost, 65
Carrot, Ginger and
Pineapple Soup, 148
Carrot, Mango, Citrus and
Ginger Smoothie with
Hemp Seeds, 81
Chocolate, Blackberry,
Banana Superfood
Smoothie Bowl, 113
Coconut Pineapple Cream
Pie, 205

Cranberry, Pineapple and
Almond Relish, 125
Cucumber Pineapple
Green Smoothie, 82
Fruit Combo Smoothie,
172
Mango, Pineapple,
Coconut and Cashew
Cream Parfait, 202
Pineapple, Avocado and
Watercress Smoothie, 76
Pineapple, Cashew and
Chile Pepper Spread,
142
Pineapple, Citrus and
Carrot Smoothie, 173
Pineapple, Ginger and
Peanut Butter Marinade,
124
Pineapple, Grape and
Spinach Smoothie, 76
Pineapple, Mango and
Bok Choy Smoothie, 99
Pineapple, Mango and
Goji Berry Smoothie, 77
Sparkling Pineapple
Mango Refresher, 98
Spiced Pineapple and
Maca Energy Balls, 188
Spinach, Pineapple and
Mint Smoothie, 106
Strawberry Pineapple
Sorbet, 195
Virgin Piña Colada, 194
polyphenols, 25, 36, 40
pomegranate powder, 36
Cranberry, Pineapple and
Almond Relish, 125
Pumpkin, Oat and
Pomegranate Smoothie
Bowl, 114
Raspberry Poppy Seed
Dressing, 119
prebiotics and probiotics,
49
pregnancy, 51–52, 213,
215, 217
protein sources, 34–35,
211, 216–17
prunes, 16–17, 210, 212–13
Blueberry Chia Parfait,
203
Garden Basket Veggie and
Fruit Smoothie, 174
Peachy Spiced Chocolate
Treat, 193
Red and Green Smoothie
with Pepitas, 70
Sliced Peaches with
Blueberry Cashew Cream,
204
pumpkin, 21, 210, 212–13
Pumped-Up Fall Harvest
Pumpkin Breakfast Bowl,
88
Pumpkin, Date and
Flaxseed Smoothie, 104

Pumpkin, Oat and
Pomegranate Smoothie
Bowl, 114
Pumpkin Cranberry
Protein Smoothie, 103
Roasted Pumpkin and
Carrot Juice Soup, 153
Spicy Pumpkin Soup, 149
Yellow Split Pea and
Pumpkin Soup, 156
pumpkin seeds (pepitas),
27–28
Berry Banana Smoothie
Bowl, 112
Nutty Date Truffles, 209
Pumpkin, Oat and
Pomegranate Smoothie
Bowl, 114
Red and Green Smoothie
with Pepitas, 70

R

raspberries, 17, 210,
212–13. See also berries
Black Forest Berry Blast,
94
Breakfast Smoothie,
Great Start, 168
Carrot, Raspberry and
Oatmeal Breakfast, 80
Hydrating Spinach, Berry
and Orange Smoothie,
106
Land and Sea Green
Smoothie with Chocolate
and Berries, 107
Peanut Butter Chocolate
Smoothie, 108
Raspberry, Beet and Mint
Protein Smoothie, 65
Raspberry, Peach and
Chia Seed Smoothie,
90
Raspberry, Peach and
Grape Ice Pops, 184
Raspberry Chocolate
Milkshake, 191
Raspberry Poppy Seed
Dressing, 119
Red Grape, Peach and
Raspberry Smoothie, 69

S

sarcopenia, 213, 215, 217
sauces, 160–66. See also
dips and spreads
seaweed, 21, 210, 212–13
Land and Sea Green
Smoothie with Chocolate
and Berries, 107
Pineapple, Ginger and
Peanut Butter Marinade,
124
Pineapple, Mango and
Bok Choy Smoothie, 99
Spicy Spinach Cilantro
Sauce, 165

seaweed *(continued)*
Spicy Tomato Avocado Smoothie, 105
Spicy White Bean Dip, 135
Sweet Chile Dipping Sauce, 127
seeds, 26–29, 211, 214–15. *See also specific types of seeds*
Berry Banana Smoothie Bowl, 112
Pumped-Up Fall Harvest Pumpkin Breakfast Bowl, 88
Raspberry Poppy Seed Dressing, 119
seniors, 9–10
smoothie bowls, 86–88, 112–14, 178
smoothies, 8, 54–56
anytime, 90–111
breakfast, 62–85, 168
kid-friendly, 168–77
soups
cold, 144–51
warm, 152–59
soybeans. *See* beans
spinach, 21–22, 210, 212–13. *See also* greens
Banana and Mango Green Smoothie, 75
Berry, Spinach and Cashew Smoothie Bowl, Bountiful, 178
Berry and Protein-Powered Greens, 94
Black Forest Berry Blast, 94
BLT Bean Spread, 180
Blueberry, Pineapple and Spinach Boost, 65
Cardinal Red Fruit and Vegetable Burst, 172
Chocolate and Almond Smoothie with Cacao Nibs, 110
Chocolate, Blackberry, Banana Superfood Smoothie Bowl, 113
Green Chocolate Milk, 176
Hydrating Spinach, Berry and Orange Smoothie, 106
Kiwi, Goji Berry and Cacao Green Smoothie, 78
Pineapple, Grape and Spinach Smoothie, 76
Pumpkin, Date and Flaxseed Smoothie, 104
Rejuvenating Spinach, Cucumber and Avocado Smoothie, 85
Spicy Spinach Cilantro Sauce, 165

Spinach, Hot Pepper and Yogurt Hummus, 139
Spinach, Pineapple and Mint Smoothie, 106
Sporty Peanut Butter Banana Smoothie, 177
spirulina, 18
Blueberry Chia Parfait, 203
strawberries, 17, 210, 212–13. *See also* berries
Avocado and Pineapple Salsa, 126
Cold Strawberry and Tomato Soup, 151
Fruit Combo Smoothie, 172
Fruity Carrot Smoothie, 173
Refreshing Mango, Strawberry and Carrot Smoothie, 97
Strawberry, Camu Camu and Oolong Smoothie, 93
Strawberry, Pear and Lime Ice Pops, 183
Strawberry Almond Dressing, 120
Strawberry Grape Smoothie, 66
Strawberry Malt Smoothie, 168
Strawberry Pineapple Sorbet, 195
stress, 213, 215, 217
sugar, 38, 55
sunflower seeds, 28–29
Banana Coconut Lentil Balls, 187
Carrot Ginger Dressing, 121
Gooey Almond Oat Balls, 186
Oats, Greens and Camu Camu Smoothie Bowl, 86
Oats, Greens and Matcha Smoothie Bowl, 87
superfoods. *See also specific foods*
health benefits, 11–36, 210–11
managing health conditions with, 212–17

T
tahini
BLT Bean Spread, 180
Blueberry Sesame Dressing, 118
Carrot Ginger Dressing, 121
Hummus, Traditional Creamy, 137
tea, 34, 36, 211, 216–17
Berry Sorbet with Ginger and Mint, Bountiful, 197
BLT Bean Spread, 180

Oats, Greens and Matcha Smoothie Bowl, 87
Pineapple, Mango and Goji Berry Smoothie, 77
Pumpkin, Date and Flaxseed Smoothie, 104
Red and Green Smoothie with Pepitas, 70
Spicy Tomato Avocado Smoothie, 105
Spicy White Bean Dip, 135
Strawberry, Camu Camu and Oolong Smoothie, 93
teenagers and tweens, 8–9
tomatoes, 22, 210, 212–13
BLT Bean Spread, 180
Cold Strawberry and Tomato Soup, 151
Creamy Tomato Coconut Soup, 154
Enchilada Sauce with Poblano Peppers and Black Beans, 162
Garden-Fresh Tomato Sauce, 160
Gazpacho, 150
Guacamole with Tomatoes and Cilantro, 141
Red Lentil, Chickpea and Tomato Soup, 157
Roasted Vegetable Pasta Sauce with Tomatoes, Carrots and Mushrooms, 161
Romesco Dipping Sauce with Tomatoes and Almonds, 128
Spicy Moroccan-Inspired Tomato Dip, 130
Spicy Tomato Avocado Smoothie, 105
Sweet Chile Dipping Sauce, 127
Tomato Vinaigrette, 116
Zesty Chickpea, Tomato and Mushroom Soup, 158
turmeric, 32–33, 211, 214–15
Ayurveda-Inspired Chia Seed and Coconut Smoothie, 100
Creamy Kale and Feta Dip, 131
Exotic Mango, Banana and Avocado Pudding, 199
Pineapple, Citrus and Carrot Smoothie, 173
Tomato Vinaigrette, 116

V
vegetables, 18–23, 210, 212–13. *See also* greens; *specific vegetables*

watercress, 22–23, 210, 212–13
Cooling Avocado, Cucumber and Grapefruit Smoothie, 102
Land and Sea Green Smoothie with Chocolate and Berries, 107
Oats, Greens and Matcha Smoothie Bowl, 87
Pea Soup with Mushrooms, Watercress and Mint, 155
Pineapple, Avocado and Watercress Smoothie, 76
Zingy Green and Fruity Energy Boost, 174
weight management, 44, 48, 52–53, 213, 215, 217
wheat germ, 36
Spaghetti Beanballs, 181
wheat grass, 18
wound repair, 213, 215, 217

Y
yogurt, 35, 211, 216–17. *See also* smoothies
Banana Cream Yogurt Shake, 191
Chickpea and Yogurt Dip, 136
Chocolate Delight, Guilt-Free, 176
Chocolate Peanut Butter Yogurt Delight, 193
Cilantro Jalapeño Ranch Dressing, 122
Mango Almond Lassi, 194
Oatmeal, Peach and Yogurt Smoothie, 72
Orange Cream Smoothie, 171
Papaya Kiwi Frozen Yogurt, 183
Peachy Spiced Chocolate Treat, 193
Pineapple, Cashew and Chile Pepper Spread, 142
Protein-Powered Kale, Berry, Hemp and Yogurt Smoothie, 83
Raspberry Chocolate Milkshake, 191
Red Velvet Parfait, 201
Spinach, Hot Pepper and Yogurt Hummus, 139